HEAT
A FIREFIGHTER'S STORY

JON WELLS

JAMES LORIMER & COMPANY LTD., PUBLISHERS

TORONTO

Copyright © 2006 By *The Hamilton Spectator*, a publication of CityMedia Group Inc.

All rights reserved. No part of this book may be reproduced or transmitted in any form or by any means, electronic or mechanical, including photocopying, or by any information storage or retrieval system, without permission in writing from the publisher.

James Lorimer & Company Ltd. acknowledges the support of the Ontario Arts Council. We acknowledge the support of the Government of Canada through the Book Publishing Industry Development Program (BPIDP) for our publishing activities. We acknowledge the support of the Canada Council for the Arts for our publishing program.We acknowledge the support of the Government of Ontario through the Ontario Media Development Corporation's Ontario Book Initiative.

Cover design: Meghan Collins

Library and Archives Canada Cataloguing in Publication
Wells, Jon

    Heat : a firefighter's story / Jon Wells.

ISBN-13: 978-1-55028-928-2

ISBN-10: 1-55028-928-4
    1. Shaw, Bob. 2. Plastimet Inc.--Fire, 1997. 3. Plastics industry and trade—Fires and fire prevention—Ontario—Hamilton—History. 4. Fires—Ontario—Hamilton—History. 5. Fire investigation—Ontario—Hamilton—History. 6. Fire fighters—Ontario—Hamilton—Biography.
    I. Title.
TH9118.S53W44 2006   363.37'092   C2006-903638-1

James Lorimer & Company Ltd., Publishers
317 Adelaide Street West, Suite 1002
Toronto, Ontario, M5V 1P9
www.lorimer.ca

Printed and bound in Canada.

CONTENTS

Preface

Acknowledgements

1. The Brotherhood	9
2. Firetown	21
3. A Mountain Boy	29
4. The Stars Align	39
5. Dragon Slayers	47
6. A Unique Connection	55
7. Near Death	63
8. It's a Boy	77
9. An Angry Flame	85
10. The Big One	93
11. Surround and Drown	101
12. The Beast	109

13. State of Emergency — 117
14. Fear and Pain — 131
15. Anger and Tears — 139
16. Badge of Infamy — 147
17. Suspects and Motives — 151
18. "I Like to Watch Them Burn" — 159
19. Final Call — 169
20. The Battle Begins — 179
21. "I'm Going to Make It" — 195
22. Prayers for a Firefighter — 203
23. The Last Fishing Trip — 211
24. "You're Done, Buddy" — 219
25. Tragedy and Honour — 227
Epilogue — 239
Afterword — 255

This book is dedicated to Mom and Dad—my heroes

ACKNOWLEDGMENTS

This book is an updated and expanded version of a series I wrote for *The Hamilton Spectator*, which appeared in the paper on consecutive publishing days over four weeks in March 2005. "Heat" is one of four (and counting) multi-week narrative stories I've written for the *Spec*, and so I express gratitude to Editor-in-Chief Dana Robbins for giving me the freedom to craft these pieces, and for his editing suggestions each time. I want to also mention Douglas Haggo, who was editor for the original "Heat" series; Doug Foley, who did the fine editing; and Bob Hutton, who was the designer. Photographer Scott Gardner has been my right-hand man, illustrating three of my series, including "Heat", and I always appreciated his talent and camaraderie at home and abroad.

    I especially want to thank all of the Hamilton firefighters who were so giving of their time and candour for this story. Henry Watson and Colin Grieve helped introduce me to the others. Special thanks to Bronco, Pepe, Dickie, Paul Croonen and Ron Summers. Among those outside the fire department who helped in my research I want to mention Paul Anderson, Warren Korol, Sid Millin and Jeff Post. I also take advantage of this opportunity to say thanks to my family, and to Scott Petepiece and Pete Reintjes for being there all down the road. Most of all, I am forever grateful to the Shaw family, for investing their trust in me and allowing me into their lives.

J.W.

PREFACE

If I could find my business cards in my desk at work I'm pretty sure they'd say my title with *The Hamilton Spectator* is "reporter," but over the past four years I have essentially authored four "true novels" for the paper. The role I have at the *Spec* is an unusual one, and it began around 2003, when the paper ran my first long-form piece, "Poison." Research took me to India and the true crime story I wrote ran over thirty-five consecutive days and 150,000 words. It won a National Newspaper Award and led to three more series: "Sniper" (which was published as a book in an abridged format and renamed *Deadly Mission*), "Post Mortem", and "Heat." They are all true stories, but each time I've been asked the question in one way or another: to what extent did I make up detail? And the answer is, I made nothing up. In *Heat*, as in each of these stories, all of the detail, dialogue, and thoughts of the characters comes from reporting.

The projects have all been wonderful adventures, but *Heat* stands apart for the emotional impact it had on me. It began when I pitched the idea of a narrative about Hamilton's infamous Plastimet fire disaster to senior editors Dana Robbins and Roger Gillespie. Plastimet had, of course, been covered in the *Spec*, but I suggested telling it from the point of view of the firefighters and describing their world and culture in great detail. The challenge was getting access to the firefighters, a tight-knit group. But over the course of six months, Hamilton's firefighters let me into their living rooms and dens for interviews, sat around the table with me over bacon and eggs at Rankin's on Main East in lower Hamilton, up at Doc's Tap and Grill for beers, and I listened to the stories. In *Heat* I have tried to let the reader hear their voices, experience the camaraderie and code of the firefighter, and get inside the gear and the fires. In addition to more than fifty interviews—half of them with firefighters—and background reading, my research included wearing the heavy firefighter bunker equipment while spending a summer day at a training tower, where I manned the nozzle to help put out a real—if modest—fire. I showered twice later that day, but lying in bed that night I could still smell smoke oozing through my pores, still feel the heat on my face.

Heat also tells a story that had never been told before—how it was that Canada's worst toxic fire was lit. My research included several lengthy interviews with an Ontario fire marshal and a former Hamilton Police arson investigator, and reviewing police investigation notes. My interviews also included, for the first time, the one who actually set the fire. As with the firefighting scenes, all of the detail and thoughts in the arson subplot come directly from reporting.

Early in my research I recognized an interesting thread within the Plastimet story—the life and career of firefighter Bob Shaw. And soon I realized his story was the most powerful of all the elements in the account of the Plastimet fire, the heart of it. I have a writing test for myself: if, after so much time researching and drafting, I'm moved by my own words in some way, then I'm on the right track. Some of the passages I wrote about Bob and his family hit me like a hammer when I first crafted them, and they hit me again when I revisited the text to polish it and add two chapters to the original for this book. The unique emotional connection I felt in writing *Heat* will always stay with me.

One final thought: the story is, of course, Bob Shaw's story, but he represents so much that I saw in the others I met who battle the fires. For that reason, Bob's story is also, quite simply, a firefighter's story.

Jon Wells, Hamilton, Ontario

1

THE BROTHERHOOD

"You fight this, you bastard. Don't give up. Don't let it beat you. I'm telling you, it will *not* beat you."

Firefighter Bob Shaw could barely move in his hospital bed. The pain was incredible. He summoned energy to force a smile for Bronco's benefit.

"Let me tell you what's going to happen," Bronco continued in his rapid-fire delivery, his face angular, eyes dark and lively. "You'll take whatever they give you and you'll get better. We've got lots of things to do, plans to make. Get back to doing what we're supposed to be doing."

Mike Horvath got "Bronco" as long as he could remember, after the 1950s NHL player who shared the same name. As a kid he had been dazzled by the sight of fire trucks, once watched in awe as firemen doused flames burning his own elementary school.

After high school, college had not been an option financially for his family. Besides, Mike's friends were getting jobs, cars. He wanted some of that. Got a job with the railway, bought an aquamarine '65 Chevy. At 27 he was hired by the Hamilton Fire Department. Loved the action, the physical nature of it. The fires. The hottest was probably the old Wentworth Street School fire in '88. Started small, interior attack. They moved deeper into the building, hit small fires. It kept getting away on them, they could hear crackling behind the next wall. Wind picked up from the west, the building became engulfed with flames and they had

Firefighter Mike (Bronco) Horvath, a buddy of Bob Shaw's, calls for a hydrant to be turned on at the old Wentworth Street School fire in 1988.

to get out or get fried. Bronco had been on the nozzle, of course. Like many of the others, he always insisted on being first in the door leading with the hose. Find the fire through curtains of smoke, hit it. Fires seemed to follow him around, no matter which station he was based at. Perfect. "Hope you boys are rested up," he said when starting at a new house. "Because we'll be going to a fire."

Bobby Shaw was the quiet one. Family man, a man with no pretense. He went about five-seven, always kept in top shape at the gym—broad chest, chiselled arms, legs thick and hard from years of running and cycling up and down Hamilton Mountain. That wasn't the Bob Shaw Mike Horvath was looking at in Henderson Hospital. He was in rough shape. But then Bob's fitness and attitude had been his ace cards. He amazed everyone with his capacity to absorb pain and bounce back.

"In no time you'll be out of here," said Bronco, who was 51 but looked ten years younger, looked like he would never stop demanding the nozzle. "Then you can get back to the poker table—the boys are ready for you to start taking their money again." Mike was really going now, as though trying to transfer his own energy into Bobby, and to make his friend believe the best—and perhaps to convince himself of that as well. Wasn't that what firefighting was all about? No individuals. You draw strength from each other, feel secure knowing that the guy beside you is just as well trained and tough as you are, that he's got your back.

"I'm already planning the next fishing trip. A little golf, a few beers. You can dust off that piece-of-crap rod again, Bobby. Remember? Remember the big one you caught with that thing?" Bob had spent his career trying to save others. Now he was trying to save himself. Could anyone be armed with a better body or attitude for the mission? "See you tomorrow, Bobby," concluded Bronco. "You hang tough, eh?" He left the hospital, heart aching but face unbroken, still wearing a tough, optimistic mask.

Naturally, Bronco had been at the fire, too. The big one. It was that perfect summer night when the history of Hamilton's grizzled North End seemed to ignite into one great black and orange conflagration. Firefighters in Hamilton and across the country would always speak of it darkly, as though invoking a serial killer—one that was never caught. Bronco had heard the *bee-bop-bee-bop* of the station alarm on July 9, 1997. You hear a short beep, it's a car fire, garage fire. But the alarm was beeping like crazy for this one, like a cluster of European police car sirens. Oh, shit, he thought. This is as big as it gets.

Meanwhile, Bob had been in Niagara Falls with his family. They drove back home on the QEW highway. It was still hot in the early evening, the heart of summer, the days impossibly long. His wife, Jacqueline, sat beside him. A classy woman was how the firefighters thought of Jackie. Petite, with blonde hair, thousand-watt smile, and kind eyes that instantly drew you in, put you at ease, as though she had known you all your life. In the back seat was their 12-year-old son, Nathan. A large cloud hovered over Hamilton in the distance. Except it wasn't a real cloud. Bob exited off the highway.

"Where are you going?" asked Jacqueline.

"Just taking a look."

Bob wanted to get closer to the fire. He exited at Burlington Street, drove through the lower city, the industrial part of town from which Hamilton got its Steeltown nickname. But streets downtown were blocked off, so he drove to their house, which was atop the escarpment locals had always called a Mountain with a capital *M*. Their home was, as usual, sparkling clean, the white kitchen floor and glass table shining. That was Bob's doing. How often did Jacqueline come home from work and find Bob waiting with Nathan picked up from school, dinner ready, the house spotless? It was just the way he was. In part it was simply the instinct of a firefighter: Maintain order, protocol, routine. The house was a ten-minute walk from the Mountain brow. The sun had started its descent, and Bob and Nathan joined a group gathered at the cliff's edge to watch the smoke over the North End, Lake Ontario further in the distance. The big one. Yes, people would say, it was just a matter of time before it happened down there. Bob and Nathan walked home.

"I hope you're not going in to work tomorrow," said Jacqueline.

"Jac," he said.

Bob was the only person who called her that nickname. He had little else to say in reply—Bob Shaw chose his words carefully. And he was a firefighter. Maybe, Jacqueline reasoned, the fire will be out tomorrow. Or Bob's station won't get called. The next morning she saw him off as always.

"Be safe. Love you." Later that day Jacqueline's office co-workers kept talking about the fire. It was still going. She phoned Bob's station. No answer. She waited a couple of hours, phoned again. It rang and rang. Nothing. And now Jacqueline knew exactly where her husband had been all day.

She had faced tough times before she met Bob. But Jacqueline was a strong woman, even though she didn't think of herself that way. She had grown optimistic largely through her husband, like a flower enriched by sunlight. Bob had faced danger on the job, been hurt. Red-hot embers fell on his neck at a house fire. Wrenched his back falling from a ladder. Bumps, bruises. He didn't talk much about it. Jacqueline had never, ever, feared for Bob on the job. Until now.

* * * * *

Fall 1992
Hamilton, Ontario

A man drove along Van Wagner's Beach Road one cold night, rain peppering his windshield, the lake along Hamilton's north shore indistinguishable from the black sky. He pulled into the parking lot at Hutch's, a local fixture that had been serving up burgers, fish and fresh-cut fries on the beach for sixty years.

Perhaps burning himself to death inside his own car didn't strike him as an especially unusual way to do it. But in fact, from a western cultural standpoint, self-immolation of any kind is an unusual suicide method. The guy was in his fifties. Life had not been good of late. He had lost his business, a pile of money. Had he heard about the story of the woman in the States? One night she drives her Saturn twenty-five minutes out of town on the interstate, stops and, with the engine running, pours fuel from the gas can into the trunk, climbs in, shuts it on herself. Flicks a lighter. As in most burnings, asphyxia killed her before the heat. Her corpse was found frozen in what forensic experts call the "pugilistic attitude," her hands and legs in a defensive, bracing posture, a result of muscle fibres contracting from the heat.

The man who parked outside Hutch's felt like he had lost his life figuratively; now he would finish the job for real. Soon after that, the *bee-bop-bee-bop* alarm tones rang inside the nearest fire station, on Woodward Avenue, the dispatcher's voice droning over the speaker. Car fire. Firefighters down the poles. The automatic station doors slowly rose and Captain Pepe stepped into his boots, which were standing at attention ready by the pumper truck. The four-man crew put on their protective bunker suits, hopped on the rig and were out, lights flashing and siren wailing. Pepe turned to a "probie" next to him and motioned to his air tank.

"Put your mask on," he said.

Car fires spew nasty, noxious emissions. Benefits of technology, eh? Same with house fires. Long ago, you got house fires where basically wood was going up. But now there's all the synthetics, in couches and so on. Cars are the worst. There's the fluids, seat coverings, and especially all that plastic. Smoke's full of the worst kind of chemicals, crap

God didn't mean for anyone to breathe. And yet old habits die hard. Some old-school firefighters avoided using their masks.

The pumper crossed the overpass over Burlington Street. Pepe could see an orange ball of fire down at Hutch's. "This is Pump 8," he said into the radio. "We can see it from the bridge. Car is well-involved."

Pepe was interrupted telling his story about the car fire.

"You want another, Pepe?"

He was hanging out with the boys at the office. Another? OK. Twist his arm. Just one more. "The office" was how Pepe and the other firefighters had christened Doc's Tap and Grill on Concession Street, near the edge of the Mountain. The place had originally been dubbed Doc's because of its proximity to Henderson Hospital up the road. Funny thing, though, while it was hoped the bar would pull in hospital clientele, doctors happened to be among the cheapest tippers—doctors, police officers, teachers and firefighters.

"Firefighters still have to be the cheapest," chimed in one firefighter.

"Next to cops," said another. "You know what they say: Firefighters want everything for half-price. Cops want it for free."

There was a mural on an outside wall depicting a group of people hanging at the bar. Pepe and his friend and fellow firefighter Bob Shaw were in the picture. The boys promptly labelled it The Wall of Shame. The bartender knew exactly what Paul (Pepé) Villeneuve was having. Labatt's Blue draft. The boys all had their favourite. Bobby Shaw was a Blue Lite man, so was Rick (Ticker) Blythe—drink lite and you'll never get sick, they joked. Mike Horvath stuck with Canadian.

Pepe, tall and burly, had a thick, greying moustache, bald head, and a round face that easily broke into a grin and gleeful laugh. He received the tall glass of beer, examined it. Sometimes they tried to trick him, tried to pass off the bottom of the keg, knowing full well that he'd catch the trick. He could always tell. He knew his Blue. He grinned. Hey, nothing to be proud of, you understand.

Pepe continued the story about the car fire that he had recently experienced. That nasty fall night, his crew had taken the pumper past the foot of the Skyway bridge, across to the beach, pulled into Hutch's parking lot, and started unwinding hose. Two of his men started throwing water on the fire. The truck had enough water on board to do the job without using a hydrant. Could the car blow up? Anything was possible, but Pepe wasn't too concerned. If he'd seen one car fire in this town, he'd seen a hundred. They never blew, not like on TV, they just burned.

Pepe had noticed a guy watching the blaze among the gathered spectators. Average height. Stocky. The guy moved closer, was standing next to Pepe, getting too close to the burning car. "Sir, would you mind moving back?" asked Pepé. The man said nothing and did not move. It was the suicidal man, the guy who had lost everything, who had tried to kill himself, but could not follow through. He had lit the fire in his own car, but the thing was, the heat was too much. Perhaps he had just enough time to think about it. Should he or shouldn't he? No. Not now, anyway. He escaped just in time. Some people, they don't leave anything to chance, put a handgun in their mouth. Others give themselves an opening for survival. And now the guy was alive and in a bad frame of mind.

"Sir," repeated Pepe. "Would you please step back?"

"That's my car," came the reply.

"Well, no point in worrying about it now."

Smack. The punch landed right on Pepe's chin, under the helmet. Radio flips, helmet flies off. Cold-cocked him, right there. Decked him, on his back. Shit, he caught me dead nuts on the chin, Pepe thought as he lay on the ground. The probationary firefighter ran over, and the guy took a swing at him, too, landed one on the head, knocked his helmet off. But the probie wrestled the guy to the ground. The fire was put out. The police arrived, took the guy away.

Back at the station, the firefighters got out of their bunker suits, someone made coffee, they hashed out the evening's events like they always did, everyone keyed up over the experience.

Phone ringing.

"Pepe—it's for you," someone said.

"Yeah," he said, taking the phone.

"Is this Pepe?" said the voice.

"Yeah."

"Well, I hear Don King's looking for you."

"Funny."

Pepe hung up.

Ring.

"Yeah."

"Is this Punching-bag Pepe?"

"Get out of here!"

The boys at Doc's bar howled at the story, Bob Shaw's infectious laugh bellowing louder and deeper than the rest.

"Why didn't you take the guy down, Pepe?" asked one of the guys.

"'Cause I was on my friggin' back, that's why!"

Everyone's best stories got told at Doc's, or at the station—also known as the house or the barn. The modern firefighter receives counselling to help deal with exposure to mortality that few other people see. The stories, often couched in black humour, serve as their ongoing informal therapy, help take the sting out of their fears. A few confide in their wives as they do in their buddies. Most are less adept at talking about it. Either way, aired or not, the experiences become part of who they are, and on occasion they wake in the middle of the night, see in their mind's eye the charred corpse from a fire, a victim's blackened skin sliding off the skeleton.

The bond between the firefighters shows in the nicknames they use. Hollywood gets it wrong in many respects. Firefighters do not walk into a burning building standing tall, looking into each other's eyes with concern. They stay on their knees or else the heat up high will melt their heads off, and there is usually so much smoke you can't see your hand in front of your face. What Hollywood does get bang-on is the brotherhood, the camaraderie. When the job runs hot, which most consider the best of times, firefighters share an intensely physical experience, testing their bodies and minds, and they do it together. They are perpetually joined, like kids, or athletes in a locker room, or warriors on the battlefield, their legal identities erased in favour of names that link them exclusively to each other, in a way they are not linked even to blood relations.

Nicknames are a rare thing in most workplaces. Nicknames are a thing of the past, of youth, high school, a college sports team where love is forged by sweat, blood, victory and defeat, a true common purpose.

THE BROTHERHOOD

Modern office-speak aims at using the language of team and mission and shared goals, but the bond is artificial. And so Richard, the office manager, is simply Richard. He is not Richie, or Dick, or Red because he has red hair, or Stretch because he's tall. The firefighters are Cruiser, Cooler, Dickie, Haggar, Hammer, Big Red and Snooze, with even the nicknames themselves having offshoots. Owing to French-Canadian roots, Paul Villeneuve became Pepe Le Pew—after the French skunk in the Looney Tunes cartoons—then just Pepe, or Pep. Nobody called him Paul. It got so guys didn't even know his real name. He was "Captain Pepe."

Firefighter Paul (Pepe) Villeneuve, one of Bob's best friends.

One day his wife, Margaret, called the station and asked for Paul.

"Paul? No Paul here."

"Paul Villeneuve—your captain," said Margaret. "OK," she sighed. "Pepe."

The names always fit somehow. Bam-Bam was the handle for a firefighter named John Gaylard, a big man, pumped lots of iron, muscles on top of muscles, busted buttons on his shirts. Good guy. The Bammer. One time, the firefighters were inside a house after a fire. Even when the fire is out, the protocol is to make sure that some flame has not hopped elsewhere in the house, is not lurking in a wall or piece of furniture. So you clear charred stuff out of the place.

"That fridge has got to go," said a captain. Maybe he meant he just wanted it slid out of the way, or for a team of guys to move it somewhere. Bam-Bam relished taking the command literally.

"Out of the way," he grunted to a probie nearby. He kicked open the door, wrapped his arms around the fridge, picked it up, the whole freakin' thing, and threw it out the door, down the back deck, onto the grass. The Bammer.

They are like families at each of Hamilton's twenty-four stations. When not on calls the firefighters sleep, shower, play cards, watch TV, clean house, do repairs, paint, cook meals. Ticker—named for his ability to tick the ball off the edge of the ping-pong table perfectly for a winner—could fire up a meal with the best of them. But Pepe was known as the best cook in the department. He'd draw up a grocery list, go to the store and load up. What'll it be tonight, boys? Steak? Lasagna? Just leave it to Chef Pepe. And stay out of his kitchen.

His start date in the department was September 2, 1975. Most of the guys remembered their start date like a birthday. Pepe was in good shape back then, 26 years old. Did the agility test, ran a mile and a half in under twelve minutes, climbed a fire ladder wearing full gear. Those that couldn't make it past halfway up the ladder were toast. No *ifs*, *ands* or *buts*. Then an interview. He quit his job at Stelco.

"Why are you leaving Stelco, Pepe?" a friend asked.

Hmm, thought Pepe, a twinkle in his eye. "'Cause it's hot and dirty and I don't like shifts?"

As the new guy he loved the excitement when the beeper went off in the station—down the poles, jump onto the back of the rig. If it was a structure fire, you never knew what you would be up against, going into a strange house filled with smoke. Could you find the fire? He met Bob Shaw, maybe around 1978, when they were both at Station 1 on John Street North. They hit it off. Bob was quiet but always willing to join in whatever Pepe had on the go. They grew very close. Ultimately, as far as chasing fires went, Pepe started to get so he deferred in enthusiasm to others. His moustache got greyer, his face and physique rounder. The younger guys wanted the nozzle. Fine, they can have it. He had seen about enough. Life was the fishing and hunting trips, getting the next deer trophy stuffed and mounted for his basement den. Like all the others, Pepe had known death. He feared finding asphyxiated bodies in houses when inching through walls of smoke. But the majority of firefighter calls in Hamilton are medical emergencies. So Pepe had seen it all, skulls crushed from traffic collisions, decomposing corpses. Crib deaths were awful. He had held a dead baby, right there in the soft pink tones of the nursery while the mother wept.

Maybe worst of all, the 15-year-old kid he found in a bathroom who had put a bullet through his own head, lying there, still breathing, blood everywhere. Couldn't get the image out of his head for a long time. Fifteen. How bad could things be?

But that was the job. You divorced your emotions from it, did your work, planned the next outing with the boys, had a few pops. Tragedy was part of other people's lives. It would all change, suddenly, one day. For guys like Pepe there was work, and there was life. Life was fishing, telling stories over a cold one, and the smell of freshly cleaned pickerel sizzling on an open fire. All of it as regular and certain and automatic as the beating of your heart.

* * * * *

Wednesday Morning, July 9, 1997
Hamilton's North End
The arsonist was alone. He loaded the movie into the VCR. How many times had he watched *Backdraft* now? He had lost count. Movie promo: "Silently behind a door, it waits. One breath of oxygen and it explodes in a deadly rage. In that instant it can create a hero—or cover a secret." The opening scene: A firefighter enters through the window of a high-rise apartment that's ablaze. The flames seem manageable, but in fact heat and gases are building to such a degree, absorbed by the walls and furniture, that the room builds to the flashover point—the temperature at which every combustible article in the room will ignite.

The arsonist watched the screen. He knew what came next. *Boom!* An explosion. The firefighter is killed as his young sons watch from the ground below. Wouldn't be much left of the guy after that, thought the arsonist.

The movie was overblown Hollywood action material. Big-time special effects, a shiny, surreal feel to the cinematography. Firefighters laughed at the over-the-top nature of it, the fictional depiction of what it's really like at a fire. But the arsonist loved *Backdraft*. Loved it. Loved all the explosions, the fire. *The fire*: It is kind of pretty, isn't it, he reflected. Beautiful, even, the way it moves, the colours. Feeling the rush through his body as he watched *Backdraft* that day, did he know what the future held?

The movie rolled on. Scene: Grey smoke creeping out under a closed door, then sucking back again; a hidden, smouldering fire gasping for a new oxygen source like a monster seeking regeneration. Scene: Donald Sutherland, the jailed Hannibal Lecter–style firebug Ronald Bartel, squirms with near-orgasmic delight talking about loving fire, contemplating the power of the brilliant orange flame, black smoke, talks about fire as "the animal." Robert De Niro, playing the cagey fire marshal whose back is a quilt of fire-burned scar tissue, asks Bartel what he would do if he were released from prison. "What about the world, Ronald? What would you like to do to the whole world?"

The arsonist could speak Bartel's line with him, mimicking the low, raspy whisper: "Burn it all." The surprise twist in the film? It is a firefighter setting the time-bomb-style backdraft fires. One of the good guys.

The movie ended. Credits rolled. Most people thought of *Backdraft* as a movie about firefighters. No, the arsonist reflected later, it was a movie about *fire*.

He got up to leave. Lived on the top floor of a duplex near Wellington Street on the edge of Hamilton's North End. Time to go for a walk. While he was walking he heard the voice.

"Wanna have some fun?"

2

FIRETOWN

Fall 1992

Doc's Tap and Grill

"How the hell are you anyway, Bobby?" asked the bartender, Mike, as he pulled on the lever to fill another glass of draft.

"Good, Mike," replied Bob Shaw.

"Want another?"

"Nah, I'm good. Thanks."

Mike had been collecting a couple of display signs for Bob to use in a basement bar he was putting together at his house.

"Got hold of a couple more. One is a Kilkenny."

"Perfect."

Doc's smelled of fish and chips, nachos. Fans rotated slowly from the green-panel ceiling. Light shooting through the front window illuminated gold inside tall glasses of beer on the counter. It felt like one of their own basement dens, the warmth of the place.

"When's the Shawzie bar going to be open, Bobby?" asked Pepe. "I'd say it'll call for a visit to the hot tub."

Whenever Bob had some home improvements on the go, the boys would do the work, then hit the hot tub in his backyard, have a few pops. Apart from the social aspect, the hot tub did wonders for Bob's back, which had been flaring up on him now and again, ever since he fell from a ladder at a recent fire.

As usual, one by one, a few other firefighters filed into Doc's, everyone talking at once, their voices melding into one rambling conversation. Laughter. Needling. Reminiscences. Fire stories. Remember our BLEVE in 1979? Boiling liquid expanding vapour explosion. At Burlington and Parkdale. That was Ticker Blythe's. Tanker truck, 4:30 in the morning, tires catch fire, heats up the tank. "We get there, grab a hydrant just before the whole thing blows. Blows the end of the cab out and the piece lands about a kilometre down the road. The concussion blows all the windows out of the gas-station doughnut shop, too."

Remember the time? What was the guy's name?

"Put it on my tab."

"Damn right it's on your tab, you cheap bastard."

Faces glowed with the perfection of the afternoon, the beers, all of them basking in the warmth of their shared history. Bob sat at the right corner of the bar as usual. Pepe beside him. Bobby didn't talk much about his fire stories. Kept most of that to himself, unless prodded. Behind the bar on the wall facing them hung caricatures of bar regulars sketched by a local artist. Bob was among them, the only firefighter up there. The drawing showed a muscle-bound Shawzie holding a keg over his shoulder.

Someone brought up fishing. Someone always brought up fishing. They were heading up to the Bay of Quinte for the annual trip in May. Someone brought up golf. Remember the time Shawzie chipped in—twice—at the scramble tournament?

"Short guy, good short game," cracked Wayne Stringer. Bob just smiled.

"Hey there, short-shit," said Garth as he walked by.

All the firefighters knew Garth Turpin. He owned Doc's and had been good friends with Bob for years. Their families met in Florida several times on vacation. You could joke with Bobby about his height in part because he was as easygoing as they came, and in part because his physique was better than all of them put together, solid as a rock. Even among a group that had its share of gym rats, Bob's physical condition was legendary. When he worked up at Station 5, on Limeridge Road East, he would bike to work from home on the West Mountain, but would actually ride down the escarpment and back up again, out of his

Garth Turpin, one of Bob and Jacqueline's good friends, who owned Doc's Tap and Grill, the popular firefighter hangout.

way, just to get the extra cardio work in, to feel his legs burning as he climbed the Mountain day after day.

"Bobby," or "Shawzie," was about as much of a nickname as he ever got. No alter ego suggested itself for him, no character trait that stood out, at least on the surface. He was his own man. Never said a bad word about anybody. Even the firefighters thought of him as a gentleman. That was the word they used: *Gentleman*. Not that he was a saint. He cursed the fates on the golf course like anyone who's ever played the damn game. He definitely had a temper if pushed far enough. Was even ready to throw 'em if need be, to scrap, because he was a loyal, fearless soldier when it came to defending a buddy—or even sticking his nose in there for some guy he had never met before who was overmatched against a barroom bully.

"Pick on someone your own size," Bobby once growled at a guy who was pushing around a smaller man outside the Jamesway bar on Upper James Street. The aggressor towered over Bob.

"Yeah?" he sneered. "Maybe I should just kick your ass instead."

And they went at it, Bob wrapping his thick arms around the guy and taking him down, hard, in the gravel, the two of them rolling in a cloud of dust. Shawzie could handle himself fine. He would not back down, even if reason suggested otherwise, was the first one in to help whatever the consequences. He led with his heart.

In Doc's he took a final sip of his Blue Lite. "Gotta go."

Bob was off to pick up his boy from school, like he always did Monday to Friday. Loved it, seeing his son's smiling face each day. Why wouldn't he? Why would anyone have a child and then not want to spend every possible moment with him? Life's too short for that, he thought.

"C'mon, he can take the bus," said Pepe with a grin, knowing full well what the reply would be.

"See ya, Pep."

* * * * *

Hamilton is Steeltown. It is also a firetown. To those who only see the dark industrial postcard view from the QEW, the flames of Big Steel lapping at the sky, it seems like the city is perpetually ablaze. But beyond the caricature, Hamilton is ripe for fires: Old buildings, heavy industry, depressed core. Not including garbage or car fires, the fire department fights more than 300 structure—building—fires each year. In 2005, the cost of structure fires was $11 million; in some years the bill has gone as high as $14 million. Chalk some of these fires up to bad wiring, routine carelessness. Most of them, though, are criminal. In 2005, 123 structure fires were attributed to arson or suspicious circumstances; the year before, that total was 141. Hamilton's arson rate has in recent years been double that of neighbouring Toronto, although not as high as in cities such as St. Catharines, Winnipeg, and Vancouver.

In March 1992, at the old Collins Hotel in the neighbouring small town of Dundas, someone poured gasoline down the stairs into the hotel basement, soaking the rug. Fumes gathered in the air overnight, gasoline molecules mixing with oxygen. All it needed was a spark and the whole thing would go. In the morning, a tenant, unaware that he was minutes away from death by time bomb, phoned 911, complaining of the smell of gasoline. A firefighter entered through the basement door and spotted two toasters on the floor each plugged in to a wall socket with a timer attached. The timers had started, the coils were turning orange, pieces of paper inside were turning brown, but remarkably there was no fire yet, no explosion. He ran to the toasters and unplugged them. The gas pipes in the basement had also been sabotaged. If it had blown, the whole building would have gone up, maybe a chunk of Dundas besides. The operators of the hotel, Pat Musitano and his brother-in-law, John Trigiani, were acquitted of charges of conspiracy to commit arson and arson for the purpose of insurance fraud. No one was ever convicted in the attempt to burn down the historic hotel.

Most arsons in Hamilton are not so elaborately staged. They are set in paper and garbage in alleyways, using matches and lighters, accelerants like gasoline. The arsonists are vandals, drunks, kids, and people disturbed mentally or otherwise. Arson is what brings the firefighters and police officers together. Firefighters put out the fire, save victims, then a fire marshal works with police to determine whether the fire was intentional. Police detectives try to identify and catch the fire-setter.

The big fire at the Wentworth Arms Hotel at Main and Hughson on Christmas Day 1976 was one of the city's worst. Ticker was on that one. Call came in at 5:00 p.m., during a Christmas dinner party at the place. Six people died. Tick drove the snorkel, the truck with the double boom on it that sprays water from a platform high in the air. Everyone was soaked and frozen by the end of the night. Down at the YMCA, police arrested the 26-year-old man who had thrown a lighted match onto a Christmas tree. He was acquitted of arson by reason of insanity.

There was a 20-year-old police cadet on duty that night named Jeff Post. He had grown up outside Hamilton, in the country, near Freelton; his father worked in construction. Went to Waterdown District High School, figured his best career options were working at Stelco or Dofasco or getting on with the police or fire department. He got a lift into the city one day and someone mentioned the police were hiring. He signed up, joined as a cadet at 17.

For years police had set up task forces and launched investigations tackling specific arsons, but the systemic plague of arsons in Hamilton continued. The opportunities were too easy, the fire-setting culture a part of the city. In the summer of 1992, firefighters reported to a late-night garbage fire in a dumpster in an alley behind a downtown bar on King Street East, just west of Union Electric Supply on Walnut Street. They put out the fire, but the officer in charge was worried about any potential spread of the heat. They checked and double-checked, entered the building, put ladders up, checking for signs of heat extension. They left. Three hours later, 3:30 in the morning, the same crew was back, this time to find the entire Union Electric building fully involved. A good fire. Took nearly three hours to knock it down. It had not been a rekindle as the officer had feared. No, someone was just determined to set a big fire that night, and so the arsonist returned to light it up again. All buildings bounded by King, Mary, King William and Walnut streets were evacuated, and so was the police station on King William when smoke entered the ventilation system. The firefighters had to protect other buildings clustered beside Union Electric Supply. Their windows were cracking from the heat, the walls glowing orange from the projection of the flames. The firefighters kept soaking the buildings, cooling brick and concrete.

The rash of alleyway fires had police referring to the firebug—or, more likely, firebugs—as the "alley arsonist." The alley arsonist and the general problem of fire setting in Hamilton prompted police to create a new position for a full-time arson investigator, who would oversee all arson cases, look for trends and patterns, and develop projects to address the problem. There was an internal competition among cops to run the unit.

In 1996, Jeff Post was appointed to set up the unit and run it. Over the years, he had worked in the tactical unit, intelligence, drugs, and vice. He was tall and lanky, six-foot-five, with a casual manner and dry wit. He disdained wearing suits or ties to work. Post studied the science of fire, how to spot the telltale signs of arson, the burn marks, evidence of accelerants. He read cover to cover a textbook called *Kirk's Fire*

Investigation by American expert John DeHaan. Page 3: "Every fire scene must be considered a possible crime scene until proven otherwise." Post figured Hamilton had all the major food groups for an arson problem. Hey, it's not rocket science, he thought. You've got your crime, gangs, a depressed downtown with a maze of alleys for easy access and concealment, and usually material to burn. Post worked contacts in the city, immersed himself in the fire-setting culture. Kept a running list of people who popped up on his radar. Sometimes, you have the same people phoning in a fire tip. Sometimes they had something to do with the fire setting themselves. Really interesting folks out there. Extortionists, fraud artists, the mentally ill. Some were just troublemakers, but the roots of arson are complicated. Some of it goes beyond mere thrill-seeking vandalism to true pyromania—those who, the textbooks say, light fires for no definable, practical reason, but who simply feel better once the flames start. For some males, it's a way to seek affirmation of their virility, potency, and power through fantasy.

Arson is sometimes merely as blunt an instrument for intimidation or revenge as a baseball bat. Or the arsonist acts for reason of fraud: Setting or arranging a fire to burn records in order to avoid taxes or audits, to clear an unwanted building from the marketplace, to reap insurance money. There are even rare cases where firefighters have been known to commit arson in order to put out their own fires and be hailed a hero. In Hamilton, as in most cities, there is the increasing problem of child fire-setters. Some of it is routine vandalism inspired by peer pressure, lighting some garbage in an alley or playground. But when devices are used—Molotov cocktails, gasoline—it suggests that the kid is using fire as a weapon against society. In some cases, committing arson as a youth is a precursor to the worst kind of criminal activity in adult life. Serial killer David Berkowitz, the Son of Sam, admitted to setting 2,000 fires in New York City.

The deeper Post got into the job, though, the more he gave up trying to make sense of the inner demons of the firebugs. He was no psychologist, and motive didn't interest him all that much. There were judges and juries to figure that out. He mostly concerned himself with proving a criminal act took place at the scene, and catching whoever was responsible. For this he relied on experience and common sense.

He would soon be assigned to crack the mystery of one of the worst fires ever in North America, to find the arsonist, if there even was one. Would experience and common sense be enough for that one? Post had three copies of the DeHaan textbook. In DeHaan's words, "As a crime scene, the typical fire scene is the antithesis of the ideal. There has been wholesale destruction of the physical material and substance of the scene. The complexities encountered in fire investigation are sometimes overwhelming."

3

A MOUNTAIN BOY

A few kilometres south of Doc's, sprawling homes and roads and strip malls and jumbo malls had forever transformed the farm fields and streams of the Mountain. But right here, on the edge, at Concession Street, with the old small-town streetscape, the past was alive. The view was timeless at nearby Mountain Park Avenue, the escarpment brow overlooking the lower city that looked still as a painting: The old houses lined up row upon row, the factories with puffs of smoke suspended in the air, and the distant motionless lake, which reflected like a mood ring the sky's ice blue or steel grey.

In his adult, settled life, Bob Shaw lived in the newer burbs on the west Mountain, an area called Scenic Woods. But his past was never far behind, his heart never left home, this spot where, in the wink of an eye, you can be propelled back in time, like walking through a tunnel into an old movie. It's not black and white; it is 1957, the colour is young and new with stark contrast. Everyone knows everyone else, and Bobby Shaw is eight. Kids' sneakers slap pavement running from the old Mountain Theatre on Concession, where a show costs five cents including the popcorn and cream soda, but where Bob and his friends still sneak in for free. One day Bob and pal Paul Anderson watched *Creature from the Black Lagoon* five times in a row before getting chased out by ushers.

Around the corner, on Upper Wentworth, sat Mountain Lanes, the bowling alley once owned by Bob's uncle, Sam Shaw. The kids hung out there all the time. Bob and his friends huddled out of sight changing bowling pins in summertime, sweating like dogs and dodging the flying pieces of wood, trying not to get plunked in the head. Uncle Sammy was a rotund gambler who looked after his friends. Used to pay rent for a homeless man just because the guy couldn't make it on his own. Sometimes the kids would collect five bucks for Sam to bet at the track for them, and he'd return and give $50 for them to gleefully split. Sammy regularly handed the keys to the bowling alley to his nephew at closing time, and that's where Bob and buddy Ricky Morton honed their skills as two of the finest young bowlers anywhere, once winning a Canadian championship representing Sam's alley, and Hamilton, out in Edmonton.

Bob's parents, Harry and Lily Shaw, lived near Concession at 44 East 21st Street. They kept the yard in immaculate shape, like most of the people on the street did. Their flower beds often won them Trillium awards. Harry was a veteran, served in the air force, was stationed in Egypt for a time during the Second World War. He was a quiet, understated man who used to bowl with Bob and his friends, did some coaching. Great guy. Lily was a tiny woman with a big heart. Any visit to the Shaws' place meant playing in the backyard with the latest blind dog that Lily had taken in from the humane society to look after. Their only son was born on February 1, 1949, the front edge of the baby boom. So much was common about him. And so much was unusual. See little Bobby, 6 years old, every time it pours rain, outside, walking through puddles, barefoot, all by himself. See him at the edge of the Mountain, alone, watching storms rolling over Lake Ontario into the lower city. He does not run, he is not afraid. He is drawn to the storm. He feels a spiritual connection and peace with the outdoors, nature, from the beginning. See Bob and Paul Anderson living a Huck Finn existence, hiking down along the stream that runs through fields and farmland farther south, where one day a huge mall and suburbia will rule. They jump on and off trains at the base of the escarpment. One day the train picked up speed, they couldn't dismount until they hit Albion Falls several kilometres to the east, and they walked an hour home again.

A MOUNTAIN BOY

Bob Shaw stands with his parents, Harry and Lily, and sister, Carol, in front of their home at 44 East 21st Street in Hamilton in the 1950s.

Another day, Bob and Paul bounced along a path on the side of the Mountain, when they heard gunshots. They heard later that a Hamilton Psychiatric Hospital patient had stolen a .22 rifle and ammunition from Nick's Sport and Cycle on Concession Street, and was taking pot shots over the edge. Perhaps it was coincidence that Bob landed on top of Paul with his arm in a protective embrace. Or maybe it was Bob's instinct. Paul never felt safer with anyone than Bob, could trust no one else quite the same. The bullet grazed Bob, but he had a thick sweater on, was not seriously hurt. He wanted to get up and circle around the shooter.

"You're crazy, Shawzie! Stay down!"

They didn't get hurt, just as they never got hurt from initiation rites and dares involving gingerly walking along the escarpment edge on the wall or on the rickety wooden landings partway down. Or sliding down the huge water pipe that ran from the top to the bottom near Gage Park. They laughed, ran, fought, broke rules, raised hell. They weren't choir boys. But it was all pretty much innocent. Nothing got burnt or broken. Nobody got hurt. (Well, maybe their buddy John's nose after he ran face-first into the glass door at the Mountain show while fleeing an usher.)

Return back through the tunnel, back from the bright primary colours to the present, more muted tones, darker, another generation, the new millennium. There are some city kids who, their lives often influenced by a toxic blend of deviant parents and a violent culture, seek outlets not just for pent energy, but for a negativity and destructive nihilism that ventures into territory that Bobby Shaw's Mountain boys would never even have considered.

*****

Bob was always among the smallest of his age, just like Ricky Morton, but he was tough as nails and did not back down. In those days, Hamilton was all ends: North end, east end, west end, and the Mountain. Bob and his buddies were known as Mountain boys. You didn't show your face in the north or east end unless you were ready to scrap. When Bob was still in public school, the Shaws moved farther south to Burkholder Drive. His father was making a decent living, he could afford a new house, a bigger one. The neighbourhood where they moved was nicknamed Little Chicago. Bob was the new kid on the block, coming as he did from the Wentworth-Concession area. He had to fight every day his first week at his new school. It's just the way it was. "Zero tolerance" was decades away from existing. You stood up for yourself or were bullied.

They were great times. "You've got it made," parents told their kids. And boys like Bob and Paul believed them. Could there be a better time to live? No fear of dying on a battlefield in Europe, always a job available if you wanted it, rock and roll exploding in the popular culture. They hung out listening to Elvis, Buddy Holly, Richie Valens. As teens, they formed a gang called the Continentals, hung out at the pool in Inch Park in the summer, went to evening dances at the outdoor hockey rink beside it. Ricky Morton was a couple of years younger than those in the group. At the summer dances Ricky stood outside the rink boards and peered through the wire screen to watch Bob, Paul and the rest of the Continentals holding court, the prettiest girls floating around them. They were the coolest thing going.

Early teens, the boys started hanging out playing pool at Mount-Way Billiards on Upper Wellington at Queensdale. They caused havoc during a show at a movie theatre once. Got booted out. With the gall only a teenager can muster, they tried to get "their" money back, even though they had snuck in.

"OK," said a manager, pulling out a sheet of paper. "Let's have your names."

The first boy, Paul's twin brother, used his middle name for his first, and made up a last name.

"Name's Tom. Tom—Trout."

Next came Bob.

"My name's Mark Marlin."

And Paul.

"Dan. Dan Dolphin."

"Get out of here!" snarled the manager.

As Bob moved through his teens, he worked every chance he got. Went to the market in the lower city downtown, battled to get on one of the trucks that took you out to a farm to pick beans, fruit, tobacco. Got a job with Paul at the CNR unloading trucks onto the cars. Got so they worked full time, after school. Get there for 4:00 p.m., work to 11:00 p.m. Bob would do anything asked of him. "For sure" was his catchphrase. In winter, the foreman at CNR, guy named Romeo, needed truckloads of frozen chickens hauled onto a train car. It was freezing cold, the wind whipping off the bay. For sure. Bob did it. They loved him, gave him extra hours; he stashed away more money, saved for a sports car, an MGB.

He thought about what the future held, because that's how his mind worked. But Bob didn't talk about his reflections. Didn't talk much about his father's work, either, although everyone in the neighbourhood knew what he did. Harry Shaw was a firefighter. His start date had been April 12, 1947. He was a good one, too. Quietly went about

Bob Shaw, second from right in front, celebrates with his bowling buddies.

his job, did what needed to be done. Harry ultimately decided that, one day, down the road, for his retirement, he would love to bring his boy, Bob, to the station on his last day of work, let him hang at the station all day, help out, ride on the back of a rig.

*****

Why does any youngster feel it? Why does the heart quicken upon first hearing the siren's wail, seeing the fire truck flash by the car window, and sensing that something special is going on? There are people out there who race into the fire while others flee. Firefighters don't parse their feelings on the question of why they gravitated towards the profession. It's not part of who they are. If they did mull it over, really thought about it, they might not choose to be a firefighter. A firefighter might cite a family connection, or a childhood fascination with firetrucks, the equipment, uniforms, "toys for boys." Sometimes the answer sounds mundane. They applied to the department looking for a career change. It pays reasonably well, good benefits. But there is also something more intangible that brings them to consider a career that most would not. It is an instinct, a gut feeling.

As with everything these days, science suggests there may be a genetic explanation. There may be a gene inherent in the "risk taker," a genetic blueprint in the soul, that reels them in, programs them with a personality that is risk- or action-oriented. The job is not always about action and danger, though. It is more often than not about preparation, waiting, boredom, hanging at the station, watching TV, making meals. But most firefighters crave the action. It is what they are trained for; they feel comfortable executing manoeuvres and using expertise that has been drilled into them.

Psychologists point to character traits that firefighters share: A desire to be needed, a strong sense of loyalty. And a compulsion for doing the perfect job. They enjoy routine and protocol, work well within a team. They embrace tradition, follow orders, are not dissenters or nonconformists. They do not have a strong desire to stand out as an individual. Some argue there is a macho element that attracts certain people to the job: The need for attention, even hero worship. It has been cited as the reason there have been extreme cases where firefighters have committed arson—that their desire to be a hero is so intense that they set fires themselves, even put themselves and innocents at risk, so they can save the day. The macho theory doesn't match the reality, though, which is that firefighters have little or no public profile as individuals. Nobody outside their immediate circle can name them. There is a group identity, not individual fame.

They do enjoy feeling appreciated. They are helping people, they matter. One of the guys, a soft-spoken, articulate firefighter named Mike Ernst—who got saddled with the nickname "Sweetcheeks" for his youthful face—had once worked at a bank. Was off sick one day, he's in the next, and someone says, "Oh, you were away?" Nobody cared. Interesting, though, he reflected: Firefighters help others, but they are only required when someone suffers misfortune. Anyway, driving in that truck and seeing the looks from people, the respect, that never gets old, it always feels good. What other occupation brings that? But most do not seek personal attention.

A scene: See four men on the tenth tee at King's Forest Golf Club in Hamilton. One of them is a guy named Paul Croonen. He knows two others in his group, but not the fourth. The fourth asks what they all do for a living. Two of them answer. Croonen, a tall, lean, lantern-jawed man, does not. "What about you, Paul?" the man asks.

"I'm a shift worker" is all that Croonen says. In fact he is a Hamilton firefighter, and an excellent one at that. Shift worker?

The job runs hot and cold. There are down times, where the firefighters are mostly cleaning the station or planning the next social event. At a house party you might get a couple of the wives teeing off on the so-called heroic image. "Work? You guys don't do a damn thing, you're too busy being off all the time. Bowling, golfing, fishing, working second jobs doing home repairs. When do you have time to put out fires, anyway?" Even some of the firefighters play it up, make their own jokes about it. There is a kernel of truth there. But the fact is, while few occupations offer the same amount of down time, few offer the same potential for physical and mental peril.

Talk to a police officer. Policing is a tough job. Never mind the risk involved. Never mind that you hold the power of life and death in your holster, yours and others. Never mind that. Listen to the cop talk about having to knock on the door of a home, pretty much like the house you grew up in, late at night, and wait for the pale, drained faces of the parents to appear. Has the officer heard anything about their teenage girl? "Yes, sir, sorry to report that she was in a fatal car collision. She did not make it. I am so, so sorry." Now listen to this same cop: He would not want to be a firefighter. Those guys—those guys have a tough job. Wouldn't do it myself.

* * * * *

Wednesday, July 9, 1997
The North End
The arsonist had risen at 7:00 a.m. to find his world wrapped in grey fog, the air heavy and wet from a steady drizzle. By noon, after he had watched *Backdraft*, the sun burned off the fog, clouds moved out, and all was clear. It had instantly become a warm summer day. The arsonist had lit fires before. There had been the one right in the neighbour's

backyard. Another one in an alley across the street. How had they happened? As time went on he thought of them all as accidents. Why did he do it? He wasn't really sure. It wasn't the liquor. He drank on occasion, yes. Downed the forty-ouncer once, all by himself. Couldn't walk after that. Just lay there on his back in a park, staring at the sky, contemplating the notion of heaven before passing out. Much later, he couldn't even remember exactly what had been in the bottle. Something clear—maybe gin? Not a good experience. Don't want to repeat that.

The psychologists could talk about family roots. But the arsonist didn't feel his upbringing was all that unusual. Thought he came from a normal family, his parents loved him. Remembered as a kid walking through a mall and literally pointing in window after window at the coolest toys. There! He wanted it! Mom bought it, just like that. He'd point at that, and that, and that, and she bought them all. So why? Why light the fires? Was it a release, was it anger? Might be. But also, he just liked fire, found it attractive to look at. That's why he never, ever tired of seeing the explosions on *Backdraft*, the raging flames, billowing smoke. He kept thinking about the movie after he had left his apartment building, walking north, towards Hamilton Harbour.

4

THE STARS ALIGN

It was midnight one summer night in 1970. Paul Anderson and a buddy nicknamed Wiener walked the streets of downtown Hamilton lamenting their plight. Plight? Oh, the 23-year-olds were only going to miss out on the biggest party in the history of the country. It was the Strawberry Fields concert festival, intended as the Canadian version of Woodstock, with at least 100,000 people expected for three days of revelry. The party was at Mosport Park, one hour east of Toronto. Paul and Wiener had no car. And it was getting late. It would probably be sold out soon. What to do?

"There's only one guy I can think of who might come through for us," said Paul. "Shawzie."

Paul had not been in close touch with 21-year-old Bob Shaw in recent years. But the thing was, even when they started travelling in different circles, their lives always intersected again. Bob always kept contact with friends he had from different scenes in his life. Paul and Wiener took a cab to the Shaw house on Burkholder. It was 1:00 a.m. by now. Bob's bedroom was in the basement, his window looking out on the driveway. *Tap-tap.* Bob's face showed at the window. Then he climbed out the window to the driveway. Shook his head at the entire notion. Mosport? Now? You guys.

"All right. Let's do it," he said.

"Really?"

"For sure."

Three of them rode in Bob's two-seat, blue, MGB sports car. The concert was in fact poorly organized, and out of control, over 250,000 people there. The gates were closed when they arrived at 3:30 a.m. As usual, Bob had an idea. He got some guys to help him lift a Volkswagen Beetle to the edge of a fence. Then one by one they were climbing on top of the body of the car and using it as a platform to leap over the fence. Bob, Paul and Wiener were the first ones over. They stayed all three days. On the way out on Sunday, the Beetle was still there, all dented-up.

"Hope that guy had a good time," said Paul.

They were great times, the late sixties and early seventies. Bob eventually bought a green Mustang to replace the MGB. Got a summer job at Stelco, along with Paul. Bob loved going swimming in quarries near Hamilton—Emerald Lake, Gulliver's Lake. He was a strong swimmer, probably could have done that competitively, too. They went on road trips to Grand Bend on Lake Huron, and down to Port Dover on Lake Erie, where they had once watched Ronnie Hawkins and the Hawks at the Summer Gardens, before the dance hall burned down.

In 1971, Bob and Paul shared a two-bedroom, clubhouse-style apartment with two other guys on Forest Avenue near James Street. Vacancies were tough to come by. The tenants on the lower floor were so unruly that no one else wanted to rent out the apartment over top, so Paul and Bob got it. Cases of beer stacked up on the balcony. They barbecued out there, too, bringing firefighters in on more than one occasion when someone phoned to report smoke. One of their roomies played Motown constantly, "My Girl" over and over, until the others couldn't take it any more, although Bob didn't much care. They told bad jokes, hung out. Bob had a deep, loud, contagious laugh. They'd all get going so hard that tears came to their eyes. And every so often, when there was a rainstorm outside, you could find Bob out on the balcony, alone, just staring out towards the Mountain at the rain. He loved feeling the air on his bare skin; even in wintertime he'd be out there in a T-shirt and shorts.

Inside, they played cards for hours. Bob loved playing into the wee hours. Even though he was physically gifted, he loved the grinding mental sports, cards, bowling, golf, pool, where you had to keep your concentration for a long time, battles of attrition. They hit the bars. Paddy Greene's, the Corktown, the Plantation, the Jamesway. Hamilton's downtown was a busy, rough place at night. There were a lot of hotels downtown back then, plenty of opportunity to get in trouble. By 1973, though, Bob was 24 and ready for a change.

"I've got to do something," he told Paul. "I think I need to move out."

"I knew you would," Paul said.

"And I'm thinking of trying for the fire department."

"What took you so long? I always thought the job was made for you."

The stars aligned for Bob Shaw. At that same time, he met Jacqueline Cannon. Their paths crossed because Paul was dating a woman named Trish Cannon on and off. Trish was Jacqueline's older sister. The first time Bob and Jacqueline met, it was at the Forest Avenue apartment. There was a group of people there. Neither made much of a move. How could it be otherwise? Both preferred listening to talking. Jacqueline was taken with Bob's warm hazel eyes, big smile. A great face, she thought. He was in excellent shape, obviously, but it was his face that stuck in her mind.

Jacqueline had blue-green eyes and the slender figure of a teenager, long, straight blonde hair, and a radiant smile. But she lacked confidence. She wasn't wearing her glasses that first time they met. Then she didn't see Bob for a few more weeks. The next time, she was at the apartment and the TV was on. She was an attractive woman, but was worried that her glasses were not flattering. Bob saw her squirming.

"Jacqueline, what's the matter?"

"I—I wear glasses now."

"So?"

"So I need them to watch TV."

"So put your glasses on!"

His attitude made Jacqueline laugh. She put on the glasses. He had done something few could do, he had put her at ease. Everything was all right. From the start Bob had this presence, like a comfort blanket wrapped around her. A few weeks later, Bob was laid up in the hospi-

Jacqueline and Bob at Emerald Lake, northwest of Hamilton, in the mid-seventies.

tal getting a cyst removed from his back. He phoned Jacqueline to ask her out for their first real date.

"Want to see a movie tonight?"

"Bob, you're in the hospital."

"Yeah. Are you up for it?"

He picked Jacqueline up at her house in his beloved Mustang. Bob knocked on the door, she walked out with him to the car. Jacqueline tugged on the Mustang's passenger door handle; it wouldn't open. It had been stuck for ages. She looked over at her date, and Bob was already in the driver's seat, window rolled down, and the engine growling. He was still a bit rough around the edges with women. Jacqueline crawled in through the window.

At that time Bob had been working with the city's traffic department. One of his jobs was working with the crew that painted lines on the roads in the middle of the night. He loved it: Straight nights, which gave him free days to play golf, go for long jogs, swim at the quarries. But he had been thinking about firefighting as the next big step. Bob told Jacqueline he had applied for a position with the fire department. His dad was still on the job. Bob had what it took inside to be a firefighter, but what about the hair? It was typical late-1970s, down to his shoulders. It wasn't curly but was as thick as a tangle of copper wire. As a practical matter, beards could never be permitted because it would prevent a good seal on an oxygen mask. His moustache could stay. But the hair was too long for the firefighter culture.

Fire departments were still very much paramilitary organizations—a culture that never completely vanished. Many of the senior officers had been hired not long after the war years and had military backgrounds. That included the chief, Len Saltmarsh, who joined the department in 1946 after being stationed with an air force radar unit in Labrador. Saltmarsh was a throwback. He was respected by his men, who, particularly when they themselves got older, came to appreciate his approach to discipline. To the chief, firefighting was a straightforward undertaking. You answer the bell, you save a life if you have to, and you do what it takes to get the job done. He knew times were always changing, jobs changed, society changed. But firefighting?

"There's the old saying: Nero fiddled while Rome burned," he said. "So they went and got the water out on it. Water's been going around for a long time. Not that I can remember back quite that far, though."

Chief Saltmarsh knew Bob was Harry Shaw's son. Bob seemed like a solid, quiet guy. On the other hand, his hair was way too long.

"Cut your hair," he told the young man.

Bob duly got it cut. He returned the next day to see the chief. Saltmarsh wasted no time in responding.

"Problem is, there are some barbers around here who forget what the scissors are for," Saltmarsh said. "You better go back and cut it again."

Jacqueline saw Bob after the second cutting of his hair.

"Oh my God," she said. "I can't believe it!"

"Jac, I had no choice," he said with a smile.

Bob Shaw now had short hair and was a probie with the Hamilton Fire Department. His start date was September 30, 1974. He had only just started, but he had already saved his first person in distress. It was Jacqueline.

* * * * *

When Bob joined the department in 1974, firemen were still called firemen, they still stood on the back of the truck when speeding to a fire, an arm sling keeping them from falling off, helmet done up by the chinstrap, riding to the emergency. Chief Saltmarsh was impressed with Harry's boy. Bob learned the ropes quickly and, like his dad, did his duty without hesitation.

There is a rhythm to firefighting. Stretches of inactivity, cleaning the barn and the apparatus, making meals, eating, sleeping, and playing cards. Then the call comes, *bee-bop* tones slicing through the peace. Down the pole, pants, boots, jacket, helmet. The driver firing up the truck, someone whipping out a map. What is in store for them? Every fire is different, and fighting them is like detective work, though the life-and-death timeline is compressed into minutes. Apartment fires? The building is made of concrete blocks, steel doors. The fire can be contained. Good. Car fires also tend to be self-contained since they usually occur on a street or an open parking lot. But they are messy, spewing some pretty toxic smoke. It gets hairy when the car fire is in an indoor parking garage.

House fires make the adrenalin pump hardest, the fires where danger runs hottest and where lives are most likely to be on the line. Smoke makes it impossible to see where anything is. What is the floor plan likely to be? Is the place messy? Make sure to stay together, use your hose line as a guide to get back out of the house. The hose couplings connect a certain way, the male end always goes towards the fire, the female end, away. Follow the female couplings to safety. Finding the fire source is the trick, because usually the house is so engulfed with smoke that the flames themselves might not be visible. Some guys seem instinctively good at finding it. In the front door, bring a Halligan tool—a big chrome-plated crowbar with a prying bar and a spike on one end. That and a sledgehammer will get you in anywhere.

As soon as you enter the building, get down on one knee. If the house is well-involved, the smoke will make it impossible to see. Stay low. The heat at two metres up will be so intense it will feel like your head is in an oven. Patience. Stop, listen for crackling. If you can't hear it, it's nerve-racking. Where the hell is it hiding? If there is some visi-

Captain Mike (Bronco) Horvath takes an axe to the roof of a home on West Fifth Street in Hamilton.

bility, consider the smoke conditions. Is the smoke at the floor level? Then the fire's probably in the basement. Is the smoke two metres up, is it banking down from the second floor? Know fire, the science of it, how and why it works, how best to attack it.

Fire is a chemical reaction. There needs to be the presence of oxygen molecules, fuel molecules (wood, paper, gas) and energy (match, lighter.) These three elements are sometimes called the fire triangle. The spark creates kinetic energy, making the oxygen and fuel molecules move faster, banging together. If they move fast enough, they will react when they collide, and light. Each type of fuel requires a different amount of energy to ignite into a fire. Once burning, a fire is like its own heat engine, a self-perpetuating process. The new fire burns vaporized fuel, producing heat, converting more fuel into vapour, and the burning cycle continues as long as there is fuel and oxygen. Take away one side of the fire triangle and you kill the fire. More accurately, the literature says that there is another part to the equation, that there is actually a fourth side—the chemical reactions taking place between the molecules. The spray from a fire extinguisher smothers a flame to separate it from oxygen, slowing down and killing the chemical reactions needed to keep it burning. Baking soda tossed on a small fire can accomplish the same thing. For larger fires, water from hoses absorbs heat. It also turns to steam as it boils, which takes air away from the fire.

Get to know the sounds. The crackling, the rumbling of water in the pipes heating up, plaster dropping. The roar the fire makes if a window is open as it gasps for an oxygen source. Find the heat. Maybe take off a glove, hold your hand in the air, feel for the heat. You sense it's farther ahead. Keep low, move along a wall, hand up again, it's hotter now; keep going, the smoke is so thick you can't see your hand in front of your face, the heat is getting worse, it's like your head is burning, you can't take it much longer. Listen. Hear the crackling, right there, open up the nozzle, hit it high, up at the ceiling, a blind shot, into the heat, turn the flame and heat up high to steam, which will knock down the blaze. Hit it again, *tissssh*, listen for the sizzle of water on flame.

Steam is a fire killer. That's why you hit the flames high, make steam to drop on the fire. Water expands 1,700 times when it turns to steam. Steam superheats the room, which is suffocating, takes your breath away, but at the same time, it rips the oxygen from the fire. Pepe Villeneuve was at a basement fire once, he hit the flame with one shot, *tissssh*, just like that, steam knocked it down instantly. You couldn't even mop up the water, he had used the perfect amount. There's a science to it. And safety. But in the heat of battle, sometimes safety loses.

5

DRAGON SLAYERS

The first time you pull on the fire-resistant bunker suit, the feeling that washes over you reinforces your instinct for the job. On go the heavy, overall-style pants, the cowl for the head, the heavy parka-like jacket made of seemingly indestructible Kevlar material, which is designed to resist ignition from direct flame. Arms through the oxygen-tank straps. On goes the clear mask, the 4.5-kilogram helmet, and now, insulated from fire and from regular people who wear regular clothes to work, you can hear your own breath as though alone inside a narrow tunnel—*uhhh-shhh, uhhh-shhh, uhhh-shhh.*

Altogether the bulky gear weighs between 27 and 37 kilograms. You are forced to constrict muscles merely to stand, it exaggerates each movement, and it means a slow turn of the head to see comrades next to you. The suit is hot, sweat crawls down your back. The gear forces you to walk like a combination of John Wayne and an astronaut: A natural swagger, adrenalin pumping before so much as a wisp of smoke is witnessed. *Uhhh-shhh, uhhh-shhh, uhhh-shhh.* You are an individual risking it all but you are also part of a team trained to save lives, to run into the fires. You have The Right Stuff. The Hot Stuff.

Up until the late 1980s, early 1990s, firefighters still wore long boots up to their thighs, a raincoat-style jacket, helmet and mitts. The neck was unprotected. When you held your arm high in the air to spray the hose, water ran down your coat and into your boots. The bunker suits improved things dramatically. In 1989, the department ordered a couple of them for experimental use. That year, a firefighter got caught in a flashover, flames all over him. The reason he lived was that he was wearing a bunker suit. Right after that, the department ordered the suits for everyone.

Next to smoke inhalation, flashovers are one of the biggest killers of firefighters. The term "flashover" is often used as a generic term to describe a burst of flame or explosion at a fire. Technically, a flashover is when an increase in thermal radiation from the combination of the fire plume and hot gases in a contained area causes all exposed combustible surfaces in the room to burst into a fully developed blaze. This differs from a backdraft, another dangerous by-product of a fire. A backdraft occurs in a room or area where the fire is poorly ventilated. Even a small fire may be producing gases containing partial or unburnt combustion products. If these accumulate, and then oxygen is introduced into the room, it can produce a sudden flame burst that races through the room towards the oxygen source.

The bunker equipment is a potential lifesaver, but the equipment is not a cure-all. The suits are heavy and very hot. And, while you can last longer in the heat of a fire, it's possible that you wait too long, so that by the time you feel hot, it's too late to get out. As for oxygen masks and tanks, in the past these were mere accessory items that were not always used. Even in the 1990s, after masks were standard issue and the new breed all wore them, there remained old-school firefighters who rarely strapped them on. A probie could be reminded of how things were done in the old days when he was inside a house, on the nozzle, down low on a knee—textbook—mask on, seeing nothing but smoke through the face-mask glass, hearing nothing but muffled voices, some radio chatter, his own breath—*uhhh-shhh, uhhh-shhh, uhhh-shhh*—and then, loud and clear, "Open it up, right now!" And the others in masks are thinking, "Where the hell did that come from?" And sure enough, there's an old-guard captain, standing straight up in heavy smoke and heat, no mask, bellowing, giving the order to open up the nozzle. Firefighters maintain military-like devotion to protocol, order, keeping a clean station, lines of command. But many also carry with them a

Flames leap out of an attic as a firefighter removes part of the roof of an east Hamilton home.

devil-may-care mentality. That, too, is part of the culture. They need it to save lives. But it can let them down, too, push them to plunge ahead when they should stop and think.

Most of the firefighters want the nozzle, want to find the fire and put it out. It's what they joined for. Did Bob Shaw demand the nozzle like some of the other guys, guys like Bronco and Dickie? Sure, Bobby wanted the nozzle, too. But with Bob it was less a hunger for danger, for action, than it was a case of instinctively wanting to do what needed to be done. He did not step on guys' toes. If someone else was demanding the nozzle, fine. The mission was everything. Bob had several key attributes for firefighting, both physically and mentally. On the other hand, he had a streak of nonconformity in him, and more importantly, there was his discomfort with confined spaces—which could be a problem while crawling down narrow smoke-packed hallways of clapboard houses in Hamilton. His real dream had been fighting forest fires.

Bob's big heart, meanwhile, was both a pro and a con. Maybe he cared too much. Early days on the job, he heard the *bee-bop-bee-bop* of the alarm at the station—down the pole, into the boots, jacket on, jumped on the back of a rig, raced to the scene. Great stuff. Structure fire. Put it out. Maybe save somebody. Who would grab the hydrant? No one ever wanted to be the one to grab the hydrant. That meant you wouldn't be on the nozzle, finding the fire inside, knocking it down. OK, if the hydrant happens to fall on your side of the truck, you grab it. The thing was, this time, when they got there, the house was well-involved. Sometimes there is nothing you can do. There would be no rescue. They knocked down the fire, worked their way in.

Inside the house Bob came across a victim. A toddler. Dead. Firefighters can take pretty much anything, can shrug off violent death and move on. But kids—there's something about kids. Innocence? Not getting a fair shot at life? Something about the weakest, who deserve protection, who do not get it. It's just different. Back to the station. Shower. Coffee. Rehash the fire. Bob said little. Later that night, off his shift, he returned to the apartment on Forest Avenue. Turned the key in the door, walked inside, then into his bedroom. He shut the door. Could still smell the smoke that dwelled in his pores. He sat on the bed, alone, in the dark. Firefighter Bob Shaw sobbed like a baby.

* * * * *

Firefighting offers rewards that even police work does not, as highly regarded in the public mind as it is. For obvious reasons, everyone is not always happy to see police officers all the time. But in firefighting, it's different, they are always perceived to be saving the day. The task might be saving a kid who has wedged his leg between the limbs of a tree. It might be racing to extricate a car accident victim, the firefighter feeling his arms burn while holding the 32-kilogram Jaws of Life spreader, wedging the nose into the crack of a car door, pulling on the trigger and feeling the device fold back steel as if it were a tin can. Most of all, firefighters are admired because they take on an enemy that everyone fears and everyone can root against: Fire. It is something both modern and primordial, a symbol of hell, a force of creation and destruction. Fire is feared and revered. A weapon of the arsonist, the extortionist, the fraud artist. A dangerous by-product of technology gone awry.

The culture hungers for heroes, real or imagined. Sometimes celebrities are beloved, but it is fleeting attention because it lasts only as long as their fame. Firefighters, nameless though they are, never vanish from the public imagination as a group. They are famous for fighting the fires of September 11, 2001; they are famous for fighting the basement fire down the street. Mere celebrity, mythologist Linda Foubister wrote, lacks greatness of soul and moral vision. True heroes in the Greek mythological vein sacrifice for something that is greater than the individual, for something like love or saving another. The true hero remains nameless. Even comic book superheroes are those who seek no recognition for themselves, they keep their actual identity a secret. They have special powers to fight evil, and courage and drive to do so. In the case of a hero like Batman, the powers are quite average, but the drive to do good and put himself at risk is extreme, verging on obsession.

Those brave enough to fight the fires have always been considered heroes, back to the slayers of fire-breathing dragons in Arthurian legend and, in Christian mythology, St. George: "As soon as the dragon saw him it rushed from its cave, roaring with a sound louder than thunder. Its head was immense and its tail 15 metres long. But St. George was not afraid."

* * * * *

May 1995
Ontario Avenue, Hamilton
Everyone at the fire was screaming—the mother, even seasoned cops and paramedics. All of them, out in front of the house, on the street, yelling their heads off. *Save him! Save Ryan! Save the boy!* It was just after 2:00 a.m., the flames and police and fire-truck flashers lighting up the street. Dickie leapt from the fire rescue truck. His heart, God, it felt as if it would burst through his chest. It was the fear. Of the fire? No. Firefighter Richard (Dickie) Sherwood did not fear fire. He respected it. Felt he understood it. Respect it or it will kill you. No, he was scared of just one thing: Not finding and saving somebody in a fire who could be saved. He would not have that on his conscience for the rest of his life, he thought. No. He would not.

Richard (Dickie) Sherwood, right, started his firefighting career in England on his 18th birthday. He worked alongside his father, whose rank was leading fireman.

The house on Ontario Avenue in the lower city, south of Main near Wentworth, was burning fast, hotter than hell inside. It was, as firefighters put it in their clinical military-style speak, well-involved. Smoke everywhere. Smoke is the real killer, blinding those trapped inside, disorienting and asphyxiating them. Ryan, who was 3 years old, had not made it out of the house. His mother was outside, screaming.

"My boy! My boy's in there! Help!"

Dickie went six-two, eighty-six kilograms, wiry and fit. He lived with his family in Burlington, next door to Hamilton. Rode his bike for fresh air, exercise. Loved that. Tried to ride every day, ride the fifty kilometres or so through the country to Cambridge. He had a British accent from growing up in Kent in southern England. As a teenager back home, Dickie left school to be a machinist. Dad had always said his boy should get a trade. But then he decided that he wanted to be a fireman—just like his father. Dickie had a practical skill to bring to the job, something he would always believe every firefighter should have. You work with tools, vehicles, and buildings: It makes you more useful on the job. Nowadays, he laments that a lot of men and women come to the job without that.

Dickie started as a fireman in England in 1980 on his 18th birthday. He worked side by side with Dad, trying his best not to let him down in front of his mates. Dickie was young, strong, thought he could do anything. He was also higher strung than his old man. That would never change. He had a passion for the job, one that sometimes rubbed some people the wrong way. Once at a traffic accident, Dickie was helping a woman, the driver, badly injured, bleeding, her legs were trapped. He held her as they tried to cut her out of the car. He's trying to comfort her—it's OK, everything will be fine, try and stay calm—and she's screaming, spitting blood in his face. A woman in another car stops alongside.

"Is anyone hurt?"

Dickie snapped. "Anybody hurt? Jesus Christ, you callous cow, how can you say something like that? You should've been here 10 minutes ago!"

Dad was there, saw his son losing it, told him to calm down. He learned from his dad, but Dickie never stopped being a hard-nosed sort who knew of only one way to do the job. The right way, and all out. There is a way to do things. Polish your boots, go by the book. You follow the book and you won't get called out. Do it right or get out of the bloody way. And he took risks at fires. Yes, he did. Always had. Always would. He had done all right so far. Dickie's temper, his refusal to accept other ways of doing things, did not change with age. He felt it in his bones: There is protocol at a fire. You follow it. No questions. They are trying to save lives and it's a serious business. Do it the right way. If you're not helping, you're putting lives at risk.

One time, at a house fire, Dickie was crawling low in the front hallway, flames blowing front to back, and he saw a man's shoes. It was the guy who lived there, trying to find his cat. If he doesn't get out, he's done. No time to argue over a cat. Out you go, mate. Dickie picked him up by the legs and threw him through the screen door.

* * * * *

At the fire on Ontario Avenue, the police and paramedics had been at the house first. Before the fire-pumper rigs do their thing, firefighters from the rescue unit are first on the scene, and first in the building—no hoses, just get on a bunker suit, put on a mask and oxygen tank, and get right into the house, if possible, to pull out anyone still alive. That was Dickie.

"The boy! Inside! Help! Help! Help!"

Dickie pulled on his oxygen mask as he sprinted towards the house. *Uhhh-shhh, uhhh-shhh, uhhh-shhh, uhhh-shhh.*

Everyone screaming, the mother beside herself with panic and grief. *Uhhh-shhh, uhhh-shhh, uhhh-shhh, uhhh-shhh.*

Dickie might have stopped, paused, weighed the situation: A well-involved house. Dangerous heat, smoke. Boy inside might already be dead. But that wasn't how Dickie worked. You wait, people die. Some of the others thought he pushed the envelope too much, was reckless. With the screams echoing in his head, Dickie was through the door and inside the house, the smoke and heat swallowing him whole.

6

A UNIQUE CONNECTION

In the couple of days prior to the big house fire, Dickie had a rough go of it. Not on the job. He was a fish in water on the job. The night before the fire, he had flown back from England, where he had attended Dad's funeral. Brian Sherwood died from cancer, a form of leukemia. Like other British firemen, he had gone maskless all those years, inhaled his share of smoke, although the smoke in the old days was less toxic in homes than now. They never wore masks in Britain, and still don't to the extent they do in North America. Maybe that's why mandatory retirement is earlier in Britain. Firefighting is considered a young man's job. Dad had been dying and Dickie rushed home to speak to him one last time. But he didn't make it in time. It was just as well. Dad was very weak at the end. So his boy remembered him the way he had been—as a top-drawer "leading fireman," which had been his rank at one time. Dad had been so calm, resourceful. It was the way Dickie wanted to bear him in his mind.

It had been in 1988, after eight years firefighting in England alongside his father, that Dickie had moved to Canada with his English wife, settled in Burlington, and was hired by Chief Len Saltmarsh with the Hamilton Fire Department. Dickie called him "Mr. Saltmarsh" from that day forward, even when the chief was long retired and Dickie was in his forties. The pay was much better in Canada but he missed some of the English regimentation and structure. He got to know and work with other longtime firefighters, men like Bob Shaw, Paul Croonen, Ron Summers. Dickie got a rep for being an excellent firefighter, one who didn't suffer fools gladly, who was a stickler for detail, order, and as someone who relished breaking windows and doors at a fire. Yes, Dickie was a door breaker. Once, a young probie asked, on the rig, if he could take down the door when they arrived at the fire. "If I don't get there first," he replied. Dickie took down the door. It had nothing to do with enjoying busting stuff up. If someone is trapped in a building, the door is bloody well going in. And breaking a window can release heat from the house, keep a firefighter from getting nicely toasted.

Inside the flaming house on Ontario Avenue, Dickie was on his knees, gloved hands slapping the floor, grabbing at furniture, searching for the mother's boy like a madman, feeling around for anything. So much smoke. Might as well be in there with his eyes closed.

Uhhh-shhh-uhhh-shhh-uhhh-shhh-uhhh-shhh.

Where is the boy? Where is he? He sucked in air inside his mask, rapidly draining his tank from the impact of the heat, his actions, and his heart rate. He would be out of air before long.

Uhhh-shhh-uhhh-shhh-uhhh-shhh-uhhh-shhh.

He heard the pumper truck hooking up to a hydrant outside, the guys coming up the step with the hose. *Find him! Find the boy, or he's dead.* Dickie's worst fear, losing a victim. Something. His hand hit something. It was a small leg. He pulled it towards him. He stared through his mask into the boy's face. The boy's skin was black from the smoke, his eyes looked grey, had rolled back in his head. Dickie cradled him in his arms, retraced his steps through the smoke-filled darkness, and carried him outside to the paramedics. Then Dickie strapped on a new air bottle, back in the house, searching some more in case anyone else was left behind, then back outside again, new bottle, and back in, on a hose this time. He was always like that, never stopping, always running into the fire, fighting the newest battle, and perhaps old ones, too.

Back inside, the guy on the nozzle, a probie, couldn't find the fire through the smoke in the house. Most of the time the fire source is not blazing for everyone to see, it is concealed somewhere in the house, throwing smoke as if to camouflage its location, as it continues to burn and spread. Dickie and the probie were on the stairs, climbing into the hottest part of the building where the heat rose. A hose from outside hit into a window, blowing flames upstairs back on top of them, fire lining the ceiling like a blowtorch, the heat incredible.

"I can't find the fire, I can't find the fire!" screamed the probie.

"Calm down, take a deep breath," said Dickie.

"We're going to die!"

"You are not going to die. Calm down, take a breath, we'll be all right. Now just give it a shot, right there, straight ahead."

"I can't see anything!"

"Just hit it."

The water hit the top of the ceiling, vaporizing into steam, collapsing down on top of flames, everything went grey-white, they felt like their bodies had been immersed in a boiling vat, but the flames had been knocked down. Later, Dickie was outside, the fire out. His eyes were burning from the heat that no mask can completely block, his nose running, body soaked in sweat, utterly spent.

And the three-year-old boy named Ryan? Dickie thought he would die for sure. But the paramedics rushed him to hospital. They put him in a hyperbaric chamber. He survived. It was a team effort, but Dickie was the hero. The boy was one of thirteen people he pulled from fires in Hamilton while on the rescue unit. Later, he received a card in the mail from Halifax, from Ryan's grandparents.

"Words are never enough, but they are all we have in situations like this," it said. "While I realize that firefighting is your job, we never stop long enough to give special thanks to those who do their job well, to those who take their job and training seriously, and who were ready last week to save my grandson's life. I know he had only at most one more minute and would not have survived. You gave him that last chance, thank you from the bottom of my heart."

Firefighting is a nasty, dirty, stinking job. That was how Dickie thought of it. Even when you wear a mask, you're always taking in some smoke at some point, you're burning skin. It's like a credit card, really, he thought. The toll keeps adding up over the years. And he loved it. There was nothing he would rather do.

*****

It was in the summer of 1974 that Paul Anderson got the hint that his oldest friend was destined to marry Jacqueline Cannon. One day, after Paul finished his shift at Stelco, he drove up Highway 6 north of Hamilton to Emerald Lake. Parked his car. And there was the green Mustang.

"Shawzie here?" he asked somebody.

"Nah. Haven't seen him."

"His car's here."

Paul went for a long-distance swim around the quarry. And as he approached a shallow part, he saw Bob Shaw standing there by himself. "Bob? What're you doing here?" And then Paul looked beyond Bob and saw the small blonde woman lying on the shore. Jacqueline.

"Ah. Not good enough for you, eh, Shawzie?"

Bob did not talk about the girl in his life, not even to Paul. But Paul could tell he was serious about her. Saw him at a party, and Bob had this look about him, this was no passing fancy. And, in fact, from Paul's memory, she was the first serious girlfriend Bob had ever had. He had no trouble attracting interest, but he had just not been into serious dating. Bob was 25, Jacqueline had turned 21 in June. They started spending more and more time together. He drove her around town on a second-hand Yamaha motorcycle he had bought. When they were dating, Jacqueline went to a party with Bob. She was chatting with a couple of women, Bob was off to the side, taking it all in, listening.

"Jacqueline," someone whispered to her, "Bob seems really nice. But he's so quiet."

Jacqueline smiled. She always smiled.

"Not with me he's not."

Shy? Wrong word. It suggests tentative, unsure. Bob was definitely not that. Nobody defined Bob for him, and he didn't try to live up to the expectations of others. He was his own man. Jacqueline was more amenable to small talk in a social setting. But deep inside, she was not nearly as self-assured as Bob, less confident of the future and her place in it. Bob was the one who gave her the direction she needed. She was born on June 2, 1953, in Glasgow, Scotland. Her father, John Cannon, worked in a shipyard in a city that was, at the turn of the century, an international manufacturing powerhouse. Shipbuilders on the Clyde River, which runs through the city's heart, produced a fifth of the world's shipping output. But Jacqueline was born at the wrong time in Glasgow's history, when tough times were getting tougher, the city falling hard from its former title as The Second City of the Empire. John Cannon took his wife, Patricia, and Jacqueline and five-year-old Trish to Canada. They would also have a son, Michael. Dad had heard jobs were booming in Ontario, Canada, in a steel city called Hamilton.

They lived on Gage Avenue North in the lower city—way north, right up by Stelco, a portion of the street that would one day not exist any more, wiped off the map by industrial sprawl. John was a career Stelco guy. The family later moved up the Mountain, the Buchanan Park survey. Jacqueline went to Westmount High School. When Jacqueline was 17, her mother got sick. The children had no idea how serious it was. She kept it to herself, that was how she dealt with it. One day she suddenly died of bowel cancer. It hit the family hard. Decades later, Jacqueline had still not come to terms with it. Jacqueline seemed so comfortable in her own skin, could engage anyone in conversation, but she could not talk about that. It was as though her mother's death put out a light in her soul, and it became a dark room she did not want to visit, and never would.

After high school she lived with her aunt and uncle in Kitchener and got a job at Mutual Life. And then, just out of her teens, she met Bob, through Trish. Jacqueline never thought Trish was setting her up. Maybe that was just her navïeté—a character trait that Bob found charming. Here was this local girl who seemed so fragile and old-fashioned, in a way, as if she had this small-town nature. She didn't drink, didn't talk much. Her face glowed, though, with the bright smile, the dancing eyes. They didn't have many of the small things in common. Bob loved to play sports, and games like cards, pool. Jacqueline wasn't into games at all. But they had a deeper connection than all that. Bob had it figured out pretty early, though he kept it to himself. He was going to date Jacqueline Cannon. And once they started dating, he knew where he wanted to go next. One day, Bob presented his plan to her.

"I've got an idea to run by you, Jac," he said one day. "I'm thinking we should get married." Plan a nice small wedding, just their closest friends. And, rather than having a big dinner, do it with just close friends and family at Jacqueline's family home. That's it. And with the money saved, take a honeymoon. Something really nice. What do you think? This was what Bob was like, what he would always be like. Planning ahead for both of them, taking care of her, leaving no stone unturned, protecting her. She loved him.

"Sounds great to me," she said, and smiled the way she did, filling the room, eyes lighting up. And that was it. Jacqueline was starting her life all over again. Bob liked that. He knew what she had gone through with her family, the death of her mother, other things in her life. He thought they belonged together, he felt a unique connection with Jacqueline, spoke to her about his inner thoughts in a way he never did with even his dearest friends. He wanted to inspire her, show her that from loss, love can still grow, from pain comes healing. Bob's favourite musician was Roy Orbison, had been since high school. Even though Orbison was no longer hip, Bob stayed with him for all time. "Pretty Woman" was a favourite, Bob delighted in belting it out with his god-awful singing voice. What was it about the sweet soaring voice, the mysterious man in dark glasses, and the melancholy lyrics? Orbison was a haunted man, his dark view of life influenced by tragedy. In 1966, his wife died in a motorcycle accident. Two years later, two of his three sons died when his house caught fire. Bob's favourite song would perhaps always be the bittersweet "Only the Lonely," a song he first heard when he was 11 years old.

"There are better things waiting for you out there, Jac," he told her. "I think we belong together. I think if we get married we'll have a great life together."

She stared into Bob's hazel eyes. She was taken aback by it, the way he talked, the look in his face. He said things like that and it felt like a guarantee. He was so quietly confident, so comfortable with himself, and with her. It helped her relax, bury her past, feel as though nothing

Bob felt a unique connection from the beginning with Jacqueline.

would ever happen to her, that she would be protected. She felt her life opening up.

Anyway, sure, Bob acted by his own light—but this was marriage. Jacqueline's family was Catholic. And so she and Bob had to go through classes in order to get married. This was not Bob's idea of a good time. Formality and structure and rules were not in him, and he would not bend to them. But sometimes "you gotta do what you gotta do." Right? And so one day Bob and Jacqueline sat in a room with several other couples and a priest. It was mandatory prenuptial counselling, the first of six sessions.

Bob could feel the room shrinking. And the topics they were discussing were ridiculous. Why were they there? Why was *he* there? Jacqueline looked over at him. She knew that look. His eyes seemed to pool, grow darker. He was not going to last. Of course, the other men in the room were feeling the same thing. But Bob was not like other men.

"Excuse me, Father. I have to use the washroom," said Bob.

He walked from the room, and looked back at Jacqueline through the window in the door as he left. A devilish grin on his face, he made a gesture with his hands that said, "I'm done. See ya." She found him sitting in the green Mustang in the parking lot. They never attended another class, but the priest was fine with it. He would do the wedding. He liked Bob. That was the way Bob had with people. He got away with things without seeming offensive. Everything was a wink and a laugh that left everyone happy.

They were married on November 12, 1977, at St. John's Church in east Hamilton. It was to be an intimate affair, but once word got out, all of their friends attended. Jacqueline's sister, Trish, was the maid of honour, Paul Anderson, the best man. Bob always preferred dressing casually, but never ragged—always a natty dresser, tidy, well groomed. Took pride in that. If he wore jeans they were always newer looking jeans, shiny belt, nice watch. But he disdained ties, and unlike men who hate ties but wear them anyway, Bob almost never wore one. He did not conform. But for the wedding, he reluctantly agreed to put one on. Or did he? Jacqueline's father was the only official photographer. And he left the lens cap on the entire time. There were no pictures.

Thanks to the small wedding, just as Bob planned, they could afford a honeymoon in Hawaii for two weeks. Rented a jeep, toured around, lay on the beach. Jacqueline felt like she had won the lottery of life. It was perfect: Bob Shaw in a heaven on earth for nature lovers, Jacqueline feeling life starting fresh in a place that at one time she could have never dreamed she would see; the two of them forming a bond that was unbreakable, their lives sealed together in paradise.

7

NEAR DEATH

Wednesday, July 9, 1997

The heat in the lower city was intense by the late afternoon as the arsonist walked north, the sun unburdened by any clouds. He watched some kids playing basketball in a park. And then the arsonist arrived at Pier 4 Park on Hamilton Harbour. Needed to cool off. Walked down the strip of sand to the lake, felt the water pool around his feet. Later, he was on the move again, walking, following the railway tracks east, in the direction of home. He wanted to go home. He was sure of that. He passed under a bridge.

"*Wanna have some fun?*"

The arsonist heard the voice. Was he really there, though? The arsonist wondered about that later. Was he a fictional character he had created? Someone he had invented in his mind's eye, his partner in crime, the one who egged him on to do things he shouldn't? If he did exist, what did he look like? Brown shoes. Blue jeans. Had a nickname, too: J-Dog. Yeah. And J-Dog knew where there was a gas can. It was hidden in some bushes near the big old building. A red gas can, half-full. *Wanna come with me? Wanna throw some gas around in the abandoned building? Light it up?* OK, the arsonist heard himself say, let's go.

The arsonist was not going home, not yet. Maybe if there had been somebody else there at the time, maybe then he wouldn't have gone with J-Dog. Or maybe he would have. He continued along the tracks.

It wasn't long before he arrived near the old factory. The can was in the bushes, just as he was told. Then he felt his hands grip the chain-link fence. There was no barbed wire at the top. Up and over. It was a dirty lot. The north end of the building was open, walls crumbling, looked like it had been bombed. There had been fires set there before. But the south end had walls, doors. Some of the doors were locked. Others were open. Did anyone work there any more? It was abandoned, probably empty, just an empty shell. Wasn't it?

*****

Uhhh-shhh, uhhh-shhh, uhhh-shhh.

Bob Shaw felt along the concrete wall with his gloved hands. Couldn't see a thing except black. He was in the bowels of a parking garage. A car fire inside had filled the place with smoke. Couldn't even see the wall he was touching. How the hell was he going to find his way out? Parking garage fires are among the most dangerous for a firefighter. The structure is all concrete and steel, not much chance for a fire to spread, but all it takes is one burning car to fill the whole place with smoke and the eerie sound of tires popping, metal bending. The building is so large, and dark, it's easy to lose your way, then have your air tank run out and you're done. The panic that sets in only forces you to drain the tank faster.

Uhhh-shhh, uhhh-shhh, uhhh-shhh.

You follow your training. It could be fatal to lose track in the smoke of where you are. Firefighters are taught to stay close to the walls inside a structure fire. The middle of the floor might be unstable if the fire is on a lower level. The wall offers some guide to get out of the building. And if you're on a hose, you follow the metal connections back out to the pumper. But Bob wasn't on a hose that could guide him back, he had gone in there on the search-and-rescue team. His tank was running low, his heart pounding.

Uhhh-shhh, uhhh-shhh, uhhh-shhh.

He heard the beeping on the alarm at his waist. It did not stop. The alarm is there to tell a firefighter when his tank is running out of air.

When he ran out, he'd be finished, the smoke would disorient him first, then kill him.

Uhhh-shhh, uhhh-shhh, uhhh-shhh.

He had seconds left. His hand hit something metal on the wall. A door. He tugged on the handle. It would not open. It was locked from the other side. He rattled the handle. Rattled it some more.

Uhhh-shhh, uhhh-shhh, uhhh-shhh.

Someone happened to be on the other side and opened the door to safety. A close call, probably the closest to death he had come as a firefighter. He got home that night and said nothing about it to Jacqueline. Much later, at a gathering of firefighters, some of the boys talked about the call and Jacqueline overheard how dangerous it had been.

Another time, Dickie Sherwood was at an apartment building on Charlton. There had been a collision in the underground garage. Gas was leaking from a car, there was a danger that it could ignite. Dickie's truck had responded to the call. So he was down there, trying to clear the area while the situation was still hot. A woman was down there offering to help. Dickie was abrasive at the best of times at a scene.

"You have to leave, ma'am," Dickie said.

"I'm a nurse, I can help," the woman said.

"I appreciate that and I know you're trying to help, but we've got a thousand things to worry about without worrying about other people being down here," he said. "You have to go. Now."

"But I—"

Dickie bristled. There was no time for this.

"Not open to debate, I'm afraid. Go."

The accident was cleaned up without any ignition. Back outside, the driver of Dickie's rig, Paul (Cruiser) Croonen, tall, square-jawed, waited. The nurse walked up to him.

"There's a rude Englishman in there who told me to get out!" she said.

Croonen grinned. Didn't surprise him. Dickie—that was just the way he was. Didn't mess around at calls. The same could be said for Croonen, too. The two of them got along well. They were both intense. Dickie was tough on others, did not mince words, took charge of most any situation. Croonen was competitive, worked hard, knew his job inside out. If Hamilton created optimal conditions for fires, Steeltown also forged the right people to fight them. Croonen was born to be a firefighter, he just didn't realize it for a while. Start with a pretty girl at a school dance in 1982—it all seemed to flow from that. Paul went to Westmount High, the same school Jacqueline Cannon once attended. A girl named Kim Smith went to Delta High School. A friend Paul and Kim had in common, Laura, introduced them at a winter dance. They talked, danced slow. Kim, a blonde, wore a velour sweater, skin-tight jeans. Paul wore the uniform of the anti-preppy tech-boy: Old jeans, a checkered flannel lumberjack shirt, Kodiak boots whatever the season. Had long hair and a beard when they were not fashionable.

He worked up the nerve to ask Kim out. Her father, Garry Smith, was a firefighter. Paul knew he needed to dial back the rebel thing, so he got his hair cut short and his beard shaved off. On their first date they saw *Raiders of the Lost Ark* at Jackson Square downtown. Later, at Kim's house, Paul made himself comfortable in one of the chairs. Garry entered the room. The last guy Kim had brought home had sat in Dad's chair, and when Dad entered the room, the guy just sat there, legs splayed, hey-how-ya-doin' attitude. Not a good approach. Garry had booted him out of the house just like that. But Paul Croonen's dad was old school, too. Paul knew the drill. He leapt to his feet.

"Is this your chair, sir?" he asked.

Garry was impressed. "That's OK. Have a seat." Paul was in.

Croonen's father was a machinist by trade. He urged his boy to learn a trade. And Paul did. Got his papers in tool- and die-making and landed a job with Wentworth Tool and Die. Enjoyed working in a machine shop, and was good at it. He had boundless energy and pride in his work. When he was dating Kim, Garry had asked him about firefighting.

"Have you ever thought of it?" he asked.

"No way. I like my job," Paul said. "I'm going to be plant manager one day where I am."

"OK."

Garry never asked him again about it. Paul and Kim got married. Over time he heard stories about the firefighters, and decided he wanted a change of scene. A few of his friends did the same thing, these guys who all had talent and passion for trades, doing work with their hands, but who were reaching for something more exciting, a chance to help people, be part of a team. They took pay cuts to make the switch. Croonen figured that the test of initiative would be one of the things that he'd love with firefighting. You're given a problem at the scene and everyone is looking at you to fix it. The team has to come up with a plan to get the thing done. Firefighters like that test, seek that test.

Paul got on with the fire department. Garry was rising through the ranks quickly, on the way to chief.

Firefighter Paul Croonen and his wife, Kim.

He made a point of not putting in a good word for his son-in-law.

"Aren't you proud?" he said to Paul when he was finally hired.

"Why?"

"Because I had nothing to do with you getting hired, and anybody ever says you got on because of me, you tell them I had nothing to do with it."

"That's great, but geez, couldn't you have made a couple of calls or something?"

Kim wasn't sure she wanted Paul to follow in her father's footsteps. She grew up sensing that her father had had some close calls at fires. She dreaded a phone call in the middle of the night that would bring the worst news. Croonen became "Cruiser" at the station where he started, Station 1 on John Street North in the lower city. He was always cruising around, on the go, bursting with energy, owing to his competitive nature: Make Garry proud, prove to his dad he made the right move, and prove to the other guys that he belonged.

"Got some advice for you, probie," one veteran told Croonen. "You want to make an impression? Every time one of those rigs leaves the station, whether it's yours or not, slide the pole. Make sure they get out and everything's fine. You hear the alarm, you just go."

"Got it."

In his first six months on the job, Croonen slid the pole for every alarm. Helped the boys get ready, closed the door behind them, washed the rigs when they returned. Some of the others started complaining that he was doing too much.

"You don't have to do that," said an officer.

"But I want to help."

"You won't get any sleep and when we do need you, you're going to be too tired."

Croonen's legwork got him on the rescue unit, working with people like Dickie who were first in at fires. Croonen became a driver. Owing to his perfectionist instincts, Croonen threw himself into keeping his truck immaculate, tools organized in every compartment perfectly, the rig spotless. And he decided to learn the city like the back of his hand. Every day after work, he rode his bike home and took a different route, memorized every corner, every landmark. This was his neighbourhood. No one would know it better. He would be prepared for anything. Just test him, anytime. Go ahead. The officers would quiz the firefighters, gather them together.

"Quick: Where's Tiffany?"

Croonen spoke up. "OK. Just go down John Street. Turn left on Barton, go over Bay, it's the first one on the right, runs from Barton to Stuart Street at the end there." And the others looked at him slack-jawed, then laughed. "Croonen, how do you know that?"

"Well you know, it's the small streets you'll get pinched on. Not John, Main or Barton. It's the little ones." Once, the call came in for 660 King East. Croonen and the others slid the pole. Croonen turned to one of the other drivers. "Just go Wilson to Wentworth, right up to King, then I think it's the first or second building on your right-hand side."

"How the hell do you know that?"

"'Cause 666 is the Toronto-Dominion Bank on the southwest corner, and right across the street are the little apartment buildings." The other guy shook his head. Croonen was young, and back then probies did not drive. He wasn't pushing for a driving job, he just wanted to be responsible, know his area. But he got so good at it that one day the officer told him: "I want you to drive."

In his early months, just like all the probies, Croonen had his nerve tested by the others. Firefighters tease one another mercilessly. If they find any chink in your armour, they'll dig into you all day. Croonen had an emergency traffic call, a drunk driver had hit a pole on Upper James, his skull crushed, he died instantly. The firefighters loaded the damaged car on a flatbed truck with the body still inside, and took it to a police garage. In the garage, Croonen had to remove the corpse. The victim's fingers still clutched the steering wheel in a death grip. Croonen had to snap them off the wheel. The coroner was there. He said to put the body into a bag. When Croonen pulled the body from the car, pieces of the brain fell out of the skull and onto the floor. Minutes later, the body cleared away, Croonen's captain took him aside, put his arm around him.

"You OK?" the captain asked.

"Yeah, why?" Croonen said.

"That got pretty messy back there."

"I'm fine."

A pat on the back, return to the station. At dinnertime, Croonen cut into a panzerotto at the table. The boys got into it pretty good. They had heard about the incident.

"That about what it looked like, Croonen? About like that?"

"Doesn't bother me, buddy," he said.

Croonen's stomach was in fact churning. But he just smiled. Do not show weakness.

It's just the way firefighters deal with the things they see. You either can make light of it, use a little black humour, or you go crazy. The firefighters used each other that way to air things out. The night after the brain incident, Croonen lay awake in bed, thinking about it. Couldn't help it. Kim knew something was wrong. He told her the story.

A lot of them did not share the stories with their wives. You don't want to put that on their plate. There was nothing worse than being at a social function, the firefighter wives get talking, and before you know it, your wife's saying, "Hey, you never told me about that." But Croonen was an exception. He always leaned on Kim, told her most everything. She could take it. She was the daughter of a firefighter. She could commiserate with him, laugh with him and take the edge off his cynicism. She was the most decent person he ever knew and always looked for the silver lining in everyone.

* * * * *

Firefighters' wives cope with unique challenges in their marriages. Their husbands work shifts, which means they are away at odd hours and off work during odd hours as well. Their husbands sometimes bond more closely with their co-workers than their family, confide in no one but their fellow firefighters. There are websites for wives to communicate with each other. Mostly American, some Canadian content. Much of the talk in the chat rooms reflects the double-edged sword of their lives, a combination of celebration and lament for the chosen occupation of their "DH," which means either darn husband, damn husband or dear husband. They tell of how bummed their DH is when there are no fires to fight, how they hunger for action, about how they are racking up the overtime.

"What can I do? I love him to pieces and he is who he is!" "My DH isn't happy unless he is going Mach 2 with his hair on fire. He is constantly waiting for the 'big one.'" Their husbands are "big kids," they get "hyped when he gets a structure fire call. Gotta love 'em." "This morning my DH said, 'I could really use a fire today. I need something to make me feel like a firefighter again.'"

There is research on the stress facing firefighters at home. Robert Smith, a therapist in Indianapolis, has studied firefighters, and says they tend to cover up emotions, focus on self-control. Others have said that the transition from work to home is not easy. Dickie Sherwood found it difficult to change gears on those days when he personally had a close call, or a front-row seat at a particularly hideous death. It played on his mind quite a bit. He didn't like to talk to his wife, Anna, about it. If she knew what he knew, it would scare her to death. The most information Anna got was when Dickie came home in obvious pain, or sporting a visible burn. One time he came through the door with both hands bandaged. She smacked him on the ear for having put himself in a risky position.

"Don't do that again!" she said.

When Paul Croonen became an officer, the toughest thing for him to do was give up the nozzle to someone else. You want it. You want to find the fire. Sometimes the firefighters would strike a deal: If the hydrant falls on your side of the truck, you take the hydrant, I get the nozzle. Other times it got more competitive, you'd have two or three guys on the end of the nozzle and no one's humping hose. When Croonen was a probie, a senior guy would tell him: "You're new, kid, you can have the nozzle, this time. But after that, you're on your own, fend for yourself." And there were still other veterans who were more than happy to let the eager probie be first in the door.

"Look, Croonen, I've had the nozzle enough. If you want it, you take it."

"OK!" shouted Croonen, his eyes bigger than saucers.

Going from the rah-rah aggressiveness of the firehouse to the home, however, can be a hurdle. Smith points out that, on the job, Dad is in control, all day, everything is by the book, clear lines of authority. And then he gets home and his 11-year-old questions everything he says. There is no more control, and after a day of keeping your emotions turned off, you have to turn that switch back on when you come home. Croonen has a reputation for being "direct" at work. Tell him what needs to be done, he'll do it. But he expects everyone else to react with the same clarity. At home, it was tough to shelve the military regimen. Once, he told his son to do something. His son delayed, wanted to show him something.

"Hey, when I tell you to do something, you do it," barked Dad.

"Paul," interjected Kim, "he just wanted to tell you about his A at school."

"Ah, geez," said Paul, suddenly pained by his knee-jerk behaviour.

There is, also, fear—of injury, or perhaps even death. Kim knew what Paul's job was like, the close calls, the gore. Maybe she knew too much. But she was confident he wouldn't get hurt, knew he would take care of himself, believed in him. On the other hand, she knew that he took risks, it was his nature. On one call, Croonen, on the rescue unit, reported to the police station downtown. There had been a fire reported in a locker room, where there were showers, a sauna. Croonen was there first, with no hose, checking out the locker room. There was a fire in the sauna area, a small one. He heard a hose crew coming up behind him, but Croonen didn't back off. He crouched low beside a glass door, felt it with his hand. The fire was inside, all right. He should have let the nozzle man go first. But he didn't. Don't hesitate.

"It's in here, boys, right there."

Croonen slowly opened the door a crack. It all happened at once. Glass shattered. *Whoosh.* A ball of fire shot out at Croonen like a blowtorch, he felt the flames right on top of him, and in one motion felt a strong hand on his coat yank him away and slide him across the floor on his back. A firefighter behind Croonen had recognized instantly what would happen and had saved him.

"What the hell happened?" yelled Croonen.

The fire in the sauna had been small, but the heat inside the sealed room had been building and building and when the door opened, it created a burst of flame that raced towards the oxygen supply. A small backdraft, what firefighters sometimes call a rollover. A very close call. Croonen had been too aggressive. His face was red from heat burn.

"You should get that checked out at the hospital," said an officer.

"I'm not going to the hospital and sit there all night," said Croonen. "Put a little cream on it at home, I'll be fine."

Another time, there was a warehouse fire on Ferguson Avenue North in the lower city. As the fire burned inside the cavernous old building, Croonen scaled the ladder, an axe and saw in tow. He was on the roof now, and moving towards the middle. They needed to put a hole in the ceiling to release some heat. As others waited to move onto the roof, he chopped a hole, started sawing.

"I'm getting it!" he said, and then he felt one leg plunge through the roof, into the heat below. Then the other. He fell up to his elbows, catching himself.

"Everyone off the roof!" called the platoon chief.

The roof held, he was able to pull himself up and crawl back to the ladder. Croonen had been too eager. He should have taken more time to feel for the hot spots, the spongy places in the roof. He learned that you always walk on the outside parts of the roof, not the middle, where the water and fire have softened the joists. But on the other hand you want to open the hole where there's the most heat, which is usually in the middle. No one said it was easy.

Ferguson North, that was in Croonen's part of town. The North End, where Hamilton's industrial soul was forged, but where beaten-down buildings now stood on dirty, unwanted pieces of toxic land that were charitably called "brownfields." The city wanted to wash its hands of the properties, investors toyed with the notion of buying cheap and rehabilitating the land, but few had the nerve to risk taking responsibility.

One old building in particular stood out as a trouble spot. There had been a series of fires at an old warehouse at Wellington and Simcoe streets, a stone's throw from Hamilton General Hospital. Out of Station 1, Croonen had been to those fires, and so had Dickie. It was the old Usarco scrap metal plant. For sixty years it hummed with production, smelting metals, brass, bronze, aluminum. In 1990, it went into receivership and was no longer operational, but the tattered building remained, free game for vagrants and vandals, a fire waiting to happen. So far the alarms had been manageable at buildings in the area. But it was a part of the city where everyone knew the big one lurked.

*****

An alarm rang just after 6:00 p.m. on June 28, 1993, a hot, sunny early evening. There was a fire in the southeast part of the Usarco building. Out of Station 1 downtown at John and King William streets, Croonen drove Pump 1 to the scene. Dickie was on board. When Croonen parked the pumper, heavy smoke was coming out the roof and windows. One hose line went into the ground floor to attack the fire. It was brutally hot in there, the boys inside were getting it bad. Dickie and an officer went up on the roof to release some heat. Dickie fired up a big power saw, started ripping a large hole in the roof to ventilate. It was a big job. He could hear the beeping on his air tank alarm. He had run out of air. He climbed down to the truck to get a new tank.

The captain did not come down with him. He still had some air left, although not much. He should not have gone off by himself into the building through a rooftop door. But he did. He became disoriented in the smoke, ran out of air inside. He was trapped. Couldn't find a way out. He radioed for help. A firefighter went in for him, found the officer and shared his air mask—a risky move. The heat, the acrid smoke. Now the other firefighter needed help, too.

Dickie went on his own search-and-rescue mission. What was it about Dickie that so frequently put him in harm's way, that pushed him to seek out danger? Where did that come from? His father had been a leading fireman, yes, but Dad was a cool customer on the job, didn't take risks like his son. See Dickie working as a young man back in England, the cries for help coming from a high-rise apartment building. The other firefighters took the stairs, there was too much fire to get in the window. Dickie disagreed. He was up the ladder and in through the window. It was the fastest way. He would not lose the people inside. Dickie and another were able to knock down enough fire with the nozzle to jump in the window—as the fire rolled over their heads like a wave towards the oxygen outside, they hit the deck just in time. Burned his hands pretty good at that one.

Dickie was not brave, he was reckless, some said. A nutbar, even. He heard the name-calling. He paid it no mind. He sized up every fire the way a boxer sizes up an adversary, and if there was an opening, he did not shrink from exploiting it. He would not put others in danger if a building was collapsing around their ears. Sometimes he was just curious, wanted to study fire at work. He was confident in his knowledge of fire, how it worked, when a risk was manageable or not. If others didn't understand that, fine. It would not change how he did business.

Dickie was back up on the roof of the Usarco building looking for the two other men, and then in through a door, into the green-black poisonous smoke and heat that had taken the other two prisoner. He found his way into an office room, barely able to see anything, and there was the captain, who was now unconscious, and the other firefighter, who was without a mask and starting to lose it. Dickie grabbed hold of the unconscious man. You don't think you can move a six-foot, 91-kilogram man, dead weight, until you have to, when the adrenalin takes over. At the same time, with his other hand, Dickie grabbed the other firefighter. *Come on, let's go!* The other man was disoriented, delusional perhaps—the smoke, the heat—he thought Dickie was going the wrong way, taking them into the fire. He thought they should go down a stairwell—right into the blaze. He fought the help. Dickie is screaming at him to come along, as he's dragging the unconscious officer, the other guy is fighting back, there's lots of hitting, kicking, screaming, both of them certain their lives are at risk. And Dickie is now fighting for all their lives, including his own. He won the fight, dragged them both to safety. The two men were rushed to the hospital. They would be OK. He had saved them both.

Outside, Dickie was badly shaken. In a lifetime of close calls, this was the closest he had come to dying on the job. They all had come close. He sat down on the sidewalk, exhausted, the adrenalin rush gone, his body aching from the fight for three lives. He thought the captain might still die. Dickie started crying his eyes out. The damage was about $200,000. The suspicion was that it was arson.

There was another fire in the northern part of the same building less than a month later, in July. And then, in 1994, again in the summertime, there was a fire in the building, on June 25. Croonen and Dickie were at all of them, the fires started to blend together. Through it all, firefighters had risked their lives to save the rest of the building. There had been no lives at risk other than their own. The remaining part of the building could still be used for a new tenant. In 1995, a new company started using the operational part of the building. It was a plastics recycling business.

8

IT'S A BOY

Springtime
Bay of Quinte
The guys trudged down to the dock, where water as smooth as dark velvet was kissing a couple of fourteen-foot aluminum boats they were using. On the dock, Mike (Bronco) Horvath looked down at the old rod and reel Bob Shaw was carrying. All the guys always had the best toys, of course, top-of-the-line fishing gear. Except Bob.

"Bobby, when are you gonna fix that thing?"

Bob smiled. It was the running joke among the boys, especially with guys who had been going on the fishing trips for years, guys like Pepe, Bronco, and Ticker. Every year Shawzie shows up with beat-up equipment. He didn't lose much sleep over it. They started going up to the Bay of Quinte area in 1980, the same year that Bronco joined Pepe and Bob at Station 1 on John Street North. They'd head to places like Picton, 200 kilometres east of Toronto, rent a boat, fish for pickerel, clean and cook the fish themselves. Beers. Poker. Sleep. Stories.

One day, out on the water Bobby was paired with Wayne Stringer. The group had decided to have a contest. Biggest fish wins. Wouldn't you know it, Bobby, with this piece-of-crap rod and reel—hell, the guy even reels in reverse, turns his hand upside-down, God knows why—catches a huge rainbow. No net, nothing, just hauls in this fish on that stick. And he attaches it to a rope off the boat, and Wayne's coming in with him, they're just talking, shootin' the shit, and the rope gets caught on the propeller or something, and they lose the fish. Who would believe his fish story?

"The money fish! The money fish!" shouted Bob. "We have to get it!" Wayne circles around, Bob's able to catch it, a second time. They bring it in and Bobby wins the contest.

Bronco was always the trip organizer, the leader. Made the plans, the calls, got everyone going, collected the money, made the reservations. One year he even gave out fleeces to the boys, with their nicknames embroidered on the sleeve. Pepe Villeneuve was the cook. That was his thing, you don't screw with that. Can put a meal on for two or 200, he'd plan the menu in advance. Even cooked one of those deep-fried turkeys once, delicious. Bob went with the flow. For sure. Get up early to fish, go out at noon, whatever. As long as he got his poker game in at night. Bobby picked his spots, and poker was his thing.

"OK," he piped up each night. "Let's get the cards out."

They'd get playing, and the boys are playing nickel-dime ante, real small change. Then it was Bob's deal, and he would grin. Firefighter Rob Kimbell shook his head. Here we go. Time for the Bobby bump. The stakes were about to rise.

"All right, Bob, what're we playing for?" said Bronco with resignation.

"Dollar ante. Two dollars a bet."

Bob usually won, the games going late into the evening and early morning. A very smart player. The master at protecting his hand, so quiet and understated that you couldn't read his face.

"I tell ya what, Bob," added Bronco. "All I have to play with is forty bucks tonight. Pepe, Kimbell, what cash do you boys have? Why don't we just save time and give you our money now?" Bob laughed.

Later in the night, Bob asked Bronco if he had any beer left. He was out of his favoured Blue Lite.

"Cripes, Bobby, every year it's the same thing. You poaching beers."

"I thought I brought enough but I'm out. Can't understand it."

"Right."

Each trip, the boys would bring a couple of cases of beer each to last them a week or so. And every trip, Bob seemed to run out early. At the end of one trip, the guys were packing their cars. Bob did one last check of his room and under his bed he found an unopened case of Blue Lite. He had forgotten he left it there.

"Ah-ha!" said Bronco. "Look here, Pepe. Lo and behold, Bobby's beer. Now I know your secret, you dirty rotten son of a gun."

"Boys, I had no idea."

Bob sheepishly loaded his new case of Blue Lite into the car as the guys kept riding him. Jacqueline never went on the trips, of course, these were guys-only. But she also didn't socialize much with the other firefighter wives. She was just not much of a joiner. The firefighter culture, the brotherhood, was Bob's alone. Socially, she and Bob often hung out with Jacqueline's sister, Trish, and her husband, Paul, Bob's old friend. Went out for dinner, drove to cottages, road trips to Montreal.

Apart from that, Bob and Jacqueline simply enjoyed each other, just the two of them sitting out in the garden, which Bob kept looking perfect, or going for walks, drives, just talking. She was a good listener, they rehashed their work days. Bob loved Jacqueline, and work, and hanging with the boys. But something was missing. He wanted a child, they both did. It had not happened. Perhaps it never would.

In 1984, Jacqueline became pregnant. She made it to term, spent extra time in the hospital near the end, the baby considered a high-risk pregnancy. The due date? Christmas Day.

When Jacqueline made the final push, Bob was there, of course, bursting with excitement, the greatest moment of his life. He wanted a baby so badly.

"It's a boy," said the doctor. A boy. A son. The firefighter couldn't contain himself, joy surging in his broad chest. There would be no immediate weighing or cleaning of the baby. Protocol was about to be broken. Bob cut the cord, picked up his new son and, as Jacqueline lay there waiting to see her newborn, Bob lifted the pink bundle in the air, grinning his biggest grin, laughing, running around the room like a football player celebrating catching the game-winning pass—running, not walking.

"OK, Bob," said the doctor, trying to talk him down. "Just—just let us have him for a minute and you can have him right back again."

He was named Nathan Mark Shaw, carrying the same middle name as Bob and Bob's father. He was actually delivered on December 20—the same birthday as Bob's father, Harry.

Their boy was born early, appropriately enough, because even into his adult life, Nathan's face would look much younger than his years. In the delivery room, the doctor asked if they could whisk Nathan away just for a couple of minutes. The reason? A woman was dying of cancer in the hospital, she didn't have much time left. Her last request had been that she hold a newborn baby. Bob and Jacqueline agreed. Nathan was that woman's last comfort, she was able to feel life blooming as hers was ending.

Fatherhood was the pinnacle for Bob. Here was his chance to care for his own flesh and blood. He would tell his wife and son for years to come, all the time: Nathan was the best thing ever to happen to him. Bob doted on the boy. When he was old enough to go to school, Bob dropped him off and picked him up every day. Went to all his school functions. Jacqueline was at work, for one thing, and for another, Bob would have insisted he be the one to go anyway. Bob took Nathan to register for swimming lessons.

"So what time is good for your wife?" said the woman taking his registration information.

"Actually, I'll be the one bringing him," Bob said.

On field trips, other school events, Bob was always the lone man among a group of mothers. Bob on the school bus with the mothers and the kids. Bob in the pool for the swimming lessons with the mothers and the kids. He knew it was unusual. He laughed about it. He didn't care in the least. In January 1989, Bob was promoted to lieutenant with the fire department. He had been on the job fourteen years. That spring, the family started taking annual trips to Florida, Disney World, hitting all the rides, Jacqueline holding the plastic bags of gifts and prizes while Bob and Nathan braved the roller coasters.

"Don't worry about me, boys, the bag lady will be here waiting for you."

It was Bob's idea to start the tradition. A couple of Bob's friends thought he was nuts. It's an expensive trip to take every year, and going on all those rides? Jacqueline was no fan of Space Mountain and the Tower of Terror. But Bob thought it was the ultimate place for a kid, their son. So they went. Bob turned 40 that same year. Jacqueline threw him a surprise birthday party. He loved it. Broke out his Roy Orbison records for the occasion. It was a great time, the collection of people from his past and present, firefighters, family. Bob had no problem turning 40, age was irrelevant to him. And he had the body of a solid 25-year-old anyway.

Bob never stopped being a little Mountain boy at heart, and it showed in quirky ways. He never got over his disdain for—socks. Hated wearing them, and so almost never did, no matter what the occasion, or the season. Developed calluses as thick as leather on his heels. Would only grudgingly put on the thinnest pair of dress socks possible at Christmastime for a formal event. In the winter you could see him out shovelling the driveway, dressed in nothing but shorts and a T-shirt, and going barefoot in his Doc Martens.

In 1989, Jacqueline, Nathan and Bob Shaw started travelling to Walt Disney World every year. It was Bob's idea. He thought it was the ultimate place for a kid.

* * * * *

As Nathan got older, into high school in the late 1990s, Bob still embraced firefighting, still spent regular social time with the other guys. But there were fewer and shorter trips for him. He was feeling more pain at work, ever since an incident in 1991. He fell from a ladder, injuring his back, but never saw a doctor for it. Two years later, he fell down stairs at a fire in his full bunker suit and mask, wrenching his lower back. In June 1995, he finally got the back checked out. The back pain would never go away completely. On October 10, 1995, he dragged a hose weighing 45 to 68 kilograms at a fire and hurt it again. Pulling hose was just instinct. Even with the bad back, others knew he could still pull the hose with his upper body strength, and so he did it. He took physiotherapy.

In the spring of 1994, Bob's father, Harry, had died after a short and painful battle with cancer, which had started in the prostate and spread to the brain. Bob had been a rock, being with his dad every moment he could, while also looking after his mother.

His devotion to Nathan, meanwhile, knew no bounds. He quit playing baseball and even his beloved bowling to spend time with his son. The guys admired him for it. Nobody else would give up so much of themselves for a child. But it was what Bob wanted to do, he didn't go halfway on things, and when it came to his family, and his boy, there would be no spreading himself thin. He was in it with both feet. He wanted to do it, wanted to maximize Nathan's range of experiences. By the time he entered university, Nathan had grown into a handsome young man, still had the angelic baby-faced appearance. Maybe that was because he never stopped being his parents' little boy. Bob never stopped figuratively holding his boy over his head, never wanted to let go. And Nathan didn't resist, didn't want him to let go, wanted things to stay the way they had always been.

Bob did not look like the retiring type, but by the spring of 1997, at age 48, thanks to time he put in as a city worker as a young man, he was just four years away from being eligible for retirement. He loved his job, loved the boys, but he was looking forward to retirement. His back continued to give him trouble. It gave way on him at home on August 12, 1996. On November 8, 1996, he hurt it at another fire, and then again on February 14, 1997.

He had big plans for Nathan and Jacqueline after his working days were over. More trips. And Nathan's career, probably in media, was ahead of him, girlfriends, one day a wife, kids. Bob was planning it already, he liked to look forward, organize. He wanted to take it all in, experience everything. Life's too short not to, he said. Some nights, when Nathan was young, if there was a rainstorm outside, Bob and Nathan would watch it from the garage on lawn chairs with the big door up. Other times, when Bob heard a rumble in the distance, to the north, he took his son outside. Just as he had done as a boy, they walked down the street from their home to the Mountain brow. They stood alone on the edge of the escarpment, watched lightning paint the blue-black sky over the lake, lower city, North End; felt the cool breeze kiss their faces and braced for the thunder.

* * * * *

Wednesday,
July 9, 1997

It was just after 7:00 p.m. Clear evening, cloudless blue sky, the sun still bright. The arsonist tried one of the doors to the old warehouse. It opened. In he walked. There was garbage on the concrete floor. Sponges, some paper and barrels of videotape, the black tangled strands from trashed VHS tapes. It was abandoned, all right. Old beat-up place. He poured gasoline on the floor. Just a bit at first. Then more. All over the place. In the barrels, on the floor, the stench strong now, the molecules hanging in the air, mixing with oxygen. In the fire triangle, oxygen and fuel are two of the points. The third is energy, the spark. The arsonist held a single wooden match in his hand. Should he? Did the question even cross his mind?

9

AN ANGRY FLAME

April 1997

Detective Jeff Post considered the question: What is the worst time of the year for arson in Hamilton? Well, the fall and spring are pretty busy. At that time of year, the days are still short, but not so cold any more, plenty of darkness. It offers more cover for arsonists, who like to work alone, in alleys and crevices of the city that rarely see light, away from the attention of others and their own self-examination. Of course, summer gets pretty busy for young fire setters, who have more time and freedom to start something up. Then again, Christmastime can get brisk, you get some fire setters feeling sorry for themselves. OK, so it's a year-round thing. Anyway, Christmas was the time of year when one arson suspect Post had followed would stare into an empty glass at a ramshackle bar downtown. The guy would get loaded, his self-hatred growing numb, then turning again to anger, feeling pissed at his girlfriend and the world, sorry for himself, and left primed to spark something up in a dark alley. Real nice case.

Post had a no-nonsense, everyman way about him. Wore casual clothes to work. Didn't like suits at the best of times, but as it happened, as a practical matter, hanging around arson scenes was no place to wear dress shoes anyway. The first week of April 1997, Post was in a familiar environment, a charred smell in the air, standing among blackened furniture. He was at what was left of the International

Modelling Search Agency on the sixth floor of the Imperial Building at the corner of Main and Hughson streets downtown. A few days before, a Saturday morning, just after 3:30, there was an explosion as the top floor of the building was ripped to pieces and rubble fell across all five lanes of normally bustling Main Street. The firefighters had poured water on the ensuing fire for several hours. The roof partly collapsed on the sixth floor below, trapping burning timber underneath. It took nearly a week for engineers to stabilize the walls so that Post could investigate on the scene.

Hamilton police have long had officers dedicated to pursuing fire setters. After a serious fire, the protocol is that the Office of the Fire Marshal is contacted. An OFM investigator, commonly called a fire marshal, studies the scene to determine how the fire was caused. The fire marshal looks for signs of an accelerant such as gasoline, or remains of matches. A police officer works with the fire marshal. By the book, arson must be considered a possible, if not probable, cause in every fire.

Arson investigations are most difficult when evidence is destroyed in the fire. But in most cases, there is something left, something to examine, test, and observe. Post poked through the wreckage, along with fire marshal Kim Ayotte. It probably wasn't a natural-gas leak—the whole place would have gone up. Any sign of an accelerant? A gas can sat among the rubble. Not typically an item you keep in the office. And in the middle of the floor, in perfect condition, was a pair of size thirteen shoes. The perp had been caught by surprise, probably had not meant to blow the roof off. He douses the place with gas, wants to start a regular fire, perhaps cover up something, destroy some documents. Except the guy's no expert. He lets the gasoline sit too long. Gas sits there long enough, the fumes mix with the oxygen, it starts to build into a ticking time bomb, it enters the explosive range and only needs ignition. Guy lights a match, *boom*. Blew him right out of his shoes. Hightails it down six flights of stairs. Post knew he needed to find the person who belonged to those shoes.

It was a busy time for arson in the city. Arson was blamed for a fire on March 11 at Just Desserts on Main Street West. The very next day an arsonist hit a vacated house on the Beach Strip, Dexter Avenue. A week

AN ANGRY FLAME

The explosion in the Imperial Building on March 29, 1997, sent debris flying onto Main Street East at Hughson. Arson detective Jeff Post investigated.

later, there was a firebombing at an Ottawa Street North building housing a futon shop, restaurant and apartments. Post was on the scene after an arsonist lit eight fires in one hour on a Saturday morning downtown, in a ten-block area bordered by Hess, Cannon, James and Market streets. Then he was assigned to investigate four garbage fires set by another arsonist. On April 6, somebody lit up part of the Burlington Sailing and Boating Club, causing $750,000 damage. The next day, some preteen kids lit a fire in a flophouse on Barton Street in the North End, killing a street man trapped inside. Post was saddened by that case. He oversaw the investigation. A *Crime Stoppers* public tip provided the lead on two kids who did it. They couldn't be charged under the Criminal Code. Too young.

Sometimes Post tried to go after the people who owned derelict buildings that were going up in flames. There was one guy who seemed to have a habit of picking up old places to use as lodging homes for the destitute, bring in people like the mentally challenged, society's throwaways. Bring them in and negotiate their welfare cheques so he gets his rent. But the buildings never met the safety requirements for a lodging home. No fire doors, or anything like that. He was nothing more than a slum landlord, let's face it. So Post and his team put together a package to charge him with negligent arson. It never flew. The Crown attorney felt there was not a high enough probability of conviction. Post lost him. The guy continued to live in the city. Wouldn't have been a big sentence, just a five-year maximum. But he deserved it—he deserved something. The experience illustrated how difficult it is to investigate and prosecute arson.

On the bright side, his most recent high-profile case was cracked. In May he got an arrest in the Imperial Building explosion fire. Police had sent material from the explosion to the Centre of Forensic Sciences in Toronto. A witness said he saw someone staggering from the building soon after the blast. He had suffered burns to his face, hands and feet. The 27-year-old was angry when he found out his former girlfriend was selling the modelling agency in which he had been involved. He stole documents from the office and tried to cover up the theft with a fire. Post got a conviction. On July 5, there was a conviction in the Burlington Sailing Club fire. That was a Halton case, though, not Post's. Turned out that two teens were responsible. One of the boys was the son of a firefighter.

The next weekend, Post started a two-week vacation. Perfect weather for it. Warm and sunny. He worked at home on a new garage he was putting on his house in Mount Hope, just south of the city. In the early evening of Wednesday, July 9, he went to the store. When he returned, he got out of his car and noticed something had fallen on the lawn. Looked like a large piece of ash. What the hell? He glanced up into the clear sky, saw there was one single mass of grey thunderhead cloud that stood out over the city, flat and broad. At least it looked like a thunderhead. Minutes later, Post was in his house watching TV. The news was not good. He knew that when he returned from his holidays he had some busy days ahead of him.

* * * * *

In all his years humping hose, Pepe Villeneuve had only been scared a couple of times on the job, times when he was inside a building and thought to himself, Uh-oh. Not good. One of those was on Wednesday, July 2, 1997. It was a fire that started in an apartment above the Yannis Restaurant on the south side of the downtown GO train terminal. Pepe was up there with Dickie Sherwood, who was on the nozzle. It was already hot outside, 27°C and humid. Inside, it was blazing. They were knocking the fire down pretty good, though.

The heat was incredible. The roof wasn't peaked, it was flat, and made of steel, so they couldn't poke holes in the top to release heat as usual. There was nowhere for the heat to go, it just bounced down again and circulated like in a closed barbecue.

Pepe felt that with the bunker suits, you're so well protected, you can get yourself into trouble. With the old black coats and rubber boots, and no protective head cowl, once you started to burn up, you got out. In the bunker suits, you feel heat, but you can last much longer. But if you wait until you can't stand it any longer, you might have hung on too long.

Pepe was looking for a window to smash. Always did that. He always figured, he didn't care how far it was to jump, if it came down to it, he was bailing. No way he's getting cooked alive. But the windows were tempered glass and couldn't be broken readily. Water dousing the flames turned to steam and superheated the place. He heard crackling behind him, turned around and saw orange flashes through the smoke. The fire was getting in behind them. *Shit*. Pepe shouted at Dickie.

"Behind us!"

Dickie turned around and blasted water at the flames up high, bringing down shards from the ceiling, and part of the water stream hit Pepe, who was standing, though he shouldn't have been in that heat. Pepe's helmet and mask fell off. Dickie grabbed onto Pepe's coat and yanked him to the ground. Bloody hell. Pieces of scorched drywall had fallen on Pepe's neck.

"Hose me down!" Pepe yelled, and Dickie turned the stream on his partner. "I gotta get out of here," he gasped.

They followed the hose line to make their way back out through the smoke, and then, to make matters worse, Pepe grabbed hold of an iron-frame bed with his left gloved hand and it burned right through.

Both of them were overheated, burnt. Dickie burned his ears, but went straight home after the shift, hoping his wife did not notice the red marks and blisters on his skin. Pepe was taken to hospital in an ambulance, paramedics took his blood pressure, treated his neck with ointment. His left hand had second-degree burns. But he would be fine. As usual, even after rest and showers, both could feel the heat lurk inside their skin even as they lay in bed in their homes that night, could still smell the smoke that had burrowed into their pores. That weekend, Pepe headed up north with his wife, Marg, to Wasaga Beach. He had some vacation time coming to him. Dickie continued to work the following week. Up at Wasaga, Pepe kicked back, had some beers. Didn't follow the news.

"Pepe, there was something on the news about a fire in Hamilton."

"Yeah? Hey, I'm on holidays," Pepe said.

"This one's pretty big. Been going more than a day."

"No kidding?" Pepe turned on his TV. Sure enough, there were the boys, right there on TV. Lots of them, too. Was a big one. Pepe instinctively wished he was there, too. Later, when he knew more about it, he thanked God he had not been. As it happened, Pepe's close call had been that fire the week before. But that fire was typical and relatively manageable. Dickie had known they were never in too much danger of burning up. Their injuries were treatable, and the fire made for a pretty good story to tell over coffee. It was over and done with. But this new fire that was all over the news? For most of the guys who were there, the big one would never be a good story to tell. And it would never be done with.

* * * * *

Wednesday,
July 9, 1997

Paul Croonen and Dickie walked up to a house on Ferguson Avenue North. They wore their fatigue uniforms: Dark pants, light-blue short-sleeved shirts. It was just after 7:00 p.m., they had started their evening shift out of Station 1. They had parked their pumper rig and were going door to door doing routine home inspections. Two other firefighters, Jeff Weiler and Paul Ormond, stayed back at the truck while Dickie and Croonen took their turn at the house.

Nice easy way to start their shift. Good community relations, get the firefighters out there in public, knock on some doors, offer tips on fire safety to enhance education. Don't keep cans of paint or gasoline in the house, that kind of thing. The morning that day had broken with fog, clouds, some drizzle. In the late afternoon it cleared. By 7:00 p.m. it was beautiful, the warmest point of the day, twenty degrees, winds light, a bottomless clear blue sky over the North End.

*****

Approximately 7:30 p.m.
Tissshhh.

The arsonist would always remember the sound at that moment, of the lit match, the tiny little mini-explosion of combustion right in his fingers, the flame sizzling. The arsonist held the burning match inside the old building on Wellington Street North. He thought it was vacant, abandoned, but it was not. It was home to a plastics recycling company. The company was called Plastimet.

Did the arsonist pause? Did he stare at the match, smell the gasoline on the floor and in the barrels, the fumes building in the air, and wonder what he was about to unleash? Why was it happening? J-Dog? His past? *Backdraft?* Anger? What was it? Much, much later he thought maybe it was the movie. Just clicked in his head, like a tape going into a player. Made him want to start a fire. Or maybe that wasn't it. One thing he did know: He wanted to see some flames. It did occur to him, fleetingly, that the room he was in was mostly concrete, the floor, the walls. Perhaps the fire would be limited. But apart from that, there was no hesitation. There was going to be a fire, the flames were about to begin. And that prospect felt good.

He made a flicking motion with the match, sending it from his fingers. It flew through the air, landed on the pool of gasoline. A flash and a sound that also stuck in his mind forever, it was like a giant propane barbecue lighting after the gas was left on for a long time—*whoosh*. The flames rose instantly up to the ceiling. He felt a wave of heat smack against his body, he fell over, stood up, shocked at the size of it, and ran, his clothes black. Over the fence. Across the street. Looked back over his shoulder, almost got hit by a car, and saw the smoke starting to blow out the top of the building. He didn't stop running.

* * * * *

The next house was a nice one, well kept. An Italian man let Croonen and Dickie inside. He didn't have a working smoke detector. The firefighters wrote up a form telling him to get one, it's a city bylaw. Sir, early detection is the key to saving your property and maybe even your life in a building fire.

Bee-bop-bee-bop. They had been in the home five minutes when the tones sounded on their radios. There was a call.

"Structure fire. 363 Wellington Street North. 7:42 p.m."

Croonen and Dickie knew the layout of this part of town like their own living rooms. Their stares bored into each other.

"That's right out here," said Croonen.

They ran out the door, looked up in the sky and could see, just down the street, a mass of orange flame angrily shooting out of the roof, hungrily clawing for new oxygen, and a pillar of black smoke pumping into the sky at least a hundred metres high, churning, twisting in circles, like a tornado.

10

THE BIG ONE

Ormond and Weiler were already stepping into their boots at the pumper. "Let's go!" said Dickie as he and Croonen ran for their gear and hopped into Pump 1. "Repeat. 363 Wellington Street North. Structure fire. Building is well-involved."

The firefighters knew where they were headed. It was the old Usarco building, again, the unsightly amalgam of brick, concrete and wood. Croonen and Dickie had been to the building several times but didn't know that the current tenant was a plastics recycler. The northwest and south ends of the building had damage from earlier fires and were mostly unused. It was the building where they had been tested before, where they had pushed it to the limit four years earlier, where three men almost died, where Dickie had saved two colleagues. At that fire, they had seen just smoke coming out of the building on the approach. This time, it was bigger. Much bigger. The central part of the plant had still been operational, processing plastics for recycling. The north section had collapsed walls and roof, it was open-ended. The fire would not be contained for long. Plenty of oxygen. Croonen hit the siren and the gas. He remembered the last fire he was at there, all the smoke hit them downwind on Wellington Street, and it had given him headaches for a month. He turned the rig around. He would pick a corner, set up, and they could hit the open part of the building.

"What the hell are you doing?" shouted Dickie.

"I know what I'm doing."

He pulled down Simcoe Street, parking upwind from the smoke, north of the structure that was raging with fire, and they jumped out of the rig. It was the first truck there. The job of the driver is to stay at the rig, ensure a consistent flow of water to the hose. Inside the building were tall, thick bales of plastic, bales as large as vans. Through the open end they could see the fire inside hopping from bale to bale, flames racing down the concrete side of the building faster than a man can run. If there was any chance to catch the fire early, this was it.

It was now 7:47 p.m. and the fire was burning very hot. Driving along Wellington Street, three lanes over, you could feel the radiant heat on your face coming right through the glass of the window. The initial bee-bops sounding in the fire stations from dispatch signalled a 5-2 alarm. The 5-alarm fire system went back at least to the 1970s. When the bee-bops were short, it meant a relatively routine call, a 5-0 alarm, with one pumper rig needed to respond. A 5-1 alarm would be either a two or three vehicle response, requiring a ladder truck, for example, depending on the situation. A 5-2 alarm was a five-rig structural fire. A 5-3 alarm, with extra long *bee-bops* sounding in the stations, was only initiated by either the platoon chief or the district chief on-scene and meant doubling the response to nine rigs and other support vehicles.

Platoon Chief Jim Warden was at the scene in less than a minute out of Station 1. Before he got out of his truck, he announced that the alarm was upgraded from a 5-2 to a 5-3. That brought in reinforcements from other stations, a command van, other senior officers and support staff. The smoke was racing in a huge, uniform column up into the sky, where a northerly breeze was blowing it over the Mountain. The radios blared with alarm tones and voices from other rigs being called in from other stations, everyone seeing the smoke from a distance.

"I see heavy smoke," said one voice.

"No kidding," retorted Dickie as he yanked hose along the ground. "The whole city can see it."

Mike Horvath was one of the first ones there, too. Fires followed him. The biggest fire the city had ever seen? Bronco would be there. He was captain of Rescue 9 out of the Kenilworth Avenue station. His job was to get to a fire first, be the lifeline for victims who still might have a hope inside a burning building. How many times had he kicked in the door, raced into the smoke and flame to save a life? But there was no one to rescue this time. No door to bust in, no rooms to search. There were men who worked at the plant, but they had escaped in time. And even if they hadn't, the building was fully involved, there would be no charge in the door. He would act as a safety officer instead, monitor the wind shifts, help move water lines and evacuate nearby buildings, like the Ball Packaging Products plant on the other side of Wellington Street. Unlike some of the others, he had never been to the property before. He had lived in the area, though, when he was a kid, at Strachan and James. Funny, he thought, back then they never had many house fires down there, even though it's a rough area of the city.

The fire was so big, the building so unstable, the chances for an offensive, interior attack were bleak from the start. Dickie was not convinced. Damned if he was not going to try to hit it hard and early. He grabbed the biggest hard line available—the biggest hose charged with water, sixty-five millimetres across—and along with Ormond and Weiler, pulled it as they stepped over a mess of rusted wire and broken concrete. They took an axe to the chain-link fence, and were right beside it now, twenty metres from the source, hearts pounding, the flames enormous, a towering wave of heat pushing them back. They didn't wear masks. Didn't need to, the

Jeff Weiler, left, and Paul Ormond were among the first few firefighters on the scene of the Plastimet blaze.

smoke was blasting straight up. Parts of the walls were starting to bow and crumble from the heat. The ceiling, made of metal and timbers, was fast on the road to complete collapse.

They opened up the hose, the best penetration available, blasted the heart of the blaze, soaking, soaking, hit it high, turn the hottest level to steam to collapse down onto the fire—textbook, the way they had always done it. Hit the bastard hard. Knock it down, win the battle and go home. But that wasn't how it was being played out. A new order came through on the radios: "All units, withdraw. Dickie! That's you! Fall back!"

A senior officer was shouting at him to follow the order, as Dickie tried in vain to blast the heart of the fire with an interior attack. He was barely making a dent in the fire, he was pissing into an inferno. It didn't help that the best penetration they had was a "fog nozzle," which blew a wide stream. Some fire departments had direct flow nozzles that let the water bore into the flame better. Hamilton did not. The stream was doing nothing. The bloody monster was toying with them all, laughing at him. Dickie knew the order to go on the defensive made sense. The Plastimet building was a write-off, it was falling apart, almost derelict to begin with. And there was nobody inside to save. Still, as the heat pounded him like a sledgehammer, Dickie did not fall back. He kept on the hose. It wasn't the first time he'd turned a deaf ear to an order to withdraw. He would not endanger his fellow firefighters, but unless the place is falling down around my ears, he thought, I'm going to make sure I've done all I can.

The fire had instantly spread, grown larger and more intense. There were hundreds of tonnes of plastic bales burning inside the building. When the temperature exceeded 507°C, the plastic hit the flashover point—it was all self-igniting. Plastics are composed of long chains of hydrocarbons linked together. When the chemical bonds are ruptured by heat, the plastic will pyrolyze into simpler, more volatile compounds, and those by-products can be highly toxic, and even more flammable. For the firefighters, this was something new. The fire was large and hot, and much of the dilapidated building was in open air. It had an unlimited oxygen supply. The water was just vaporizing in the flames.

* * * * *

"Welcome to Hamilton."

The man wearing the white fire-chief's helmet and clean, new bunker suit had to laugh ruefully when he heard the greeting in passing from Acting Lieutenant Bill Pittman. Wes Shoemaker had been on the job as Hamilton's fire chief all of five days, and was faced with perhaps the worst toxic fire ever in North America. Good thing he had been there long enough to know the colour of the fire rigs, he thought dryly.

When the fire started, Shoemaker, who had just come east from Edmonton, had been out house-shopping with his wife. He was driving in the chief's vehicle on the Mountain towards the lower city when he saw the plume, then heard the radio buzzing with voices and orders. He whisked his wife back to their temporary home—the downtown Sheraton Hotel—and then headed to the scene. He arrived, and the size and heat of the fire, the monstrous plume, hit home. Oh my God, he thought.

The new chief met his senior people who were already on the scene, Deputy Chief Gil Desjarlais and Assistant Deputy Chief Jim Cardwell. From the start there was a sense that this one would not be doused quickly. It was an unusual fire, with the size of it, the huge volume of fuel—the plastic bales—that would not go out easily. The building was beginning to collapse, the rubble would make it harder to get at the fire. Shoemaker started thinking ahead to broader decision-making that he would need to be part of, in addition to fighting the fire itself: Safeguarding other buildings, the safety and health of the community and the environment. His first decision was appointing Desjarlais and Cardwell to be the incident commanders overseeing the fire. They would make the call on tactical decisions for fighting the fire, in consultation with Shoemaker.

The new chief barely knew anyone in the department, had only started a few days before to make his introductions. Unlike seemingly every previous Hamilton fire chief, he was no grizzled veteran of the local fire scene. He was just 36 years old. If the city had followed precedent, Desjarlais probably would have been the chief. He had been with the department for twenty-four years. He had applied for the position.

Tradition, routine, protocol: These are elements deeply ingrained in any fire department. The rumour among the firefighters was that some of the senior people were not pleased that some golden-boy MBA from Edmonton had been parachuted in to run their fire department. Had they not always hired from within? Had they not always hired guys who had fought the local battles?

Shoemaker was no Reg Swanborough, who had been chief in the 1950s and stayed in the office for seventeen years. He was no Len Saltmarsh, the old-school chief who also led the department for seventeen years, retiring in 1989. George Baker had been the most recent long-term chief, from 1989 to 1995. A real hands-on guy, well respected. Garry Smith—Paul Croonen's father-in-law—had been the last chief before he retired, and like those who came before him, Smith had humped hose in Hamilton. Was Gil Desjarlais bitter to be serving under the new guy who hadn't paid his dues in Hamilton? Desjarlais said no, he was not. He had tried his best to be hired, gave it his best shot, it didn't happen. His position was, whoever comes on board from the outside, you support that individual. You have to be professional about these things. You have to support the new chief or else there's chaos.

Shoemaker did not have a conventional fire chief's resumé, but that is what the city at the time was looking for. This was the dawn of government restructuring, municipalities looked for "efficiencies" and "harmonization of services," "doing more with less." And so in the spring of 1997 the city hired Shoemaker, who had been fire chief in Edmonton and overseen the amalgamation of that city's fire and emergency services departments. The expectation was that he'd do the same thing in Hamilton. Before coming to Steeltown, Shoemaker had been the only Canadian invited for a fellowship for senior executives in state and local government at Harvard University's John F. Kennedy School of Government. He was described by the former Edmonton fire chief as "a brilliant young man," a quote that made it into the pages of the *Hamilton Spectator* in a story announcing his arrival. It all gave Shoemaker an aura far removed from that of an in-the-trenches smoke eater. The fact was, though, while he had a strong academic resumé,

Shoemaker's roots were in hands-on firefighting. He started his career as probie firefighter like all the others. Wore the bunker suit, was on the nozzle, knew what it was like to feel fire rolling over your head when you hit the deck inside a burning house.

But Shoemaker was personable and articulate and possessed an analytical mind. He was clearly an ambitious man who wanted to lead. He was perhaps the perfect candidate to transform Hamilton's emergency services. But something more pressing had come up: Plastimet. Some who saw Shoemaker early on at the fire thought he had a deer-in-the-headlights look. He was overwhelmed by it all—but so was everyone. It was the biggest fire in the city's history. Shoemaker did not panic. He organized his men and planned. It was as if someone had drawn up a nightmare emergency scenario: Huge toxic industrial-plastics fire, and in the immediate area there is a harbour in danger from contaminated runoff, plus there is an old residential neighbourhood, a jail on one side of the fire and a hospital on the other—one that has some of the most sensitive cases in southern Ontario, as a regional centre specializing in trauma, neurosurgery and cardiac surgery. You are the brand new chief. Solve the problem.

11

SURROUND AND DROWN

The bloody thing was laughing at them. That's how Dickie Sherwood thought of the fire that was not going out. It was clear, early on, that an offensive strategy was not going to work, at least not the way they were going. Dickie and the others stayed with it, on the attack. But the bales of plastic were like self-mutating monsters of flame, as though perfectly created to beat the firefighters. When each plastic bale caught fire, the separate sheets of plastic melted and fused together to become one hot blob. If the water hit the bale before it fused, the water could get in between the sheets, perhaps put it out. But once the sheets fused, the water would hit one side of a bale, the flames retreated in behind the stack and continued to feed off it. And then you moved the stream, and the entire bale ignited again. Even when a blob of burning plastic was extinguished, the cooled crust of melted plastic would hide heat still lurking inside the bale, which was ready to ignite again.

"Dickie! Withdraw!"

He heard the order once again. This time, finally, Dickie pulled back the hose. The attack was over. The fire was winning. This would be an exterior attack. Surround and drown, they call it. Set up the pumpers around the building, pour and pour, soak it with master streams. They were digging in. At 8:33 p.m., the city's water works confirmed that they had increased water pressure. Dickie, and a few others, made a pitch to take a different approach.

"What about foam?" he said.

One tactic for fighting hazardous-material fires is using foam. Each pumper truck had a five-gallon drum of solution. You attach a conductor to the hose, it forms bubbles and a blanket of foam. The molecules of the foaming agent absorb the air molecules, killing the fire. "Just one can, why not give it a go?" Dickie said to an officer. The answer was no. Dickie shook his head. Why not just try it? You have to get your suggestions by the white hats, the chiefs who were distinguished by their white helmets. You try and put your best case forward. If they go for it, great, if they don't, they don't. Sometimes those in the higher ranks don't want to hear suggestions, he thought.

Upon hearing the advice from his incident commanders, Chief Shoemaker agreed it wasn't a viable option. Could they even get fire apparatus close enough to lay a blanket of foam? And what about the topography of the fuel? With the plastic bales you would need a foam blanket to cover the entire material and smother it, but the bales were too high to accomplish that. And with the roof collapsed, there were too many hot spots that couldn't be hit at all. Plastimet firefighters would talk about the foam option for years to come. Some argued that it might have worked, or it was at least worth trying. Even after the roof collapsed, the foam was designed to seep through the cracks in the structure and get to the hot spots more effectively than water. But there was no time to sit down and have a debate on the subject. The strategy would be water. Surround and drown.

* * * * *

Wes Shoemaker had agreed that a command post must be set up at the scene to co-ordinate the emergency. Bill Pittman, a 38-year-old acting lieutenant, was seconded from his position at the fire to set up the post in a large box-like van on Wellington Street. Make sure it has power, operational communication lines. Just before 9:00 p.m., more than an hour after the fire call, Pittman walked towards the command van in his bunker suit. He happened also to be a member of the department's haz-mat (hazardous materials) team. Like the others, he had felt the burning on his skin from the toxic mist in the air. This was no ordinary fire. But what was burning? He thought the building had been vacant. The fire had not been declared a hazardous-materials fire, which would necessitate fighting it differently, taking special safety precautions. Pittman knew the van had a library inside, manuals. If he could find out what was burning, he could do some quick research on the danger involved. He had heard the firefighters talking, rumours spreading. The bales on fire looked like plastic, but what were the by-products being burned off? Acronyms were being tossed around. PCBs? PVCs? What the hell was it? As Pittman made his way to the van, a firefighter called over to him. The firefighter was standing beside a man with greying hair and glasses.

"Bill," said the firefighter. "This is the owner of the building. He knows what's in there."

Pittman walked over to the man. The fire was still roaring like a volcano right in behind them, smoke pumping and twisting high into a deep blue sky that was lit by the late evening sun. The air reeked of burning plastic, mixed with the smell of old wooden timbers burning in the building and diesel fuel from the rigs. Everywhere you could hear radio chatter, orders shouted, and the constant sound of water blasting from hoses, and the whir of pumps running at high RPMs. Pittman looked through his helmet visor into the face of a man named Jack Lieberman. He

On Wellington Street North at Simcoe Street, firefighters pour water onto the northeast end of the Plastimet building as the fire pumps thick smoke into the sky. To the left is the Ball Packaging plant, which had to be evacuated.

was the operator of Plastimet Inc. Minutes after the fire call went out, the phone had started ringing at Lieberman's home in Westdale, a well-off community bordering the campus of McMaster University in the city. He had just sat down to dinner with his wife, Lynne. There was some bad news. He called the fire department to let them know what was in the building.

"So what's burning in there?" Pittman asked Lieberman. "PCBs?"

"No, no," Lieberman said. "PVC. Polyvinyl chloride."

Lieberman explained that his business recycled plastic car parts. Dashboards, that kind of thing. Shredded plastic. The operation used machines to flatten and bale the plastic. There were also quantities of polyurethane foam. The material inside had been collected, ground up and stacked in large bales, but hundreds of tonnes of it had not been moved anywhere. It hadn't been recycled. Instead it was all just sitting there, most of it in the closed portion of the building, and some outside.

Pittman walked past Lieberman to the command van, climbed inside, took off his helmet. Then he rifled through manuals and textbooks in the mini-library. He learned that PVCs, when burning, give off highly toxic substances: Hydrochloric acid, chlorine, benzene, dioxin, and phosgene. All bad things. And why did phosgene stick out, he wondered? Pittman was a history graduate from McMaster. Had once thought about teaching for a career, but wanted something outdoors, more exciting. Canadian history had been his specialty. Vimy Ridge. The gas attacks. Phosgene was first used by the Germans in the First World War, was considered more lethal than chlorine gas. No, this was no ordinary fire.

* * * * *

It is a curious relationship firefighters have with fire. No one wants fires to happen at all, but they are trained to go where it's hot in a hurry. Everything they do in between fires is biding time until the next call. It is not only a job, but also a calling. They seek the action, hunger to go into battle. Early on at Plastimet, the firefighters had been excited. That first night, in the initial stages, the fire was enormous, hot, a striking visual. So many were involved fighting it. But it wasn't long before it started to sink in: Something dark was happening. There were no doors being kicked in, nobody was being saved. And the fire was not going down.

The television cameras were arriving, North End residents gathered to watch the fireworks. It was a surreal situation. The fire was so big it was being beamed on TV across Canada, coast to coast, the industrial-plastics fire in Hamilton, Ontario, and even carried on CNN in the United States. Firefighters are usually not watched on the job for long. At most fires they arrive quickly, hit the fire, and it's done with. But this was different. It was an event. And that did not sit well with the men.

An order was given that all firefighters should wear their masks and air bottles because of the toxic fumes. Ontario's Ministry of the Environment was notified. The MOE's air monitors were needed on the scene, now, to determine the air quality. Officials from Hamilton General Hospital and the Hamilton-Wentworth Detention Centre, both sitting nearby on Barton Street, huddled to talk about potential dangers. Hospital brass was out on the roof of the General, craning necks to watch the plume churning into the sky above them. Hospital staff engineers monitored the smoke to determine when the building's air-intake valves would be shut. There was no immediate danger to the hospital and its staff and patients as long as the plume kept blowing up and away from the lower city. But if the wind changed, all bets were off.

* * * * *

The firefighters weren't making a dent in the blaze. It was too big, too hot, and the fuel—the plastic bales—seemed limitless. They had to get right on top of the monster. They needed the snorkel. The crew of Dale Burrows, Ed Stanisz, Greg Phillips and David Harbottle had been up at the training tower facility on Stone Church Road. When the 5-3 Plastimet call had first gone out, they knew they'd get the hook, and soon. They suited up and jumped on their rig. The snorkel truck has a hydraulic lift arm, like a hydro truck's but much larger, that elevates two firefighters at a time in a basket-like platform, with a jumbo nozzle attached. Unlike a ladder, which is stationary, the snorkel platform can manoeuvre back and forth at altitude.

The crew's drive down the Mountain was difficult. Traffic was bottlenecked at the brow, with hundreds stopping their cars and getting out to watch from Sam Lawrence Park. The plume was more than thirty storeys high, dwarfing the lower city. People as far away as Guelph, fifty kilometres away, could see it, figured it was a storm cloud.

The snorkel crew heard a platoon chief come on the radio to announce what was burning in the factory. They would need to have their tanks and masks ready. The snorkel truck parked on Wellington Street. Burrows and Phillips were in the basket, lifted up, up and over top, the inferno right under their feet. It was quite a sight, the biggest fire they had ever seen. And very hot. The wind was blowing hard over top of the flames. The fire was so enormous it was creating its own weather system, sucking in air, hungry for oxygen, whipping up a breeze.

Burrows and Phillips felt the wind at their backs, this fresh air whistling past them. It helped keep them cool, because the heat rising from the fire was so intense. They had to stay low in the protected basket. If you put your hand outside the basket, it was like sticking it into an oven. Black smoke was rushing up in a column, drifting towards the Mountain, turning lighter when it cooled up high. But at first, around the basket, the air was remarkably clear because the plume was blasting upwards in such a uniform shaft.

As long as the basket was kept out of the plume, the firefighters didn't need to wear their masks. In the middle of the black smoke column—which was so powerful and thick it was carrying chunks of plastic high into the air and onto the Mountain—they could see orange flashes, tiny fires from gases and particles combusting within the smoke. It was, at first, a spectacular site, an interesting place to be. This is what they were trained for. But over time, it got hairy. Every so often, the wind shifted slightly and the smoke plume would move, and the basket had to moved or else be engulfed by smoke. Phillips got caught during one shift. He heard the beeping sound come from the monitor on his hip. He was out of air, just as the plume blew into the basket. They kept fresh air bottles in the basket, and he struggled to get on a new tank, sucking in the fumes. He nearly retched as his lungs rejected the poisons.

The water pounding on the sizzling bales of plastic from the snorkel and ground hoses, meanwhile, evaporated in the heat and turned to a mist of hydrochloric acid that rained on the firefighters. Burrows and the others could feel burning on their faces. They thought it was airborne embers stinging exposed skin, which would not be unusual. Then they realized that wasn't it.

"Holy smokes," said Burrows. "It's not the embers. It's the acid."

The burning was inside their clothes, too, as the mist—this poisonous fog—percolated through openings in their bunker suits. Burrows' snorkel crew was over top of the fire for 10 hours that night.

* * * * *

The entire area was in chaos. Residents were flocking to the scene, motorists trying to get closer like rubberneckers passing a car accident. Thirty-five police officers were dispatched to the scene for crowd and traffic control. The fire had knocked out hydro, lights were out at several intersections. Police phoned CN Rail to advise they should stop all trains running in the area, because there were tracks just south, west and north of the property—tracks that would soon be under water from the runoff. At 8:33 p.m., Hamilton-Wentworth Detention Centre was advised to close its air intake, and five minutes later, police asked Hamilton General to do the same. Even on the Mountain, Henderson Hospital closed its intake, reflecting the speed and strength of the plume. All the city's hospitals were placed on a Code Orange alert, meaning they should be prepared to receive some of the General's 218 patients on a moment's notice. Joseph Brant Memorial Hospital in Burlington was also on standby. The General had to clear its emergency department to be ready for a possible influx of patients suffering smoke inhalation.

It was crazy just outside the General. Police had the whole area closed off in front—fire trucks, crowd-control barriers, and the fire blazing right next door. None of that stopped one woman from walking through the entire bottleneck in through the doors of the ER—because she had a toothache. Nurse Jo Kolonics was in charge at the emergency department that night. She knew the firefighters had arrived before she saw them. It was that familiar burnt smell—more like hotdogs cooking at a summer barbecue—that, for her, always heralded the arrival of the boys in their bunker suits. Some firefighters began to report to her department because of heat exhaustion, smoke inhalation. Nurses gave them oxygen, tested their blood to make sure their carbon monoxide levels were not too high. They showed up in their full gear, faces dark and wet with soot and sweat. She had seen firefighters in the ER many times, but never so many at one time. But firefighters were always the best patients. No whining. In groups the boys' camaraderie always came through, she thought. Just fix them up, and off they go.

"What's it like out there?" she asked.

"It's a big fire. Lot of smoke."

In the first few hours of the fire, the air wasn't too bad at ground level, not with the smoke shooting high into the sky. But the peculiar chemical odour from the burning PVC plastic was oppressive, it felt like needles poked inside your nose and right down into the back of your throat. Mike Horvath had been to many fires, but this was unusual. He allowed himself to reflect briefly that whatever it was, the fumes would not be the best things for their lungs. The sunset at 9:00 p.m., the black smoke set against a navy sky, while near the ground, the smoke was lit grey by the orange of the angry flame and the flashing lights of the rigs.

12

THE BEAST

At 10:38 p.m., Hamilton Police Superintendent Tom Marlor got on the phone. He requested that an arson investigator respond to the scene. Detective Jeff Post was on vacation, someone else would need to be seconded. The arsonist, meanwhile, was right there, at the fire, watching the action. He had fled as soon as the fire went up in front of his eyes, blackening his clothes, melting his shoes. Had run home to the duplex where he lived a few blocks from Plastimet. Up in his room he could smell the gasoline on his hands and feel his heart pounding. From his window he could see the smoke whirling high into the sky, he thought it looked like a twister. He was frightened. He cried. His emotions were mixed, though. He didn't expect the whole building to go up like that, but he had wanted to light a fire, hadn't he? And it was just so massive. He watched some of the coverage on TV. He had to get closer, had to return.

So here he was, outside, on the perimeter, the smell of the burnt plastic and the charred building ripping through his nose, a stone's throw from the firefighters who were trying to put out what he, the arsonist, had done. That was the kind of fire it was, you could get close. Adults were milling around, kids were running in and out of the smoky mist like it was some kind of game. The arsonist had to see it. *I have to see the beast I created.* A terrible thing. He couldn't take his eyes off it.

Members of the public gather to watch Plastimet burn in the city's North End. One of the spectators who came to watch the fire was the arsonist.

* * * * *

Bill Pittman had finished setting up the command post van. He had to return to his men at the fire. It was just before 10:00 p.m. But before he left the van, he placed the books and articles open to the important spots—information about PVC fires—on the table for the senior officers and chiefs to see. He phoned dispatch. There were CDs on file with more information on PVC and its properties. Could you fax the articles to the command van? Pittman turned to the man running the radio room.

"There will be more information coming on the fax machine," Pittman said. "Put it over with the rest of the information." He returned to the fire. An hour later, he returned to the van. It looked to him as if none of the books had been looked at. Looked to him like the faxes sent by the dispatcher were on the floor with footmarks on them. He couldn't be sure if senior officers were ignoring the information. But that's how it felt, and it bothered him.

Yeah, he was a lowly acting lieutenant. But he was haz-mat trained and he was raising important points. Perhaps his warnings had, in fact, been heeded, because at about 11:00 p.m., firefighters were given a blanket order that they all must wear full bunker gear at all times. It was warm outside, and with the radiant heat from the fire, the men had been taking their bunker coats on and off, dumping heat whenever they could. But now the order said: Bunker gear on, and masks.

Pittman's concerns were not isolated ones. As the fire wore on, doubts started to grow in the minds of the firefighters, decisions were being questioned. Chief Shoemaker knew that morale could become an issue. This was going to be a long fight, it would be frustrating for the firefighters. At most fires, there's no time to mull over strategy and other issues. You do that well after the fire, back at the barn over coffee. But the debate was happening right at the fire scene. Was it being fought the way it should? Why hadn't they tried foam? Should they just be letting the fire burn itself out? Should it have been declared a haz-mat fire in order to widen the area of evacuation and intensify the decontamination measures for firefighters?

The chiefs did not declare it a haz-mat fire. By the book, a fire containing PVC plastic was not listed as a haz-mat situation. But when the material burned, that's when it got hazardous—the by-products created by the fire, and the hydrochloric acid created by the water combining with hydrogen chloride. Maybe Shoemaker wasn't getting the best advice from his senior people? Shoemaker didn't buy any of that. The fire was being fought as it should be. And he felt his incident commanders Gil Desjarlais and Jim Cardwell were professional and did their best. There were no games being played.

Shoemaker called a briefing at the command van at 10:13 p.m. There had been talk about evacuation. Should the entire area be cleared? If the jail was evacuated, should it be done in daylight for security reasons? And what about the hospital? To that point, at least, the weather was co-operating, sending the smoke plume away to the south, over the Mountain. A change in the wind would dramatically change the conditions, but so far they had been lucky.

There were a variety of officials at the scene who could weigh in on the evacuation issue. But the person who became the most visible figure in protecting the health of the North End was Dr. Marilyn James, the region's medical officer of health. James, 48, had been on the job for two years, and in Canada for eight. She had an impressive resumé, was licensed to practice medicine in the United States, Britain and Australia. Her second husband was the CEO of the Royal Ontario Museum. Travelled the world, had a passion for listening to classical music, never watched TV. Born in Australia, she spoke with an accent.

"This is a 5-3 fire," said Shoemaker. "The by-product consists of plastic toxic fumes, dangerous by-products, and dangerous smoke content that is still unknown. There is agreement that more specialized equipment is required to measure the air."

He said the MOE was en route with equipment to check the air quality. He advised that people should keep away from the area and that residents should keep their windows shut. He adjourned the meeting. At that moment, the MOE officer speeding to the scene from Toronto was stopped in a traffic jam on Highway 403. He finally arrived at 10:30 and began testing.

* * * * *

At midnight, Shoemaker held a second briefing. The MOE representative said he could test for only about four chemicals in the air out of a possible three hundred. He'd have results in about twenty minutes. Greenpeace was on the scene, too, warning that dioxin produced by the burning PVC plastic was an immediate danger, and that heavy metals in the runoff water were endangering the water supply because the treatment system was not designed to filter them out.

"This is an environmental disaster of large proportion," said Greenpeace's Matthew Bramley, who was everywhere on television, interviewed live on the local news as well as CTV, CBC, and Toronto's Citytv. Residents in the North End, and on the Mountain, where the smoke was drifting, were worried. The police were taking calls just after midnight from Mountain residents worried about the quality of the air.

On the ground, the fire suppression was still going slowly. The runoff coming back at the firefighters was getting deeper, covering hoses and starting to inch up on the tires of the rigs. At about 1:00 a.m., a veteran firefighter named George Cooke tripped over one of the lines and fell face-first in the runoff, swallowing a mouthful of the toxic soup. The scene had turned into a nightmare.

*****

The police officer stood before the emergency officials at the closed-door meeting.

"The first question is, 'Should we evacuate?'"

That was the way Gary Ostofi began every meeting of the emergency operations group that was gathering regularly to talk strategy. Officials continued to meet from the General, Hamilton-Wentworth Detention Centre, regional health department, MOE, police, fire, and the city. Ostofi was a veteran police officer on secondment to work for the region as its emergency preparedness co-ordinator. The Mississauga train derailment in 1979—when a chlorine gas leak forced 250,000 people to leave their homes—had led to the creation of his position. Municipalities wanted to be ready to manage large-scale emergencies if they happened in their backyard. Ostofi had co-ordinated three other major emergencies over the years: The St. Joseph's Hospital fire in 1980, the Hagersville tire fire south of the city in 1990 and the mercury spill scare in 1993 at the Usarco property—the same place that was now ablaze. The St. Joe's fire had so shaken him up that he had been diagnosed with post-traumatic stress disorder. When Ostofi first saw the Plastimet fire, he likened it to staring into the jaws of hell. His job was to keep officials talking to each other, co-ordinate information between different agencies. He remained at the command post that had been set up near the fire for nearly the entire time. Evacuation wasn't Ostofi's call to make, but he made sure that it remained at the top of the agenda at each meeting.

Early Thursday, well before sunrise, fire, police, health and government officials continued to talk about the air quality. The firefighters were making some headway cooling the fire, but as they did so, it was producing more noxious smoke, which was starting to drift back on top of the scene and the North End. The situation could get much worse.

There was plenty of debate on evacuating the hospital within the General, among senior officials including CEO Scott Rowand. The hospital had set up a command room to plan strategy. Hospital staff inside continued to stay on the job and work, but the mood was anxious, they were only hearing news about the fire in bits and pieces. The air intake had been turned off, but everyone could smell the acrid smoke inside the hospital. And with the air conditioning off, it was getting hot inside, patients were complaining, staffers were getting worried.

Were they in danger? When was the fire going to be out? Word was not getting out to staff as well as it could have about what to expect.

The General had already cancelled all elective surgery and outpatient visits and had moved out any patients who didn't need to be in the building. But a minimum of twenty-five patients remained who were considered too sick to move. Should they try to empty the hospital of those patients as well, along with all staff? That option was being debated. The hospital was put on a Code Green, meaning stand by for evacuation. The most important question was raised: Was moving patients worse than any exposure they might get from Plastimet? Without better data, was a decision to move justified?

"If we don't evacuate ICU patients, they may die," Rowand said bluntly at one meeting. "If we do move them, they will die."

*****

The collective decision so far was not to evacuate, pending further details of what was in the air. Everyone was still waiting for the MOE's best air-testing unit to arrive, the Toxic Atmosphere Mobile Unit. Acting Hamilton Mayor Dave Wilson wanted it there, now. At 1:39 a.m., Wilson asked that a police officer be sent to Ontario MPP Lillian Ross's home to wake her and get the wheels turning faster. Ross then got on the phone to Environment Minister Norm Sterling. Two hours later, the MOE reported that their air-monitoring unit was on its way and should arrive in ninety minutes.

The air was getting worse, for the firefighters and everyone else on the scene. At 3:00 a.m. Police Constable Cathy Summers felt sick from the fumes and was walked to General Hospital to get checked. At the same time, Gary Ostofi, the emergency co-ordinator, also felt sick and was taken to the hospital. At 4:41 a.m., the MOE contacted officials to say they had made a wrong turn and ended up next door in Dundas. They were turning the trailer around and heading to the scene.

At 5:30 a.m., the MOE announced the results of its air tests: The nitrogen oxide level was ten times higher than normal—even on the Mountain. There were high levels of metals such as lead reported in the water runoff. Just before dawn, everyone's worst fears started to come true. The beneficial wind direction started to change. The smoke and toxic mist were blowing back on top of the fire, the emergency personnel and the neighbourhood, and the plume looked even darker.

Plastimet was not the first PVC plastics fire Chief Wes Shoemaker had encountered. In Edmonton, he had been in command for smaller-scale plastics fires. But the weather had not been a factor, it stayed consistent, the plume stayed airborne. Not in Hamilton. The police and fire command vans were moved farther north on Wellington Street, out of the gathering smoke. A police unit was sent to the Beach Strip on Lake Ontario to monitor conditions there as the smoke blew back towards the northeast.

Everyone grew more anxious. Deputy Police Chief Ken Robertson was concerned about the safety of his officers. He asked if air tanks for police should be used, and wondered about evacuating the neighbourhood. At 6:00 a.m., a police officer wrote in his notes that there would be no decision made on evacuation "until Dr. Marilyn James makes her decision." There were sixty officers on standby awaiting that order. Around sunrise Thursday, the twelve-hour night shift came to an end for the fifty or so firefighters that had been the first on the scene. They all went back to their stations, and then home, exhausted, remnants of the fire branded on their bodies and minds.

13

STATE OF EMERGENCY

On Thursday, snorkel crew leader Dale Burrows sat in the bathtub at home trying to scrub the black grime from his skin. Most of it wouldn't come off. And when he drained the tub, a black ring was left that couldn't be removed. In fact, for the snorkel firefighters, a film of black soot on their hands and face would remain for a couple of weeks, rather than wiping off within a couple of days as it usually did.

As Paul Croonen was leaving his post at the scene, the next shift showed up to find his pumper truck—the one that had been first at the scene Wednesday night—standing in water. The runoff was now covering the exhaust pipe. They were pouring 10,000 gallons of water on the fire every minute. The floors of the building were concrete, with no provision for containing water runoff. When the steel roof collapsed, the water pounding on top of it just flowed right back at the firefighters, gathering in the hollow area by the train tracks.

"Hey, thanks for leaving the rig in Croonen Lagoon," cracked one firefighter.

"Any time, boys," Croonen said wearily.

Like many of the others, Croonen had got his feet and legs soaked walking through the hydrochloric acid–laced water. His skin was burning. He changed back at Station 1 and rode his bike to his home in the east end, as he always did, but completely spent. No matter when he got home, no matter what he encountered at work, he was always in the mood to chat a bit with his wife, Kim, catch a little news on TV. Not this time.

"Going to bed," he said. "Don't wake me up."

As his head hit the pillow and he drifted off, Croonen pondered what was to come in his next twelve-hour shift the following evening. There would be overhaul: The process of cleaning up the mess left behind after a fire, when you ensure there is no fire hiding behind walls or among debris. Usually overhaul is done on the same shift the fire is fought, but not with Plastimet. His final thought was that there would be so much debris to clean up, kilometres of hose to wind. Will take forever. Another long shift. But at least there wouldn't be a fire to fight any more. Right?

* * * * *

From an air-quality perspective, Hamilton is not a good location for an industrial city. On occasion, warm air flows off the escarpment, meets cooler air coming off Lake Ontario, forming a lid that traps pollution over the lower city. It is called an inversion. Hamilton's topography, and the wind change, were now sealing the Plastimet smoke in. By Thursday afternoon, the smoke was even worse, blowing back entirely on top of the firefighters and the neighbourhood. By Thursday night, the smoke and toxic fog were so thick that firefighters arriving at the scene held hands walking down the street trying not to lose one another or trip over a hose, followed lines to locate their crews. There was no escaping the smoke now. They were changing their air bottles inside rigs, trying to get out of the smoke.

By 10:25 p.m., the smoke was covering Hamilton-Wentworth Detention Centre and staffers were threatening to walk out. Police officers and MOE officials went to the jail to try to defuse the situation. One inmate was moved out. That night the General and the jail had activated early-stage evacuation plans, but backed off when MOE air tests suggested the contaminants remained within acceptable limits. At the hospital, ER nurse Jo Kolonics was ordered to go home, and stay there until it was over. She was six-months pregnant.

STATE OF EMERGENCY

"A range of chemicals have been identified in the smoke plume," Marilyn James told gathered journalists. But concentrations ranged from "barely detectable to well below threshold" of danger to health.

* * * * *

Bob Shaw had not even heard about Hamilton's biggest fire. He was off, had been with his family. Nathan, 12, was on summer vacation, and the three of them often just hit the road for a day or two. This time they were in Niagara Falls, walking around, had dinner, as usual, at Friday's Restaurant. As the sun started its descent Thursday, Bob drove Jacqueline and Nathan home on the QEW. As they got closer to Hamilton, they could all see the dark smoke against a dark-blue sky. Bob wanted to drive closer, see what was going on, but the streets in the area were closed.

When they arrived home, Bob and Nathan walked from the house down to the Mountain brow. There was a group of people there. In the day's last light they watched the smoke hover over the lower city. Bob was due back at work the next morning. He knew Jacqueline did not want him to go to the big fire. He knew there was no question that he would.

* * * * *

Late Thursday afternoon, Paul Croonen left home to return and work the night shift. When he arrived at the station at 5:30 p.m., his pumper rig wasn't there.

"What the hell is going on?" he said.

The fire was still going. Croonen got into a Suburban with the others and drove back to Plastimet, the entire scene in a fog. When he found the pumper, Croonen was shocked.

"Nothing's moved," he said with resignation. "Everything's exactly where we left it. Oh man. This is unreal."

Croonen knew his rig like no one else. Knew every inch of it. He noticed that cap screws in the cab were rusting, and so was the exhaust.

"Look at this," he said, his eyes bugging out. "The rig's three months old. It's brand new."

Dickie Sherwood was there with Croonen. The fire had long since passed the point of attack that he craved. Surround and drown. The worst bloody kind of fire. You're standing there hour after hour, in the smoke. You always think you're going to win, you're going to beat it, put it out. Not this one. Even for Dickie, it was pretty demoralizing. He watched the water gushing out of the rubble back at them, flowing over the ground towards Simcoe Street. As it passed over rubble and earth that had long since been contaminated by smelters on that site over the decades, you could see the water turn myriad colours. And it smelled, too, like burnt rubber.

The stinking poison in the air was already playing havoc with their health, causing their skin to itch and burn. The water pooled on Simcoe Street ("Lake Simcoe") was up to their thighs. Croonen could feel it burning his crotch. As firefighters felt their skin and throats burn, and saw the fire rigs breaking down before their eyes, it started to get to them mentally. There was too much time to think. Plastimet had become a full-time job. What was going to happen to them?

Something is definitely not right here, Croonen thought. He saw the maintenance-truck guy deliver fresh air cylinders for them to change their tanks—and that guy was wearing a mask, just to drive in and out again. They were eating snacks and drinking bottled water right there, at the scene, fumes in the air, and Croonen was thinking, why are we eating here? And yet, there was no thought of refusing to wade through the water, or of leaving the scene—even though no lives were immediately at risk. Croonen was 33, had been on the job seven years. His officer had maybe a year or two on him, everyone else was junior. They were pretty young. Tell them what to do, they'll do it. It was Croonen's motto, and they all shared it.

* * * * *

Late Thursday night, MOE air tests showed the situation was worsening. Benzene and chlorobenzene levels had risen. The air quality was clearly not going to get better, if anything it would get worse with everything trapped in the lower city, and the air about to get warmer. Three industries along nearby Burlington Street had reported employees becoming sick with headaches and throat and eye irritation.

At a meeting at 3:30 a.m. Friday, fire department officials were repeating their position that an evacuation was needed. To the firefighters, that move was a no-brainer, and long overdue. North End residents were taking it on the chin. The order should have come already. Residents didn't have masks like the firefighters and police officers. What had the health and environment officials been waiting for?

Captain Bob Shaw in his bunker gear at the Plastimet fire.

That morning, Dr. Marilyn James heard the latest information—that there had been a fivefold increase in the benzene levels. Now she was concerned. She had preached caution to that point, saying the levels reported in the air were manageable, not dangerous. But to her mind, that had now changed. She agreed with an evacuation. At another meeting at 4:00 a.m., an evacuation was proposed. It was decided that police would carry it out after 8:00 a.m. when their staff levels would be highest. First, a state of emergency would need to be officially declared.

* * * * *

5:30 a.m.

"Daddy? Daddy?"

Dave Wilson squinted towards the bedroom doorway at his young daughter.

"Yes?"

"There's a police officer here to see you."

The acting mayor rolled out of bed, reached for his housecoat and walked to the door. There was a uniformed police officer in the front hall.

"You need to come with me," intoned the officer.

"Excuse me? I'm not even dressed," said Wilson. "Let me get some pants on, anyway."

The first night of the fire, Wilson had been at his son Ian's soccer game at Churchill Park in Westdale. He had walked across the field to say hi to his son, when he turned around to the east to see what everyone was staring at—the monstrous plume. He noticed a city truck beside the field. He walked over to them.

"Hi, I'm Alderman Dave Wilson," he said, "the acting mayor."

"We know," said one of the city inspectors. "They're looking for you down there."

When Wilson arrived at the scene Wednesday, he met with Chief Shoemaker. Wilson had been on the hiring committee that brought Shoemaker to town, and now the chief had this to deal with, less than a week into the job. Here was Shoemaker, reflected Wilson, wearing this white—virginally white—bunker suit and having to face this. Kind of like going from the minor leagues to the bigs, thought Wilson. Was Shoemaker over his head? Everyone was, Wilson thought. Everyone was overwhelmed.

Mayor Bob Morrow had gone on vacation and left Wilson in charge. Wilson was a bearded, stocky career man with Bell Telephone, worked as a lineman for years. Wilson was also a political animal, glib, quick on his feet. Each alderman had a place in the rotation for taking the mayor's place if he took a vacation. Perhaps, reasoned Wilson, July was a safe time for Morrow to leave, knowing that Wilson, an alderman for six years, would sit in his chair.

After the police officer rousted him, the next thing Wilson knew, the cruiser was screaming through the city, lights and siren going. Wilson felt his sleepy heart leaping, the car must have been going, what, 140 km/hr? At the command centre off Wellington North, Wilson met with the emergency operations group at 6:15 a.m. He declared the fire site an official disaster area at 6:40 a.m. A state of emergency was declared. The city announced a voluntary evacuation.

"It is with the assistance and advice of the emergency operations group that I have come to the decision that we do have to declare a state of emergency at this point in time," he told a news conference.

The evacuation covered eleven blocks: 650 residents and 35 businesses. It began at 10:30 a.m., as police officers went door to door, wearing light-blue summer police shirts, as well as air-filter masks, urging people to leave. Three families refused to budge. The hospital was not to be evacuated, and by noon Friday, it had been decided that the jail would not be evacuated, either. At a meeting Friday evening at 8:00, Dr. Marilyn James was considering expanding the evacuation area.

* * * * *

The media had been all over the Plastimet story from the start. It was precisely the story that Hamilton's image did not need. Friday's evacuation order gave the story new life. It was in all the Toronto newspapers and national TV broadcasts. Greenpeace's Matthew Bramley was popping up on every newscast, the fire scene in the background, talking about dangers from dioxin in the air. The story had everything. It was just what the doctor ordered for the much imitated, flashy, *live! everywhere*! style of Toronto's Citytv, which was, of course, on the scene. Their Friday dinner-hour news coverage led with the Plastimet evacuation story.

Six o'clock: See Citytv anchor Anne Mroczkowski in studio, live, standing. Never sit, this is news. Live! Now! She's framed from the waist up in a collarless, form-fitting, black jacket with a deep scoop neck, arms at her side, breasts pressing against the sateen finish, then *zoom*! In half a second the lens is in closer and higher, her face filling the screen. Her head and shoulders are back, shoulder-length blonde hair, red lips and rouged cheeks: The pose, the look of authority, no clipboard or notes, and:

"Good evening. A state of emergency tonight in Hamilton where a voluntary evacuation is under way after that huge plastics fire. Live to Kevin Frankish for the latest."

The entire intro takes five seconds. And now here is Kevin, live!, his trademark light-blue, pin-striped dress shirt with white collar, dark tie, dark suspenders, no watch, sleeves rolled up—we're-getting-down-to-business-in-the-trenches—and holding a reporter's notebook. He is on the Mountain brow, the fire behind him in the background. The time flashes on the bottom right corner of the screen. 6:00:05, :06, :07.

"Anne, believe it or not, 46 hours and still counting, smoke as you can see, still being belched out of that recycling plant that went up in flames on Wednesday. The weather has now trapped that smoke"—hand gesture over the skyline—"into north Hamilton, as a result, prompting the evacuation of an"—lowers voice—"entire neighbourhood."

Now to taped footage: Cut to Dave Wilson declaring the state of emergency, and then to police officers wearing air-filter masks knocking on doors. Cut to Marilyn James addressing media: "The fire is still burning, putting out copious amounts of smoke and fumes, despite all the efforts to date, and clearly conditions will change over the day and we may be chasing a moving target at ground level."

Visual: A woman leaves her home, holding her cat. Kevin is with her, wearing a surgical-style mask tied around his neck, but not covering his mouth.

"So you're getting outta here," says Kevin.

"Getting out of here," she says.

"Don't know if your cat's too happy about it."

"Cat's been scared all day, he knows something's going on."

Kevin to another man at his door: "Are you scared?"

"Yeah. For the children."

Visual: Woman being loaded into ambulance on stretcher, with oxygen mask on. Visual: Vans taking away "some of the real bad boys" from Hamilton-Wentworth Detention Centre, says Kevin. And now see him on camera wearing his surgical mask over his mouth, and also sunglasses while in the shade of trees in a parkette near the fire scene, his sleeves still neatly rolled up. He crouches down like a baseball catcher and stares into the lens, then lights a match and starts burning a small piece of garbage on the sidewalk. This material, he tells us, is ground-up dashboard plastic. Camera zooms on the burning flame.

"As it burns it is sending dioxins and furans into the atmosphere. And now firefighters add water"—Kevin pours water from a plastic bottle onto the little flame—"and voila, all of a sudden you get hydrochloric acid."

Cut to Matthew Bramley: "This should be treated as a serious chemical accident because we're not burning wood here, we're burning synthetic chemicals and plastics, and it has to be treated in a different way from an ordinary fire."

Big finish: Back to Kevin, live!, again on the Mountain brow. 6:02:29 p.m. Sleeves still rolled, he stares directly into sunlight, but is no longer wearing sunglasses.

"In order to better orient you, I'm going to take over the camera work, I hope our cameraman doesn't mind," and now Kevin takes the camera in his own hands—and this could have been done earlier, off camera, the picture is herky-jerky, jarring, as he takes the helm, and this is live!, great stuff, Kevin doing it all. He points with his finger to the evacuation area in the North End. He dutifully returns the camera—perhaps the cameraman can handle it from here—and looks into it again for his finish.

"Now, if you are trying to get in touch with a loved one in the evacuation zone, the Red Cross will try and do it for you. Call their hotline. That's it"—drops voice again—"live from Hamilton. Back to the newsroom." 6:03:10.

Back to Anne Mroczkowski, shot from just above the knees up, in the long, black, form-fitting, scoop-neck outfit, a red background and a banner that says Toronto Everywhere. She has a pen in one hand, she is walking right towards the camera, movement, right into your living room.

"All right, Kevin. Thank you."

* * * * *

While Jacqueline was at work on the Mountain Friday morning, she didn't want to think about it. Didn't want to think about whether Bob was at Plastimet. The thing about Bob's job had always been that, while she knew there would be risks at times, she didn't need to dwell on it.

An aerial view of the Plastimet fire from southeast of the site. On the right is the Ball Packaging Products plant; at the top of the photo is Simcoe Street East, part of it underwater. Some of the firefighters dubbed the street "Lake Simcoe."

When Bob came home, he talked little about his work. There were times she learned more about a fire he had been at while at a party, when other wives were talking, than she learned from Bob. Every so often, one of the women Jacqueline worked with asked if she ever felt fear for Bob. The truth was—on the surface, anyway—she did not. She knew he was an excellent firefighter, did not take unnecessary risks. He was in top shape.

But Friday morning, the women were all talking about Plastimet. It was still going, a day and a half after it had started. Jacqueline said nothing. She phoned Bob's station. Maybe he was there, maybe their crew had not been called. The fire was being put out, wasn't it? There was no answer at the station. She knew what that meant. He was on a call. And she was pretty sure what that meant.

"Jacqueline, is Bob at the fire?" asked one of the women.

"Yes."

Just after 7:00 a.m., Lieutenant Bob had reported to work at Station 1 downtown. He put on his bunker suit, boots. But there would be no ride to the fire on a rig, sirens blaring. All the rigs were already at

Plastimet. So he hopped into a yellow fire department SUV that took him and others down to find their rig, Pump 12. He sat next to Matt Madjeruh, a 32-year-old firefighter with dark hair, a broad, gym-forged physique, Popeye forearms. The two of them sometimes crossed paths in the gym, where they both worked out regularly. Bob was 16 years older, but Madjeruh marvelled at his lieutenant's fitness. He rode the bike like crazy, worked out hard. Madjeruh had been at the fire the day before as well, had seen the rigs parked in runoff water. They didn't say much driving down to the site.

"Wonder where the rig is," Bob said.

"I know exactly where we're going," said Madjeruh ruefully.

The SUV parked. It was 7:30. The whole area was a scene out of Dickensian London. You couldn't see more than a metre, because of the inversion layer. Bob couldn't believe the scene. He looked at Madjeruh.

"Let's go."

They walked through the mist and smoke to Pump 12 at the corner of Wellington and Simcoe streets. The visibility was maybe two or three metres. Bob's crew was to operate the pumper and a ladder truck as well. They walked past the rig through knee-deep water. It was as bad as Bob had heard. Worse, probably. Wednesday night had been the most spectacular stage of the blaze, but it was also the safest time to be down there on the ground, because the plume blasted straight up and drifted away. The heat inversion Thursday changed everything, trapping the smoke at ground level. And now, on Friday, the air remained nasty, it instantly burned eyes and throats.

The main blaze had been knocked down, but firefighters continued to pour water on the smouldering rubble, to extinguish bales that stubbornly refused to go out or were reigniting, still spewing poisons into the air. Bob and his crew were to extinguish spot fires that continued to flare. The air was toxic and hot. They had been ordered to keep their bunker gear on as protection, which generated even more heat, suffocating their skin, sweat pouring down their backs.

Bob and Madjeruh checked hose lines, moved them around, hit hot spots. Madjeruh was a gung-ho firefighter, on the job since he was 25. Enjoyed the action, working with the boys, they were all good guys. The camaraderie—it was like being on a hockey team. But Plastimet was not action. It was not fun standing around or moving lines through the water, in the smoke, no end in sight.

"This is brutal," he said.

Bob nodded. "Can think of a few places I'd rather be," he said.

Bob didn't say much else. That wasn't his style, even in a hellish situation like this. Do the job. The assignment was nasty, probably not even productive. But the firefighters kept showing up, kept working. Even under orders to use air masks at all times, most of the firefighters wore them sporadically. The masks were hot, they dug into your face. They were used to wearing masks for quick bursts at most fires, not for entire shifts. And even those firefighters who always kept a mask on inhaled their share of the smoke. Each firefighter had a thirty-minute tank. But when the smoke was heavy at ground level, it could take fifteen minutes just to move into position, and that long to move back out.

Tanks got used quickly, and they were frequently changed in the smoke. When the wind changed direction and blew the smoke away, Bob and Matt removed their masks, could talk a bit. Then the wind changed again, brought back the smoke, the masks were back on. There were a couple of chances to grab a sandwich and water. They took off their masks to eat, drink bottled water provided by the Salvation Army. Sometimes the air was bad when they did. Was it the best thing to do? No. Consequences? You do what you do. Can't worry about it.

The fire department called in twenty off-duty firefighters to help out that day. Bob Shaw's crew worked until 2:00 p.m. before being reassigned. Bob arrived home at the end of the day. He was utterly exhausted, the toll from sweating in the heavy bunker suit for seven hours, but more than that, he was drained from something else that was going on inside him. Jacqueline saw it in his face. His eyes were dark, there were rings showing stress and fatigue. His eyes stung, his nose and throat burned. Mentally, he was shaken. He was not himself.

For once, Bob could not stop talking about the fire. His words spilled out in excited, fearful tones. Jacqueline wasn't even asking him about it, he was just talking. He was disturbed, worried. Not like him at all.

"Jac, it's awful, the mess, you wouldn't believe it, never seen anything like it. I mean the water is up to our knees, and then the wind, it changed direction—I guess it hadn't been too bad last night, but the wind changed and the smoke came right down on top of us, you couldn't see a thing in the whole area. They're going to have to move the command van because now it's right there in the soup."

Bob kept coughing. Not unusual for a firefighter to cough after a long day at a fire. Except that Bob almost never did.

"Bob, don't go back," she said. "You don't need to."

"The worst part, you know, the rig, the stainless steel on the truck? It's corroding, it's wearing down, on the spot. That's not normal smoke up there. It's a plastics plant, they still don't know what kind of chemicals are in the air."

"Bob, please."

"It's OK, Jac. It's my last shift tomorrow."

Bob went to bed. Jacqueline turned on the news. The fire was all over it. The evacuation, the toxic smoke, Greenpeace on the scene warning about dioxin. She turned the TV off. She couldn't take it, she didn't want to know.

14

FEAR AND PAIN

Morale among the firefighters was not good. They were doing as they were told, setting up apparatus, moving hose lines, hitting hot spots. But the conditions were taking their toll, and so was the workload. Every so often, a firefighter would leave his post by the stationary hoses, pick up a hand line, drag it up and try to extinguish a bale by himself. Dickie tried it, so did some of the others. They might even put out a bale, feel some accomplishment. Then move on to the next bale, look over their shoulder, and see that the first bale had caught fire again.

Firefighters like starting a job and finishing a job. But there was no end in sight with Plastimet. Sure, they were getting some relief, being sent off site for an hour to get a break at a fire station. But that meant going out to regular medical calls, and backlogged calls caused by Plastimet, as their "break." Don Angle, who drove Ladder 7 to the fire, got called while on break to a playground fire on the Mountain. Some kids lit a plastic play apparatus. Angle had to chuckle at the whole thing. He was now on break from Plastimet and he was putting out a fire of burning plastic. Mini-Plastimet. Perfect!

Angle didn't like how the big fire was being fought, either. Thought they should have explored the foam approach. Why not see if they could bring foam trucks from the airport? Seemed to him like the chiefs were fighting the fire on the cheap. On the other hand, the chiefs had never seen anything like this before. He had sympathy for their position. You could hardly blame them for not knowing how to handle it.

Late Friday night, area hospitals reported an increase in admissions of people with respiratory problems, including at least eight firefighters. Some were experiencing nausea, burning, headaches. Dale Burrows' snorkel crew was back at the fire. Four hours into their night shift, at 11:00 p.m., Burrows, Ed Stanisz and Greg Phillips all felt sick. Wicked headaches, dizziness, nausea, burning skin.

"We're not doing well, Jim," Burrows said to Platoon Chief Jim Warden.

Warden said they should get to the hospital. Medical staff was expecting them at the ER. The firefighters took off their clothes to reveal open sores the size of nickels on their necks, faces, hands, but mostly on their legs and feet, from the water that had soaked into their boots.

"What have you guys been exposed to?" asked a doctor.

The crew was hosed down, their contaminated clothes taken away. They were dressed in hospital greens and released around 2:30 a.m. They returned to the fire hall, showered again, went home when their night shift ended a few hours later. Don Angle was also on the night shift. By 5:00 a.m. Saturday, he couldn't take it any longer. His night shift would be over in two hours. His skin was burning, it felt like bacon grease constantly splashing on his skin. His eyes were stinging. He wanted to get some treatment before he went home. He turned to an officer at the scene.

"I gotta get to the hospital," he said.

"We don't want to send anyone over there right now," said the officer. "They're overwhelmed with fire people, can't take any more."

Angle was a twenty-year veteran, a lean firefighter with a thick moustache whose nickname was Big Red, from the old *Red Fisher* TV show. He was devoted to his job, but was also a plain-spoken guy who didn't take crap.

"Well, I'm going. I'm either driving or walking, but I'm going."

The officer drove him to the General. The nurses in the ER welcomed him in right away. Angle went into a shower room, stripped, someone hosed him down and scrubbed his skin with a brush on a stick, special soap. Put him in scrubs and sent him back to his station, then home. Angle was bitter. Felt to him like he was being discouraged from leaving his post, seeking medical attention. What's going on? Was it just an old-school, suck-it-up mentality?

When he got home, he changed, didn't tell his wife a whole lot about his night. She didn't need to know, he thought. Yeah, it's not too bad down there, I'm kind of off to the side from the main action, he told her. Don't worry. But Angle knew it was nasty stuff they were working in. Who knows what it might do to you, long term? Can't be good, that's for sure, he thought. But, he reflected, when your number's up, your number's up.

*****

Bob Shaw was back at the fire at 8:00 a.m. Saturday. The morning broke sunny and hot, it was 23 degrees by 9:00 a.m. It was suffocating under the heavy bunker suit, sweat immediately started crawling down his back like insects. About twenty firefighters had booked off sick after the first two nights at Plastimet. By 10:00 a.m., the main fire was officially declared out. But spot fires continued, and not just minor sparks, either, but big fires in the rubble where firefighters had to wade in with hand lines.

The voluntary evacuation order was lifted that morning, and hundreds of people returned to their homes. By the fourth day, the fire department had brought in heavy machinery, backhoes, tractors, and dump trucks to separate the smouldering piles and extinguish each separately. Stelco allowed the department to use two of its front-end loaders that could withstand intense heat. It was a lesson learned at the Hagersville tire fire. Rather than trying to put it all out at once, it's better to separate and fight several smaller fires. Some firefighters felt this was a step that should have been taken earlier.

Bob thought the air seemed slightly better than the day before, at least to the naked eye. But the building and plastic bales still smouldered, toxic smoke rising evenly and steadily from the rubble as if from dry ice, colouring the air like a dream. In some ways, this was the type of atmosphere that was most dangerous for firefighters. When a building fire is put out, the "overhaul" process begins. Firefighters rip down walls, toss out furniture, appliances, ensure there are no other fires hiding. It is often the time firefighters let down their guard, toss aside their air masks, because there is little or no smoke visible in the air. But it is during overhaul that the fumes still lurk. Some of the firefighters continued to wear masks. Some did not, including some white hats, the chiefs. Most of them picked their spots. They had air tanks strapped to their backs, but masks dangled uselessly to the side. They were, after all, outdoors. The air, free of the pollution-socked inversion, did not look as dangerous any more.

Yellow fire-scene tape surrounded the scene, what was left of the black and dirty copper-coloured walls, mounds of twisted, scorched metal and concrete. Outside the tape, kids continued to run and play in the green grass, lawn chairs were still up for residents to watch. Little girls in pink and blue tank tops, boys in ball caps. Some of the kids wore surgical-style masks.

Bob and his men were still trudging through the poisonous water that was knee-deep in spots. The runoff continued to pour through the foundation, back at them over top of their boots, rivers of the stuff, making small waterfalls off the concrete and wire, and drywall and plastic, then changing colours, a mix of grey, brown and green as it ran over the toxic soil. Bob was shaken by the experience, thinking too much. He had time to notice things. His eye caught the pumper and aerial trucks. The chrome was pitted with acid, the rigs covered in a black-green goo. Even the shiny silver firefighter badges on formal caps had turned green. Every time he swallowed, it hurt, he could barely manage it. He was worried. Eight hours later, at 4:00 p.m., Bob was off the job. He showered at the station and went home.

* * * * *

In the end, 264 of Hamilton's 400 firefighters played at least some role at the scene. Nearly 99 million litres of water was poured on the fire. More than 400 tonnes of plastic burned. It would go down as a fire that

FEAR AND PAIN

By the fourth day at Plastimet, the fire department was using power shovels and other heavy equipment to separate smouldering piles and extinguish them separately.

burned four days, although it would burn in spots for three weeks. Vacationing mayor Bob Morrow flew into Hamilton for the weekend to visit the site, and chat with building and fire officials.

Saturday night, Paul Croonen reported to his station for his night shift, still tired, and hurting. The word was, they wouldn't be going back to Plastimet. Relief. His squad had got it in the face Wednesday night, Thursday night and Friday night. Platoon Chief Jim Warden, whom all the guys respected, a real people-person, asked if they had any physical ailments. Croonen, Dickie, and several others had the same symptoms. Nasty rash, bloodshot eyes, wicked headaches. They were tired and sore. Croonen, for all his rah-rah attitude, his sir-yes-sir instinct, was upset. He was broken down, and had rashes on his feet and legs and even his scrotum. Skin on his toes was peeling.

"You guys go to the hospital," said Warden. "Get it checked out."

A doctor at Hamilton General took Croonen, Dickie and a few others into a private room at about 8:00 p.m. They were asked to strip down to their underwear for a brief physical, do respiratory tests, give blood samples. The doctor examined their peeling feet, the rash.

Matt Madjeruh moves a hose in the heat and toxic smoke at Plastimet, where he worked alongside Bob Shaw.

"It goes all the way up to the crotch, Doc," added Croonen. He looked at the doctor. "What is it?"

"Well, you've been exposed to a chemical," said the doctor in a matter-of-fact tone. The rashes and headaches are basically a chemical reaction, that's all it is."

"But what does that mean?" asked Croonen. "Are we OK?"

"Well, time will tell. I can't tell you what will happen, I don't even know what these chemicals were. It was probably a corrosive agent of some sort. Let's get the blood work done and see what it turns up."

"OK," said Croonen.

A training officer entered the room. He said that a platoon officer had ordered Croonen to return to Plastimet.

"All of us?"

"No, just you."

The rescue unit was doing work at the smouldering remains with a thermal energy camera, trying to find more hot spots as they dug and separated the wreckage with backhoes. Croonen, for once, hesitated upon hearing an order. One, he was getting checked out at the hospital, two, using the thermal camera did not make any sense.

"It's plastic, you won't see anything through a thermal camera," Croonen said.

"I'm just doing what I'm told, and I was told to pick you up."

Croonen was tired and angry, not normally one to complain.

"Come on," he protested, "I'm getting checked out in the hospital."

"I'm not pleased about it, either. But you have to go down."

"Fine."

Croonen arrived to find a senior officer walking around the site with no mask on. There's smouldering piles everywhere, the stench was still strong, and it just about made Croonen vomit.

"Croonen, we need you to go in there with the camera," said the officer.

"Just a sec. Have to put my mask on first."

"What?" said the officer.

"I have to put my mask on, I have headaches, this stuff is making me sick," said Croonen.

"OK, fine."

Croonen argued that they didn't need him there. Another officer intervened to argue with the one who was giving orders. They butted heads. And the second officer took Croonen away. The next night, Sunday, Croonen was back at the station. He was supposed to be off, but was working a "trade." He had no energy left, but felt he had to go in. He still could not shake the ghost of Plastimet. He looked at his assignment card. It said he was on the next pumper, Pump 12.

"Can you just put me on the ladder? I'm working a trade and just had four nights at Plastimet."

The officer told Croonen that what was needed was a thorough cleaning and decontamination of the Pump 12 rig, wash the exterior and interior, it was covered in toxic filth. None of the other guys were assigned to that duty. Why Croonen?

"You've already been down there," the officer told Croonen, and one of the other Plastimet firefighters assigned to the task. The rest of them hadn't. So Croonen was the logical choice. He was already screwed.

"Gee, thanks, guys," said Croonen.

He loved his job, but this was not what it was all about. This fire had been botched. The firefighters were hurting, he was hurting. The fire was dividing the team.

"You also have to go to Station 11, too, because it hasn't been decontaminated either. You can help them out."

Croonen was pissed off, but he was also always among the first to tell the others: Suck it up and do the job, boys. So he followed the code, did the work, then had a shower, his skin itching everywhere, feeling tightness in his chest. His shift got a call that night, and then another— to a spot fire at Plastimet. Got there, needed to hump ninety metres of line out there to the spot, wet it down. The hose had been dragged through contaminated water and debris. An order was given to roll it up, loaded it on a supply truck for decontamination. And the officer ordered all their bunker gear into the supply truck as well. Croonen was shocked. These firefighters, new to the scene, were treating the site—after the fire was out—like it was laced with nuclear waste. So what was to become of the firefighters then? His fear level rose right at that moment. So *now* they're taking care around everything to do with Plastimet, now that the grunts have bathed in the poison for four days.

15

ANGER AND TEARS

For some, the Plastimet fear had dramatic, lasting effects on their mental health. Firefighter George Cooke, who had landed face-first in the runoff, was haunted by Plastimet in his dreams. He had sucked in a lot of smoke over his career. But this was different, all that plastic, the hydrochloric acid, the dioxin. Everyone was talking about it. Cooke had actually swallowed that noxious, multicoloured water, sucked some into his nose, it seeped into his ears. He hadn't thought much of it at the time, but then he started hearing how dangerous that water might be, and it tore him up inside. He wondered about the future, his wife, and their life together. He had nightmares where he saw cancerous lumps growing on his skin. At first Cooke didn't say much about it, didn't want to come off like a sissy. But he was only human, whatever the macho image of the firefighters. He had shortness of breath he never had before.

The checkups showed nothing, but when he biked or went for a fast walk, he was gasping for breath. What had happened to him? Was he destined to die an early painful death from his exposure to the Plastimet fire? Had the city's worst fire consigned him to a life sentence? He had seen death on the job over his twenty-seven years as a firefighter. Was he now looking at his own death? Am I, he wondered, a walking corpse? Cooke had been one of the guys the young firefighters went to after a fire for wisdom, for stress relief. He joked around, a senior guy. But Plastimet had changed him, maybe forever. He never returned to work.

A survey done after the fire showed that 86 percent of all firefighters who were at the scene reported some health effects. The majority reported throat and eye irritation, headaches, and coughs that lasted several days, in some cases up to two weeks. Many also complained of burning nasal cavities, stinging skin. Other symptoms differed from person to person, but included skin rash, speaking discomfort, stomach aches, chest tightness, odd taste in the mouth, runny and plugged noses, diarrhea, phlegm, itching, shortness of breath, wheezing, nausea, peeling skin, tingling hands, arms and feet, fever, and vomiting.

More than twenty-five firefighters lost time from work because of their symptoms, more than a hundred and sixty sought medical attention for their ailments. The toll on equipment at the scene scared them as much as anything. Their equipment is supposed to be their weapon against fire. But rigs that had been at the fire fell apart. A chunk of a radiator fell out of one of the pumpers. They had to sandblast the trucks. The seemingly indestructible bunker suits, made to withstand fire, dried up like paper, ripped and had to be thrown away, a highly unusual procedure.

The fear, the sickness, it meant that Plastimet became in some ways a revolutionary event for the department. In the paramilitary culture, Plastimet galvanized political action. Many of the firefighters felt mistakes had been made, their health had not been properly protected.

It turned firefighter Colin Grieve into the department's new compensation claims representative—and later he became one of the highest-profile firefighters in that position in Canada. Grieve had been at the fire the first two nights, came down with breathing problems, tightness in the chest, rashes on his feet. He was already a cautious person, health-conscious. The union asked if he wanted to take over the claims position. He submitted a claim for compensation for his days missed because of Plastimet, and won. Then he began a never-ending campaign to advocate for all of the Plastimet firefighters filing claims.

* * * * *

For residents who lived in the North End, fears about the after-effects of the Plastimet fire continued for days, months, and years. Was their long-term health at risk? They had to scrub black soot off their garden furniture. And what about their kids? All this talk of firefighters and police officers getting sick—and they had air masks. Residents did not.

Gary Ostofi, the police officer who had co-ordinated the Plastimet emergency group, had pushed to have a community information centre set up in the neighbourhood after the fire. Have a storefront, or a trailer, something, anything, where residents could drop in and vent, ask questions. But that didn't happen. It was a big mistake, he felt. Communication was poor. Residents stewed, foremost among them, a woman named Ann Gallagher. The night the fire started, she had been in the CIBC office tower downtown where she worked as a legal clerk part-time. Her husband, Clive Jones, had called her about a fire on the Plastimet property. It didn't strike her as that unusual. There were always fires in that building. But then she heard it was big, and she went to an office window to have a look. Like the rest of the city, she could see the plume. Her parents, who lived in Grimsby, told her that they could see the smoke as well.

Gallagher came home later that night to her husband and their children, who were 2 and 4 years old. The next afternoon, Thursday, day two of the fire, her son was having his nap. When she looked out the window, there was so much smoke in the backyard, you couldn't see six metres. Gallagher had shut all the windows of her house, they had no air conditioning, and it felt like thirty degrees outside. It was stifling in the house. She was upset. She phoned her husband at work and told him enough was enough. She packed up all she could, all the kids' things. Clive came home and they headed for her parents' in Grimsby, about twenty-five kilometres to the east. They lived there for a month, even after city officials said it was safe for North End residents to return home. She didn't consider herself a political person, but the fire radicalized Gallagher. She had been raised to believe that if something is not right, you make it right.

In the fire's aftermath there were too many unanswered questions. She felt the residents' health had not been the priority it should have been for the emergency response. She wondered, why had they not been ordered to evacuate sooner? Residents had been directed to see local health officials, the Victoria Order of Nurses, if they had health concerns, tangible symptoms. But, Gallagher wondered, what if you had no symptoms? Did that mean you were OK? What were the long-term impacts from breathing in that vile air? She heard local and provincial health officials say the pollution exposure levels fell within the acceptable range. For adults, maybe. But what about for kids?

And in addition to the health issues, there was the Plastimet operation itself. How was such a fire hazard allowed to exist? Gallagher was certain the community wasn't getting the whole story. She and Clive rolled back into town for neighbourhood meetings about the fire fall-out, left the kids with their grandparents. Then they would return to Grimsby again. One of the meetings was held at the Bennetto Recreation Centre, with speakers from Greenpeace, the Ministry of Environment, and public health. The room was packed with men, women and children, it was hot and sticky, everyone dressed in shorts and sweat-stained T-shirts, fanning themselves with the meeting's agenda, faces worried and tired and angry.

"We shouldn't have waited to find out how much dioxin was in the air, any amount is dangerous, and we should have been evacuated right away," said a McMaster University student. "That's what I want to know—why we weren't evacuated."

An elderly man at the back spoke up. "I'm tired of this city looking at the North End as some kind of dump."

In August, Gallagher happened to turn on the TV and came across the CPAC channel. She never watched it, but she heard a reference to Plastimet and tuned in. "Nobody has brought any hard evidence to me . . . the medical officer of health has made a statement that there is not a long-term health problem with this and I must accept her professional advice." Environment Minister Norm Sterling was talking about measures taken after the Plastimet fire, arguing against the need for a public inquiry into the disaster. Gallagher heard him mention her by name in the course of his comments. Gallagher, who did not hold the Progressive Conservative minister in high regard, was furious that he was citing her. It was an emotional time. She phoned Sterling's office, angry, crying.

ANGER AND TEARS

A North End resident asks a question at a meeting of concerned neighbours after the Plastimet fire.

In the years that followed, Gallagher and several others in the neighbourhood agitated to have a community health study done by the public health department, and to get the debris left from the fire moved off the site, have the site turned into a park. The fire would always burn in her psyche. For years she wouldn't let her kids play in their own yard, not while they were still little and rolling all over the ground. No way. In winter, yes, but not in summertime.

In the November 1997 city election, she actively campaigned against veteran North End aldermen Vince Agro and Bill McCulloch, who had been in power when Plastimet hit. She felt they had not been responsive enough to the community. She went door to door campaigning against them. "Remember, what did they do for you?" she would tell voters. "They did nothing. *Nothing.*" McCulloch, with thirty-one years in office, and Agro, with twenty-five, were defeated by newcomers Andrea Horvath and Ron Corsini.

The political battle did not end there. Hamilton East MPP firebrand Dominic Agostino hammered on the provincial government to fund a public inquiry into the fire. The Liberal environment critic was not known as one who minced words. "What does (Sterling) need, a body count?" he asked. "Do we need people to die before he decides there is a need for a public inquiry? I cannot believe that he would have the gall to stand there—after all of the evidence of people getting sick—and say he hasn't been convinced."

Plastimet became an issue in the 1999 provincial election. NDP candidate David Christopherson promised that his party would initiate a public inquiry into the fire. But the PCs won, and the inquiry never happened. The government's position was that there was no need for it.

Another official whose performance Gallagher and other angry residents found wanting was Marilyn James, the medical officer of health. Part of it was due simply to her personality. Even officials who had nothing negative to say about James' performance during the emergency pointed out that her less than diplomatic approach had something to do with enmity some felt towards her. Dave Wilson felt she received an unfair amount of anger, given the stress and uncertainty of the situation. James had tried to allay fears in the aftermath of the fire, in an effort to calm fears of North Enders. But her words were construed by Gallagher as being unfeeling, unconcerned. Some interpreted her words, and tone, as condescending and that she did not take their health concerns seriously during and after the fire. As usual, Gallagher did not couch her language.

"A figurehead like that should be like Mary Poppins," she was quoted in the *Hamilton Spectator*. "She should give you the warm and fuzzies." On August 10, 1998, exactly one year and one day after the fire, James announced her resignation from her position as the region's medical officer of health. There was restructuring going on at the region.

*****

The arsonist pulled the home-rolled cigarette out of his coat pocket, lit it with a match, felt the flame singe the tip of his finger, just a bit. Flinched.

"You pyro," said a friend.

The arsonist smiled. They were outside, on Main Street East downtown. The arsonist inhaled on the cigarette, which looked like a wad of paper hastily rolled into a ball, felt the smoke fill his lungs. He brought up *Backdraft*. He always brought up *Backdraft*. Loved watching it repeatedly since he was a kid. Loved the explosions, the colour. Sure, he loved the fire, "the animal" as Ronald Bartel called it in the movie. Enjoyed watching it. Had gone on some camp trips recently, set some bonfires, the biggest bonfires you can imagine. No one got hurt. But he didn't feel he was in the mould of Bartel, the jailed pyromaniac in the movie who taunts firefighters. No way. Bartel says he wants to burn up the world. Kind of had a few screws loose upstairs, thought the arsonist. He would never want to burn the whole city. At least not intentionally.

The arsonist had wept many times over what he had done at Plastimet. Told himself that he hadn't meant to do that, to light it up so big. He didn't know the place was packed full of plastic. Didn't know it would be so toxic. Fire's a dangerous thing, he reflected. No one knew that better than he did. He had heard that people got hurt, sick. The environment took a beating. He hoped no one had died at the fire. If he killed someone, he'd probably go and do something stupid. Probably light another fire. Why? Because it would have made him angry, knowing he had killed someone. Fire, yeah, it did feel like a release, draining the anger from his soul. That's why he had always liked going camping. He'd build a nice big fire. Loved that. No one got hurt. He did light up some trees one time, when things got out of hand a bit. He didn't mean to.

16

BADGE OF INFAMY

There are always going to be disputes in the department about working conditions, tactics at fires. But the Plastimet fire had been so long, and brutal, that it generated a lot of bad blood. It was a difficult time. Firefighters are a proud, passionate group, most of them love their job. Everyone had an opinion, many had concerns. Some felt that senior people weren't listening, and some senior people felt the complaints were misplaced. In the fire's aftermath of Plastimet, some firefighters took it upon themselves to investigate how the fire was fought, what mistakes were made. Firefighter Ron Summers was one of them. The secretary of the Hamilton Professional Firefighters Association had been off during Plastimet, but studied the incident reports and interviewed firefighters. Summers had started with the fire department in 1990, was a former Hamilton Hurricanes football player with a bodybuilder's physique. He did not shy away from doing what he thought was right. As a young firefighter, Summers, a black man, had once prepared a paper on systemic discrimination in the fire department. He ended up in a private meeting with the chief and a human resources official at City Hall.

Summers felt the department's administration botched Plastimet, believed that there was a lot of politics going on, egos getting in the way of the safety of the men fighting the fire, and that new chief, Wes Shoemaker, had been hung out to dry by his senior people.

Summers helped write a detailed complaint sent to the Ministry of Labour about how the fire was handled. It listed "a number of contraventions of the *Occupational Health and Safety Act* involving the firefighters." The report didn't name names. The union just wanted to have some recommendations come out of it, some recognition that Plastimet was not fought efficiently or safely. But nothing came of the report.

Some firefighters and senior officers bristled at repeatedly revisiting Plastimet. Yes, the fire was overwhelming, ugly. Yes, most of the firefighters suffered health impacts. But it was a tough fire. And they put it out. It's what they do. Dale Burrows, who took the fire head-on in the snorkel rig, fell into this second school of thought. He had suffered after the fire. He experienced severe headaches, a condition that never really went away. But the Monday-morning quarterback stuff bugged him. They did an exceptional job, he thought. They put it out, didn't they? Not too many fire departments would have gone to the wall like that to get it out in that window of time.

Summers knew it was a tough, unprecedented fire. But he also felt much better safety measures should have been taken: There should have been full decontamination facilities on site, and hot and cold zones where firefighters were given the chance to fully rehabilitate, or at least a clean place to change their air bottles and get a drink. And you don't send them away on a "break" to fight fires elsewhere in the city. They just treated it as a regular large fire, he felt. "And it simply wasn't. We knew within 15 minutes exactly what was burning in there."

Summers wondered how the department would react if there was another large-scale polyvinyl chloride fire. Would they be ready for it? Had they learned lessons about how to fight them? In the wake of the fire, Wes Shoemaker spoke at conferences out of town on the subject of PVC industrial fires. A few Hamilton firefighters raised eyebrows about that one—"What, so now he's an expert on how to fight a plastics fire?" In his presentations, Shoemaker trod carefully when it came to talking about how the fire was fought. He focused on how communities could prevent a fire like that from starting. He did not address what went wrong suppressing it. For one thing, doing so would encourage legal action from anyone looking for a scapegoat for fallout from the fire. For another, Shoemaker believed they had made the right decisions.

Firefighters always relive their fire and emergency calls, tell the stories for years. But most of those are about jobs gone right—hairy experiences, certainly, close calls, but jobs that got done. The difference with Plastimet was, the stories often focused on questioning how the fire was fought, and how their safety was compromised. The issues remained the same: Why didn't they have decontamination areas completely free of the smoke? Should they have moved in the heavy dozers earlier? Should they have at least tried foam? Should it have been an "unmanned" fire, where you just set the hoses up and withdraw? Maybe they should have just let it free-burn itself out—you wouldn't have had the same problem of the smoke inversion from the rapid cooling of the blaze.

All those points had counterpoints. Gil Desjarlais, at the time the deputy chief and appointed the senior incident commander, had no regrets, even seven years after the fire. In retirement, he bristled at the criticism over Plastimet: "I won't get into debate on operational tactics. In retrospect you can always say you should have done this or that, but that's the easy way out. We made decisions we thought were sound, and we'll stick by those now. At that time, we did a good job."

Some of the more vocal firefighters lamented the fact that Plastimet was fought like a conventional big blaze, when it was nothing of the sort, because of the volume of burning PVC plastic. Fire Chief Wes Shoemaker had not declared Plastimet a "hazardous materials incident," which would have meant a precautionary evacuation, outfitting firefighters with extra protective equipment and using special decontamination procedures. Shoemaker said that on the question of hot and cold zones, and declaring it a haz-mat fire, "they involve the tactical decisions made by the on-site incident commanders. As I was involved in the interagency efforts that were not on site and my role was not to make those tactical decisions, I am at a disadvantage to comment on some of the specifics."

Plastimet was a long, drawn-out, ugly war, and the firefighting operation wasn't always running as smoothly as it usually did. There were stories of infighting at the scene, officers foot-dragging on orders from above. Maybe it was resentment of Shoemaker, some of the firefighters speculated. An order was given to rotate one crew in a hot area with another, and the officer at the scene refused to do it. For his part, Shoemaker always said he felt he got solid help, his commanders gave him their best effort and advice. He did have a penchant for assuming a diplomatic approach. Years after the fire, when told by a reporter that Acting Mayor Dave Wilson suggested Shoemaker was overwhelmed by Plastimet, Shoemaker made a point of asking the reporter to emphasize that Wilson had done "a great job," that he was an "awesome and tremendous support to managing the incident."

The fire took its toll on everyone. Not long after Plastimet was done with, one cold, dreary, rainy night, Wes Shoemaker was on the scene at a fatal fire. The fire marshal's investigator at the scene looked into Shoemaker's grey, weathered face and did not see the young climber who had first come to the city from out west. Shoemaker looked like he had aged ten years. His tenure in Hamilton started with a bang, but didn't last long. An opportunity came up in Winnipeg to do what he had been brought to Hamilton to accomplish, which was consolidate the city's emergency services. In Hamilton that consolidation did happen, later, after Shoemaker had left. On September 28, 1998, fifteen months after he arrived in Hamilton, the City of Winnipeg announced it had hired Wes Shoemaker as its new chief. He started fresh. And he never had any regrets about how the fire had been fought, how his senior commanders had advised him, and would always be proud of how his men had battled.

For the city, meanwhile, Plastimet had become a badge of infamy. It supplanted the 1990 Hagersville tire fire as the biggest, dirtiest, most memorable blaze in the area. The tire fire lasted seventeen days, but Plastimet was right in the city's heart, a stunning visual for TV coverage beamed across North America. Amid all the politics and controversy, the one question that few seemed to focus on was, who set the thing in the first place?

17

SUSPECTS AND MOTIVES

·

Tuesday, July 15, 1997
Click.

The fire marshal's investigator walked along a ledge atop the roof of a building across the street from the wreckage. He focused the lens and took another photo.

Click.

On the sheet of paper headlined Fire Investigator Photograph Register, he wrote "East view, south side." Bill Osborne continued taking photos of the mass of blackened rubble and shattered concrete and twisted wire that, in black and white, looked like archive photos of an industrial area bombed in England in the Second World War. Osborne had officially taken control of the Plastimet site, and it was his until he chose to release it.

Click. "East view, middle."

Osborne was a former cop, his body fit and hard from the gym, with dark eyes and a dark moustache. He shaved whatever hair was left on his head in favour of the bald look, which further toughened his aura and made him look like he was in his forties rather than fifties. Years ago, fire marshals had the power to arrest arson suspects. But the fire marshal's role evolved into investigating how a fire started and, if criminality was suspected, sharing information with police. Osborne had been the fire marshal who arrived on the scene after the Collins Hotel nearly blew up five years earlier, when toasters had been rigged with timers and gasoline-soaked rags. Osborne investigated, along with Hamilton police, under the name Project Toast. It was a good case. Nothing had burned, so Osborne could effectively gather evidence.

At the Plastimet scene, there wasn't much to investigate. Just huge piles of rubble that had been shuffled around with dozers—toxic rubble, Osborne grimaced. One of the Ministry of the Environment guys told Osborne he personally wouldn't set foot on the site without wearing a full rubberized protective suit. Osborne did not take such precautions, but then he wasn't getting too close to the rubble. As it happened, he already knew the layout of the building. Osborne had been inside before, from one end to the other. It was one of the most notorious fire sites in the city so he had been called to the scene several times. In the previous four years there had been ten fires.

Click. "East view, north side."

Osborne looked over the site and shook his head. Some scene. There was nothing much he could do with it. Sherlock Holmes would throw up his hands with this one. Still, headquarters had been hounding him for answers from the get-go, even as the thing was still burning. The media were all over the story, environmental groups on the case full-bore. What was burning? How did it start? Was the company operating legally? During his investigation, whatever information he gleaned from talking with fire officials, police, he faxed to the Office of the Fire Marshal in London, Ontario. He had started his investigation reading fire department reports. The owner of the property was a man named Frank Levy. The operator of the business on the site was Jack Lieberman.

* * * * *

The Plastimet site was a historical relic of the boom and bust of Hamilton's full-contact creative-destructive world of recycling. In the beginning, at the turn of the century, a man named Moses Levy arrived in Hamilton from Brooklyn. He built 120 homes on Sherman Avenue North for workers at the nearby International Harvester factory, which started life as a Deering Harvester plant in 1902. He went on to build houses elsewhere in the city and named Gertrude Street, Morris Avenue and Peter Street after family and friends. The Levys were a success story. The family businesses included the United Smelting and Refining Company, later known as Usarco Ltd., at 363 Wellington Street North. At its peak it comprised four divisions and employed 300 people. The family bought mothballed 15,000-tonne ships, which were towed into Hamilton Harbour, stripped, their parts swallowed by two 50-tonne furnaces melting $30,000 worth of metal in a twelve-hour shift.

After the Second World War, Moses' son, David Levy, ran the company and was a local giant at the top of his game. He was dubbed "the admiral" after buying twenty navy corvettes from the government and having them sailed into the harbour. David and his wife, Ida, threw the best parties in Hamilton, platters of the biggest shrimp passed around, titans of industry and Ontario politics closing the evening puffing on the fattest cigars in town.

David had an international reputation. In 1971, he was awarded the Israeli Independence Award, from the State of Israel, for his leadership selling bonds to strengthen the country's economy. David Levy died in 1977. His son, Frank, would eventually run Usarco. But by the late 1970s and early 1980s, metals recycling, while still potentially lucrative, had become a remnant of the city's past that had lost its lustre. Environmentalism was in vogue. Entrepreneurs who could bring great slabs of metal to the city to burn were no longer placed on a pedestal. Instead, citizens complained about the pollution. In 1989, charges were filed against Frank Levy and his son, Monte, on ten counts of violating Ontario's *Environmental Protection Act* for air pollution. They paid $20,000 after a court hearing in which the Levys' family business was reprimanded for environmental degradation over the company's sixty-five years of operation.

Usarco was forced into receivership, with 240 workers owed almost $1.4 million in severance, termination and vacation pay. Receivership meant Frank Levy could not run the business, but it also protected the receiver and mortgage holder from responsibility for the site. And the City wanted nothing to do with it. Abandoned and polluted, the Usarco property was plagued by fires. On June 28, 1993, a major fire severely

Jack Lieberman, the operator of Plastimet, speaks to a senior fire official at the scene of the big fire.

damaged buildings on the site. It was the first of ten fires there in four years. On July 17, there was a three-alarm blaze. And then in September the property was the site of the city's first-ever state of emergency. Some kids broke into the building and found some mercury, tossed around containers of it in a playground. The City paid $80,000 for the cleanup.

Jack Lieberman was one of the players in the local recycling industry. He grew up on Sanders Boulevard in West Hamilton, not far from where Frank Levy lived. He managed Hamilton Iron and Metal, a company that had been run by his father, Benjamin, at Barton and Caroline streets. For years, neighbours complained of pollution that they said showered upon them sometimes as thick as snow. The company ran aground in 1993. In July 1994, Lieberman got in trouble with the law. The Ontario Provincial Police's antirackets division charged him with fraud. He was sentenced to six months in jail for defrauding the Ministry of the Environment and Ontario Development Corporation. One of his companies had sought and received a government grant to import recycling equipment, but in the application he had inflated the cost by hundreds of thousands of dollars. In 1992, another of Lieberman's companies, CanAm Plastics Inc., had closed operations and left a warehouse packed with 4,000 tonnes of scrap plastic. In October 1995, after striking an oral agreement with Frank Levy, Lieberman moved his new company, Plastimet Inc., into the old Usarco building.

*****

Bill Osborne worked for the Fire Marshal's Office, but he would always have the mind of a cop. He had been a police officer in Port Credit, got the Hamilton fire marshal's job in 1989. Back then most of the fire marshals were former cops. That would change. Eventually fire marshals had to go through a year of training, but when Osborne started, they put you through three months' training, gave you a car to use, assigned you a territory, and off you went. Osborne knew he'd have plenty of work as Hamilton's lone fire marshal. He considered the city a firetown.

He had first heard about the Plastimet fire on TV, then gone outside his home on Flatt Avenue to see the plume. He knew that, unfortunately, he'd be getting hooked for that one. He kept an open mind about the origin of the fire, but from the start Osborne knew he would need to interview Frank Levy and Jack Lieberman. The first night of the fire, Lieberman had been there. He sported fashionably longish salt-and-pepper hair with a small bald spot, wore wire-rimmed glasses, a beige golf shirt, jeans. Around midnight, he left the scene, walked back to his SUV-style vehicle with a man waiting at the wheel. You could see orange flame reflected in pools of water gathered on the ground at his feet. Reporters were there peppering him with questions. Any comment on the fire? How do you feel? Aren't you concerned?

"I'm concerned, believe me," he finally said. "Let's leave it at that." He climbed into the passenger side of the vehicle and it drove away. Osborne had phoned Lieberman as the fire was still burning. They met at a Tim Hortons in the Dundurn Street plaza. The fire marshal listened, observed, studied Lieberman, and took notes as the interview subject talked. Plastimet was still burning, and its operator looked upset. Osborne had been to the old Usarco building before, but not since Lieberman had taken over. Osborne wanted to know how Plastimet worked, what kind of material went into the facility, what came out. He learned that Plastimet recycled scrap plastic, primarily from junked cars. It worked like this: A tonne of plastic costs $600 to be deposited in landfill. Plastimet was paid $400 a tonne to take scrap plastic off another company's hands and recycle it.

Red flags had repeatedly been raised about the site, including a litany of fire code violations—as many as twenty at one point. At the time of the fire, fifteen of those violations had been dealt with. Among those that had not was an order to install a sprinkler system. Plastimet was supposed to process scrap car plastic and move the bales out. But the scrap was piling up, more was coming in than was going out. Plastimet still made money simply by collecting it, since the company was paid by other companies to take the garbage off their hands. Ontario's Ministry of the Environment knew about the problems. A Hamilton MOE officer named Carl Slater had been worried about the buildup of scrap plastic. After the big fire, Slater was interviewed on the television news show *W-5*. He explained that he had been so concerned, he had sought an order from the MOE for Plastimet to obtain a Certificate of Approval to continue operating. He was overruled by the Toronto bureaucracy. Plastimet didn't need a Certificate of Approval. Six months later, the fire hit.

Ontario law said companies didn't need COAs as long as they were recycling, not polluting. Plastimet was considered part of the new breed, preventing scrap from taking up space in the province's landfills. This wasn't an old Steeltown smelter, it was an environment-friendly, green operation. This was recycling, after all. Recycling—an ideology, a god worshipped in Ontario. Recycling good, landfilling bad. But at Plastimet the bales of plastic were not being moved out of the building for reuse with any frequency. Instead the plastic was accumulating in a derelict facility—one that had a history of fires but no sprinklers.

There were many mistakes made by many people prior to the fire. But did that mean Lieberman, the operator, or Frank Levy, the landowner, had any interest in seeing the building burn?

Osborne's meeting with Lieberman at Tim Hortons ended after about an hour. The fire investigator would need to explore the site, take pho-

SUSPECTS AND MOTIVES

tos, and try to determine how the fire started, whether it might be arson. The field was wide open for suspects. And that included anyone who had anything to do with that building. Osborne thought Lieberman seemed upset about the fire. Angry, in the way anyone would be if their home or place of business had burned down. Osborne left Hortons keeping all his options open. It was too early to think otherwise.

Later, once the fire was extinguished, Osborne visited the site to take his photos, and he continued interviewing. He spoke to Levy. He was the site owner. Wasn't he? The issue seemed, to Osborne, at least, a bit murky. He interviewed about eight Plastimet employees. The workers were from Honduras and Nicaragua. Osborne had been an "uneven" student in high school in Port Credit. His guidance counsellor suggested he take his SATs. Later, he saw the list of schools ready to take him, and one of the names jumped out at him. Mexico. Sounded about right to him. Universidad de las Américas, in Puebla, just southeast of the capital. That was where he picked up some Spanish. It came in handy interviewing the Plastimet workers, although the men spoke fairly good English. The foreman, Jose Vargas, had just come off his shift, was outside the building and walking home. Inside the central area of the building, four workers were shredding and packaging scrap plastic. One of them ran out, yelling that there was a fire. It's noisy in the plant, the grinders that process the scrap plastic make a hell of a noise. If you were working, you probably wouldn't even notice if a fire started. But one of the men had gone to use the bathroom, or something, in the north end of the building. He had noticed smoke.

Osborne worked on the case for nearly a month. The Office of the Fire Marshal kept on him for answers. The media wouldn't let it go. Geez, every time Osborne was at headquarters, he got the feeling his boss looked at him and all he saw was Plastimet. The big one, the one where there were no answers. At the end of July, Osborne filed his report. He listed the property damage at $500,000, the content loss at $250,000. He wrote that the scene was altered so much by the blaze and by the fire department's separation of rubble into piles that "scene examination was not a viable means to determine the cause of the fire."

He felt the fire had started not in the occupied, working end of the building, but in the unoccupied north end. "The employees working in Plastimet observed no fire in the central area of the building and there was only the odour of smoke. The first indication of this was at about 19:30 hrs. By the time the fire department was called and the first truck arrived it was 19:42 hrs. By this time the fire had progressed the entire length of the building and was also back to front. . . . There were no heating systems in the building and no gas supplies to the building."

Under the heading Fire Alarm System Data, Osborne wrote: "No fire or smoke alarms. No sprinklers." He noted in his conclusions: "Accidental sources of ignition in the north end of the building such as electrical components or natural gas did not exist. None of the witnesses interviewed could supply information as to the presence of any substances that would be subject to spontaneous heating, and none of the products that were being recycled were subject to spontaneous heating."

Osborne's task, as always, was to try to come to a conclusion about how the fire started. And on that question, he had no answer. On his Fire Investigation Report, dated July 31, 1997, in the blank next to the heading Fire Cause, he wrote "Undetermined." He also couldn't say whether the fire had been intentional. If it was arson, though, Osborne had, in his own mind, ruled out Lieberman and Levy. Osborne wrote: "There have been 10 reported fires on the property since 1993. All these fires have been the result of trespass, break and enter, and arson. There is no evidence to link the cause of the fire with the recycling operation."

Since Levy collected rent money from Lieberman, Osborne thought, what would Levy have to gain from the building burning down? Levy is an elderly gentleman. Doesn't get around very well. He had co-operated, at least with Osborne. And Lieberman? Again, no motive, thought Osborne. The fire had caused the man a lot of pain—it was his business, a source of income. So why torch the place? Lieberman seemed like a nice guy. Osborne liked him. He's a guy just trying to make a living. Other suspects? The case was mostly out of Osborne's hands now. It was up to the police to go further down that road.

18

"I LIKE TO WATCH THEM BURN"

Monday, July 21, 1997
The air was already humid before first light, the morning broke cloudy and it rained. Bob Shaw drove to the office of his family doctor in Ancaster, a suburb of Hamilton. His experience at Plastimet had ended just nine days earlier. Mentally, the fire was gnawing at all the firefighters who'd been there. Nearly everyone was talking about it, the stuff they had breathed into their lungs, and the water they were exposed to. The guys talked about it at the barn, at Doc's, on the golf course. Bob walked into the doctor's office, sat down and talked to her. He said he had suffered eye and throat irritation ever since Plastimet. "My eyes are feeling better. But my throat's dry." The doctor noted that Robert M. Shaw was a nonsmoker. No medical history, apart from treatment for a bad back. Was in excellent health otherwise, worked out regularly. She examined his throat. The only positive finding she could note was that it looked slightly red. Bob left the office.

At a party, a firefighter who had been at Plastimet got talking about how nasty it had been, telling stories for some friends, wives. Bob, off to the side, heard what was being said. He turned to a friend. "Yeah, it was bad," he said quietly, out of earshot. "Fine. But it's our job," he added. "You know? It's what we do. What we're paid to do." Bob had always felt mastery over his body, and his profession. But while he said nothing to anybody but his doctor about it, he had felt a change in his body, and his mind, from that first day at the fire. He was worried.

That same morning, detective Jeff Post returned to work after two weeks' vacation. He started his day following up another arson case, and then met an assistant Crown attorney at the courthouse to discuss another. He returned to the police station early that afternoon, parked his car, walked into the station through the rain that been falling on and off and sat down at his desk. There was a file waiting for him. It was about the investigation into the worst fire in the city's history. He opened his daily log book and made several notations.

"Notes on the Plastimet Fire, 9 July 1997 / 14:00 hrs. Review Det. Martin files." When Post was on vacation, Detective Mike Martin had been seconded from auto division to begin the arson investigation until Post returned. Martin had first noticed the fire on his way from an interview in the Stoney Creek rapist case. Martin had already done strong work on the Plastimet case, conducted interviews. Post reviewed those notes, and spoke with Bill Osborne about the fire marshal's findings. Post was up against it. Arson investigation is always difficult. But this time, the scene was destroyed. It wasn't even clear if it was arson, or if the cause of the fire could ever be determined.

But Post did agree with Osborne's intuition that the fire was most likely set by someone. It had started in the north end of the building, where there were no machines operating, no electrical sources. Motive? Motive usually offers a road map for a detective to crack a crime. In murder or violent crime, the motive probably involves love, money, and revenge. But fire setting? More complicated. Post had read page 325 in John DeHaan's seminal textbook, *Kirk's Fire Investigation*:

> There are many motives for fire setting. Some psychologists argue that all fire setting is an irrational and therefore pathological act. However, from an investigator's standpoint, it may be more useful to consider two basic categories: Rational, in which some specific benefit is seen by the setter as accruing to him or her as a result of setting the fire, and motiveless or patho-

logical fire setting, in which the fire is set only in response to an internal impulse or urge.

Plastimet? If the arsonist was a vagrant there was no benefit to burning it to the ground. It was, like most of the arsons Post saw, impulsive. Who could figure out the mind of someone with that kind of urge? Post's task wasn't to unravel that mystery. It was to find the one who lit it up. He left the office and got into his unmarked police pool car and hit the streets in the North End. Whoever set the fire probably lived near the Plastimet site. Post wore plain clothes—or "old clothes," as the detectives called them—a golf shirt, running shoes. No weapon, either. In summertime, the piece would stand out. You don't see many people wearing suits or dress shoes in that part of town. Post stood out enough from his height alone. You have to look like you belong, fit in. Plus, as it happened, Post hated wearing suits as a matter of course.

He went knocking on doors, going street to street, alley to alley, looking up old contacts, gathering eyewitness details of what people saw and heard on the day of the fire. If anyone contradicted facts he already knew, it raised a red flag. One group he needed to explore was local youth. The best way to arrange for interviews with "the kids" was going through their families. Some parents were cooperative, invited Post in. But it wasn't always easy. The police were not always welcome in that part of the city.

Once Post was with a kid, it was about getting down to their level, talking to them in their

Hamilton arson detective Jeff Post was assigned to investigate the Plastimet fire.

language. They'll tell the truth more readily than an adult, usually. And you can read them pretty quick if they lie. The chronic offenders get better at it, though, he reflected. They learn to lie at those schools of lower learning, youth detention, jail. Every time they come out, he thought ruefully, they get a bit smarter. Post pulled his car in front of a house on Burlington Street. A teenage boy who lived there had been a suspect in a 1994 arson in the area. Post was greeted at the front door by the boy's father.

"I'm here to speak to Rick about the plastics fire," Post said.

"You might as well just leave now," he said. "My son's been accused before for fires and the police found the right guys, and we never got an apology. Never."

"I just need to speak with anyone who might have been a witness, or who had been a suspect in the past," said Post.

"He's away at camp. And anyway, he won't talk to the police again."

"Thanks for your time."

* * * * *

It was not his fault, not his alone. The arsonist was sure of that. If that other guy had not been with him that day, the big factory would not have gone up in flames. When he was younger, it was the same thing. Sometimes ran with the wrong people, or was in the wrong place at the wrong time. Really. One time, he was hanging with some other guys, smoking cigarettes in an alley in the north end of the city, and one guy flicks his butt into a little pile of trash, starts a little fire, it's out in no time. But the arsonist? He flicks his cigarette and it sets off a lot of garbage, then the flames climb up the wall of the building, and pretty soon the whole thing's on fire, he hears the sirens. The arsonist ran away from that one, too, dropped his lighter down the sewer. The cops wouldn't understand: It had been an accident, was not intentional.

There was another time, though, he lit a ratty bed on fire in an alleyway. The bed was leaning against the garage of an old house. That was no accident that time. He wanted to do it. Wasn't sure why. He just wanted to see the fire. So the bed is flaming, it catches on the garage.

Later, he found out there had been a car with a full tank of gas inside the garage. The firefighters got there in time to put it out before the car blew up. Would've killed the arsonist, he stood right beside it, watching. Death? The arsonist didn't dwell too much on that. His mother had once told him the story: As a newborn, he almost didn't make it. Lapsed in and out of life five times, on the incubator. They brought him back each time. Mom said it was a miracle he ever lived. As for the biggest fire of all, the one at the old factory, the arsonist continued to have mixed emotions about it. There was a part of him that was proud of what he had created, Hamilton's biggest fire ever. Perhaps he craved recognition. But you can't have recognition if no one knows what you did, if the police don't have a clue. And they didn't.

* * * * *

On Monday, July 21, 1997, at 4:30 p.m., Post visited the fire scene. The Plastimet foreman, Joe Vargas, was there. He was there with a man from Certa Inc., an emergency services company in Burlington. The detective had just missed Jack Lieberman. He had just left. Vargas recounted what he had seen the night of the fire. Around 7:30 p.m., Vargas got off work, left the Plastimet building, headed for the bus stop. He heard someone yell, "Fire!" Vargas ran back into the building and told the others, who fled. Vargas had enough time to shut down the plastics compressor machine. Post took notes as Vargas spoke, and made a freehand drawing of the plant layout at the time. He toured what was left of it.

At 5:00 p.m., Lieberman arrived and handed Post his business card. Lieberman said that just hours before the fire, he had had an engineer in the plant to assess how the fire regulations could be met. Lieberman told Post that there was no power in the part of the building where the fire started. And you'd need an accelerant to get that kind of plastic going, he added.

"The fire was deliberate. It couldn't have started by itself," Lieberman said.

"What about kids on the property?" asked Post.

"The building was secure, but we were still experiencing some prob-

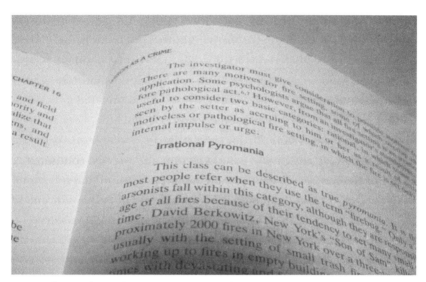

A page from Kirk's Fire Investigation, *a textbook by John DeHaan. Arson detective Jeff Post knew the book well.*

lems. A while back we had a phone in the office stolen. No one uses the north end of the building, no one really knew if kids were getting in or not."

"Was your company making any money?" Post asked.

"Yes. I was looking for more space."

Post got back in his car and drove a few blocks away. At 5:15 p.m. he was at the door of a house on Mars Avenue, northeast of the fire scene. Inside, he sat down with a 14-year-old boy and his mother. Detective Mike Martin had already interviewed him once. The teenager had been involved in fires before, had a probation officer. Martin had asked what he was wearing the night of the fire. Answer: Tiger-Cats football shirt, white. Emblem on the front. Baggy blue jeans.

"Why did you light fires in the past?" asked Martin.

"'Cause I like to watch them burn," he replied.

The boy had been spotted at the fire scene, but had given some conflicting information to Martin. His mother told Martin that her son has trouble telling the truth. On the day of the fire, he had gone to Bennetto school during the day. Sat around his house until 6:30 p.m. Played basketball at Robert Land school until 7:45 p.m.—the time of the fire. He was walking home with his buddy P.J. when he saw the smoke. Went and checked it out. Was home by 11:00 p.m. Later, though, he changed the story, said that he played basketball and also went to Birge Park in the afternoon, and to his sister's house. He was home by 7:05 p.m., and at 7:30 p.m. P.J. rode by on his bike to tell him about the fire.

Now it was Post's turn. As he started asking questions, the boy on Mars Avenue appeared calm. But there was obvious tension between mother and son. She was not defending her boy, quite the contrary—she seemed to believe that he could well have been the one who lit up Plastimet. "Why did you give different versions of your whereabouts to Detective Martin?" Post asked.

"Because he kept asking questions," the boy replied.

He was familiar with the Plastimet building. Been in and out of it many times before with other kids. Can't remember the last time. Everyone could sneak in and out. Had he been involved in a previous smaller fire at the Plastimet site? No, he said. His mother interjected: Her son was in fact responsible for that one, she volunteered. Post asked the teen if he had witnessed the Plastimet fire. "I was there all night watching," he said. "A cop came up to me. I only told him my first name. The cop smelled my hands and stuff and then told me to get out of the area."

Post pointed out that he had been violating his 9:00 p.m. to 6:00 a.m. curfew that night. And he urged him to come clean about what he knew and did. Told him about the *Young Offenders Act*. There were options there that could help. "But none of that can be considered until a person accepts responsibility for their actions," Post said. "You ought to be truthful with your answers."

The teenager on Mars Avenue was a suspect. And his mother shared that view. Post handed each of them his business card and left the house at 6:00 p.m. Over the next two days Post was working other arson cases. On Thursday at 4:15 p.m., he answered the phone in his office. It was Jack Lieberman, returning a page.

"I'd like you to do a video witness statement, how about tomorrow?" Post asked. Lieberman said he had a funeral to attend in Toronto the next day, but he could do it right now. Lieberman would come down to Central Station within the half hour. Post set up the video equipment. Ten minutes later, Lieberman called. He had spoken with his lawyer. The lawyer wanted to speak with Post. At 4:50 p.m., the lawyer called. He wanted to know about Post's investigation to date.

"At this point I have no evidence of a suspicious or criminal act of arson," Post told him.

"I want to make sure this isn't a witch hunt for my client," the lawyer said.

"I need to speak to him to establish the nature of his business," Post said. "And I need to determine how the fire occurred."

"Can we set up a meeting with my client for next week that I can attend?"

"That would be no problem. Call me tomorrow."

Ultimately, Lieberman decided to only answer questions that Post submitted through the lawyer. Post was fine with that. It was the prudent thing for Lieberman to do. The next day, Friday, July 25, Post reviewed notes on the fire code violations on the property, including the failure to reduce storage piles of plastic and install sprinklers. Post reviewed criminal incidents at the Usarco/Plastimet property in recent years. They included:

1993: Arson/hazardous material.

1994: Arson/trespassing/trespassing/arson.

1995: B&E/B&E/B&E/Fire/Fire.

1996: B&E/Arson/B&E.

Post left a message with Frank Levy to call him. Levy returned the call at 10:25 a.m. "I need to speak to you regarding your position as owner of the site," Post told him.

Then he called the 14-year-old suspect on Mars Avenue. He wasn't home. His mother said her son had spoken to a lawyer, who advised him not to speak to police any further. "The only real suspicion about him is that he was in the area when the fire call was received, and was there afterwards as well," Post told her. "And that he seems to have four different stories in response to simple questions we've asked him."

"What would happen to him if he had any involvement?" she asked.

"I'd like to get a videotaped statement from him under oath so we can check his statement," Post said. The next day, he talked to the teenager's mother again. Her boy did not come home last night. She didn't know what to do. She would call his probation officer.

*****

On July 28, Post met with Bill Osborne and Ministry of the Environment investigators Anthony O'Grady and Lynn Kergan, Environment Investigation and Enforcement Branch, to discuss the Plastimet operation. Had Plastimet Inc. violated the *Environmental Protection Act*? No. Plastimet did not have to be registered under the EPA. In January 1997, the MOE had deemed Plastimet a recycling enterprise, which made it exempt from licensing requirements. It had met four requirements under the act: It was processing a waste product, the product could not be used for landfill, there was a market for the recycled product, and the process did not involve combustion.

The meeting ended at 1:20. Ten minutes later, Post met with a fire prevention official from the Hamilton Fire Department and reviewed the history of the site leading up to the fire. Back on October 1, 1996, nine months before the fire, Plastimet was ordered by the fire department to meet twenty fire code requirements. The city's fire prevention officer met with Lieberman on November 14 to discuss compliance. Some improvements were made. Five months later, on April 23, the fire prevention officer inspected the building and found that several requirements still needed to be met. Lieberman was given thirty days to comply. A week later, Lieberman went to the fire department and said he was being forced out of business by the requirements. He said he'd have to close shop and would seek legal counsel. On May 2, Lieberman sent a letter advising that an engineering firm had been hired by Plastimet, and Frank Levy, to help them comply with the requirements. On May 6, Alderman Marvin Caplan, who knew nothing about the nature of the plant, phoned the fire department asking about an extension for a compliance order for Plastimet. Lieberman had phoned him complaining that "he was having some problems with the fire department." On May 22, Lieberman asked for an extension. One was granted by the fire department a few days later, giving him until June 9. On June 9, the engineer said he was close to completing his report on Plastimet. On July 3, the engineer outlined several options for dealing with outstanding issues. A meeting with fire officials was scheduled to take place on July 11. On July 9, the plant went up in flames.

Plastimet was supposed to be a recycling business, with material shuffling in and out. But the plastic had simply continued to mount. If a substantial fire started, it would go huge, and would be highly toxic as well. But fire code enforcement and environmental violations were not Jeff Post's focus—criminality was. Who set the fire? Post had pursued the usual suspects, and that included the owners. Could it have been a crime committed for monetary gain? There were rumours floating around the city to that effect.

But Post found there was no evidence to suggest Lieberman or Levy was responsible. When it came down to it, Post reasoned, neither man had motive to light it up—the place was a cash cow. The fire did nothing but stop the cash flow. Since Post came to the conclusion that there was no gain to be had from burning Plastimet, what was left, perhaps, was the motive of the pyromaniac: There is no rational motive. *Kirk's Fire Investigation*, page 325: "The true pyromaniac receives no material profit and sets the fires for no definable, practical reason. They are merely set for the release of tension or anxiety. The subject simply 'feels better' once the flames are started."

19

FINAL CALL

Bob Shaw was back in the heat of the action on August 14, about a month after the Plastimet fire. His station was called to a structure fire. As they knocked the fire down inside a building, pieces of the roof broke off, fell on the back of his neck, burning him, heat blisters bubbling on his skin. He saw his doctor for treatment and was off work for a week. When he returned, the blisters had healed nicely. But at that visit, it wasn't the blisters that had Bob concerned.

"My throat still feels dry," he said. "Dry and raspy now and then. I always have to clear my throat, it drives everyone crazy." The doctor took a throat swab. The test results were negative.

On October 7, at a building fire just after midnight, he lugged thirty-four kilograms of hose up a flight of stairs. Felt a twinge in his back. Finished his shift in pain. Bob returned to his doctor for treatment of the spasm. And he expressed concern, again, about his sore throat. He asked her directly: Was it Plastimet? A few days later, his back was spasming badly. He saw the doctor on October 13. Again he brought up his throat, and some flu symptoms he was having, and Plastimet. But in February, while he mentioned Plastimet again to the doctor, he didn't seem quite as anxious. He had been feeling a bit better. He was regularly taking lozenges for his throat.

* * * * *

Jeff Post continued to investigate the fire as he worked on other arsons in the city. A letter was circulated in the North End, asking anyone with information about the Plastimet fire to call *Crime Stoppers*. Towards the end of the summer of 1997, Post talked to more than a dozen adults who at one time or another could be considered suspects. The fourteen-year-old boy who lived on Mars Avenue was still the best suspect. There were rumours going around that he had actually said he lit it. Post spent a lot of time on the file, clearing individuals, chasing a lot of leads into a lot of dead-ends. There was one guy that it took two years of checking to clear. You track down one group of teens who heard something, you get their story, confirm all of their whereabouts and check the timelines to see if their involvement is viable. Most of the investigation was eliminate and eliminate. It takes time.

A year into the investigation, Post had nothing else to go on. He had suspicions, but even as his instinct and common sense said the fire was arson, he couldn't be 100 percent sure. There was not enough tangible evidence to even prove a crime had been committed, much less point a finger at anyone for setting it. Eventually Post was moved out of the arson office. With retirement just over the horizon, he worked in intelligence, monitoring high-risk offenders and parolees, pedophiles. And Plastimet?

Police never close a case until someone is charged or caught. The fire was a cold case. The file sat under Post's desk, a reminder of the big one that may have got away. Post didn't know it at the time, but while he had talked to many people, cleared many leads, there was one person he had not checked.

* * * * *

It was in the months following Plastimet that Bob started to seriously consider taking early retirement. He was still young, 48 years old, and his body was as muscular and fit as ever. But he had nagging health concerns. There was the bad back, which had been a problem for years. He twisted it and hurt it running to the rig on a call. At a medical call the back went again when he lifted a patient. He saw his doctor, physiotherapist, and chiropractor, took anti-inflammatories, stretched regularly, did all he could, but the back never really got better. Still, he stayed on the job. In January 1998, he was transferred to Station 5 on Limeridge Road East. Like all the firefighters, Bob had been moved around over the course of his career—east end, downtown, east end again, back downtown, up the Mountain, downtown again, back up the Mountain. On November 25, 1998, he was promoted to captain.

The firefighters at Station 5 knew about Bob's back. He wasn't a complainer, but you get to know the guys pretty well in the house. They knew it was killing him. But he could still pull his own weight—his upper body and legs were so strong that he could compensate for the back. He was still fanatic about exercise, he would ride his bike from his home in Scenic Woods, down the rail trail, along the escarpment and back up again, just to do the Mountain, then to the station on Limeridge. Just to get a workout in. The back, Bob could deal with, he could manage the pain. The nagging cough was more of a concern. It would not go away. At the station, guys who knew him well, like Ticker Blythe, would comment on it. It was a persistent hack, like he had an obstruction in his throat he couldn't get rid of.

"Bobby, that cough bothers me," said Tick. "You ever get it checked out?"

"I have, Tick."

Bob talked it over with Jacqueline. It was tough to focus on the job, enjoy it, with his health issues. It was time to hang up his helmet for good, concentrate on getting well, to start taking some of the trips they had always dreamed about—Vegas, for sure, and maybe someday visit Scotland and play St. Andrews, the ancient home of golf. On February 1, 2001, he turned 52. It had been on New Year's Day 1979 that Harry Shaw and Bob rode on Pump 4, two working firefighters, father and son, together, on Harry's last day before retiring. On his own last day at work, a night shift on June 16, 2001, Bob took Nathan to Station 5. Nathan, who was now 16, got to ride on a rig, slept right at the station. They both beamed.

Bob enjoyed his daily retirement routine. He started the day checking on his mother, Lily, who was not well. Every day it was pretty much

Like his firefighter father before him, Bob Shaw spent his last day at work with his son, Nathan.

the same thing: Bob would see Jacqueline off to work in the morning. Have a great day, Jac. Love you. Then he would take Nathan to school. Love you. Love you, too, Dad. Then he'd run errands, buy groceries, plan and make dinner. Find time during the day to visit with the boys at Doc's, or in summertime get in a golf game, and of course do his daily workouts at the gym. He picked Jacqueline up every day over her coffee break, took her to the Starbucks on Upper James, sat down for their butterscotch scone, coffee with milk. She joined Bob for workouts when she could, followed him around doing his routine but with much lighter weights. She marvelled that Bob never did leg weights, even though his legs were so muscular. He did the treadmill, StairMaster. Loved staying in shape, loved the control he felt over his body as he aged.

As a family they had for several years visited Disney World in the springtime. But in 2001, to celebrate Bob's retirement, they went to Las Vegas in August. Stayed at The Flamingo. Great time. Bob was in his glory in the gambling mecca, hitting the blackjack table hard.

They went out for dinner, Bob dug in to a mammoth slab of ribs. Later, back at the hotel, Nathan and Jacqueline put on their pyjamas, sat down with some chips and watched TV, while Bob gleefully headed downstairs to the casino. Just as he had always done with his buddies for years, Bob played cards for hours, late into the night, then into the morning. At 5:00 or 6:00 in the morning, Bob was in bed. Couple of hours' sleep.

"All right, let's start our day!" He was the first to bounce out of bed. Downstairs to get a coffee for Jacqueline, and then while Jacqueline showered, he hit the treadmill in the gym.

* * * * *

"So, Bobby, you let any of the high rollers in Vegas leave with their shirts on, or what?"

Bronco Horvath grinned. They were at Doc's, as usual, telling stories, having a couple of beers. Bob laughed. And coughed. Damn tickle in his throat was still there. He popped another lozenge into his mouth.

"Bobby, did I tell ya about New York?" Bronco said. He had arranged to go down to New York with some of the guys to attend funerals for firefighters who died in the terrorist attack. Bob wanted to go too, but Jacqueline was not keen on the idea. It was a nerve-racking time, people were afraid to travel, and Jacqueline wanted him to stay home, stay safe. So one night Bronco goes to a Rangers game at Madison Square Garden, wears his dark uniform fatigues. A security usher leads them through the arena, walking along ice level. They will be special guests at the game.

"So get this, Bobby," Bronco continued. "The usher says, 'Follow me.' So we're walking, each of us carrying a beer, 12 of us, right behind the glass in the Garden, and the crowd looks and sees the fatigues. And then they start." Bronco paused, started demonstrating the slow, deliberate, respectful applause he heard that night. *Clap. Clap. Clap.* "And geez, you look up at all these people, thousands of them, and you feel like trying to hide, because hell, we haven't done anything. Right? Then the people stand—stand! Clapping as we walk by. Going crazy, the whole arena." It took an awful lot to get Bronco choked up, but his eyes started to glisten as he told the story.

"And it's like, we're saying, 'Thank you, but we didn't do anything.' And the security guy says: 'It doesn't matter. You're here. You came. You came here from wherever. And we know it and appreciate it, and what you guys do.' A standing ovation, Bobby. In Madison Square Garden. Greatest story of my life." One of the New York firefighters Bronco got to know mailed him a keepsake, a framed piece of twisted iron from the collapsed Twin Towers. Bronco proudly hung it in his basement den.

Bob Shaw wasn't big on formalities, but he thought the Americans knew how to do it up right. There was an event held each year in Colorado Springs honouring firefighters who died from their work. Each fall new names are added to the Fire Fighter Memorial wall. After September 11, the gathering of family to honour the dead was massive, more than 10,000 people were there to honour 499 firefighters who died in New York. Bob and the others would attend line-of-duty firefighter funerals whenever they could. They are emotional, military-flavoured rituals. They reflect a brotherhood that knows no national boundaries. They are cause for much sadness, yet also a kind of solemn, white-gloved celebration of honour, duty, bravery.

* * * * *

In May 2002, Ticker Blythe retired, twenty-eight years, to the day, after he had started. Bob and the boys gathered at Doc's for the occasion. Tick was happy to be hanging up his helmet. Had loved the job, but had also seen enough. It was a good chance to spend more time with his family, his 14-year-old son. But there was one call he went on not long before he retired that would stick with him forever. It was a car accident. One of the vehicles had been on fire.

Once they had the fire out, Tick and the others tore the car apart to get to the victim. They used the Jaws of Life, but this time, there was no life to save. The pincers of the jaws bit through the black metal, twisting it, snapping it off with loud cracking and popping sounds.

The car was burnt so bad, you couldn't tell what kind it was. Tick thought from the structure that it was probably a Ford Tempo. The person in the driver's seat looked like a blackened mannequin, you could

Bob Shaw, left, Paul (Pepé) Villeneuve, middle, and Rick (Ticker) Blythe celebrated Ticker's retirement party at Doc's Tap and Grill.

barely tell it was a person. The firefighters slid the corpse onto a tarp. The only thing that wasn't burnt to crisp was the seat of the pants, and so the wallet survived. A police officer on the scene reached over and pulled the wallet, and some ID. It was a male.

"He's 14," he said.

Tick felt the skin on his face tighten. Fourteen. A boy. The same age as his own son. No, Ticker would not miss calls like that. At the party at Doc's, the stories were considerably lighter. The boys hoisted a few in Tick's honour. All the guys were there, Bronco, Pepe, and Bob, who had recently returned from Disney World. Bob wore dark jeans, shiny belt, casual grey and black shirt, tucked in, hanging perfectly on his lean, muscular frame. Bobby always looked sharp. But he was still coughing.

"Cripes, Bob, that damn cough," said Ticker. "You still got that thing? I thought you were getting it checked out."

"I did, Tick. They don't know what it is."

That spring, Bob visited the doctor. He was worried. It had been running through his mind, and for some time now: Cancer. What if he had cancer? Bob was 53 now and Plastimet was still haunting him, just as it had for the last five years. What if Plastimet had done it to him? Jacqueline urged him to ask for a colonoscopy. It was the typical litmus test for a man of his age to determine if he had colon cancer, a common form of the disease. His doctor noted that he had had no change in bowel function. Due to his obvious concern about his exposure at Plastimet, she ordered the test. Given his lack of symptoms, there was no rush. The test would not happen for a year.

Life went on. The cough, the sore back. Bob squeezed in some time with the boys while spending every possible moment with his family. Every day he drove Nathan, who was 17, to Toronto, where he had a part-time job working in media. Bob was so proud of him. The family watched movies at home all the time, and never missed *The Simpsons*. Well, *The Simpsons* was Bob and Nathan's thing. Bob sat on the couch, feet up on pillows, supporting his back, the cat on his lap. He'd roar in his deep, contagious laugh, Nathan joining in, Jacqueline wondering just what was so funny about it all.

On September 30, 2002, he was back to see his family doctor. Bob told her he was still worried about the impact Plastimet was having on his body. He had the cough, as always, and a postnasal drip. The doctor recommended he see an ear, nose and throat specialist. The specialist suggested changes to his diet. Bob told Jacqueline the specialist said he was to stop drinking caffeine, eating spicy food and sucking on lozenges. It was, Bob and Jacqueline felt, great news. Jacqueline had tried to keep worst-case scenarios out of her mind, but you can't help wondering. She told the women about it at the office. It was just Bob's diet. Nothing to worry about. "Jackie, that's great news!"

That winter, on Christmas Eve, Jacqueline's sister, Trish, complained of having headaches. They didn't improve much over the next few days. Three weeks later she lapsed into a coma from a cerebral aneurysm. They tried in surgery to clip the aneurysm, but missed it. They couldn't bring her out of it. She died. It was a devastating loss for her husband, Paul Anderson, Bob's boyhood friend from the old Mountain days. It was another tragedy in Jacqueline's life. She had always been so close with Trish, they looked alike. Life is so short. Bob managed to make Jacqueline smile at the funeral, though, when he refused to wear a tie.

"Jac, Trish of all people would understand," he said.

In the spring of 2003, Bob visited a gastroenterologist about having the colonoscopy he had requested. How was Bob feeling? He had the cough, still. Bob thought the doctor was a nice man, great guy. He talked with Bob, this retired firefighter with the perfect physique.

"Any other problems, Bob?"

"I've had this cough for a long time. Irritating. Saw a specialist. It's still there."

"How long have you had the cough?"

"About six years."

"Six years?"

"Yeah. Since '97."

"Well, I tell you what, Bob. I think that since we're examining one end of you already, we might as well do both. Do an endoscopy as well. What do you think?" Bob agreed. They would use a flexible fibre-optic instrument to check his colon, and also put one down his esophagus. On Tuesday, May 27, Bob had the first test at 7:00 a.m. Jacqueline came to the hospital with him. After both tests were over, a nurse could see that Jacqueline looked worried. "Will you be phoning us with the results?" Jacqueline asked.

"Don't worry, they only call if there's something wrong," she replied.

20

THE BATTLE BEGINS

Pepe Villeneuve walked through the doors at Doc's. It was May 30, 2003. On the phone Bobby had told him he wanted to sit out on the patio. Patio? They never sat on the patio at Doc's. Shawzie did love the outdoors, though, and it was a beautiful sunny day. So it made sense. But cripes, had Bob forgotten that Pepe had just had the melanoma removed from his skin, the cancerous growth? Pepe was going to be OK, but the doc said to stay out of the sun, or at least slap on some sunscreen. He'd have to ride Bobby for that oversight. And nail him down on setting their next golf date. Pepe had parked, walked along Concession Street to Doc's. It was the kind of day that heralded a new season, people surfacing from winter, feeling a warm breeze on their bare arms for the first time in months, dry pavement under their cars that now move a little faster, with a bit more insouciance, a carefree, life-is-forever ethos, renewal. Bob was already at Doc's, holding down a table outside in the bright sunlight.

"Geez, what the hell you trying to do, kill me, you stupid ass?" said Pepe as he approached the table. "I'm supposed to stay out of the sun."

"Sorry, Pepe."

"It is nice out here, though, eh? Give me a second." Pepe went back inside and returned carrying a glass of Blue draft. Sat down across from Bob. Took a sip.

"I gotta tell you something," said Bob. "I went for some tests at the hospital. They say I have cancer."

"Esophageal cancer," Bob continued. Shock. Pepe froze. He replayed their conversation from minutes before. *What are you trying to do, kill me?* Nice. Well done, Pepe.

"I guess I put my foot in it before, eh?" said Pepe.

"Don't worry about it."

Pepe stared at his best friend. Bobby? Cancer? It didn't make sense. Later, thinking about that moment would bring tears to Pepe's eyes, but at the time he was too damn numb to feel much of anything. And Bob did not appear emotional, he talked about it matter-of-factly. And so they sat there talking about it almost as though it was someone else they were discussing.

"When did you find out?" said Pepe.

"Couple of days ago."

"What are you supposed to do?"

"I have to go for more tests. But at this point it looks like I'll have surgery, then chemo and radiation."

"Surgery?"

"They can go in there and cut it out, cut out the cancer. Get rid of it all. They think they've caught it early enough. Everything's going to be fine."

It had been two days earlier, the day after the test, that the gastroenterologist's office called Bob at home. He was alone. They said he should come in. Bob didn't show up to meet Jacqueline for her coffee break at work as usual. She kept phoning him, there was no answer. He didn't want her to worry at work, but couldn't bear lying to her about the call. That night, Bob told Jacqueline they had to go in to see the doctor. Jacqueline felt her stomach tighten. The nurse had told them not to worry, they only call if there's something wrong. And they had called. She was shocked. Jacqueline went to the bathroom and vomited. The rest of the night, they didn't talk much. They just stared into space. The next day, they went to see the gastroenterologist. He had the results of the colonoscopy and endoscopy.

The colonoscopy showed nothing abnormal. But the endoscopy appeared to show two small esophageal tumours. The biopsy on the tumours confirmed they were squamous cell carcinomas. Cancerous.

THE BATTLE BEGINS

At 54, Bob was young to be diagnosed with it. And it was a rare form of cancer besides. Bob and Jacqueline left the doctor's office. They were frightened, but Bob took a business-like approach to it. We'll be fine. Jacqueline fed off his optimism.

But Bob's face turned serious as they reached the car. "We gotta tell Nathan," he said. It was the worst part for Bob. In the kitchen that night, everyone was standing. Bob did not tell Nathan to sit, did not say he had some bad news. He just looked into his eyes.

"Nate, we got the results back today from my tests, and I have cancer. They're going to do some tests, and we'll get busy on the treatment and beat this and get on with our lives, OK?" And everything felt OK, too. Nathan hugged his father. There were no tears. The way he talked about it, matter of fact, no emotion. Bob had never stopped being a firefighter. Got a job to do, do it. Some danger involved, yes, but don't think about that. His priority was protecting his wife and son.

Bob saw the surgeon the next morning. A vigorous attack on the cancer was recommended. First, surgery to cut out the cancer. Not just in the esophagus, but the stomach as well.

To go through that kind of surgery, you have to be in top shape, and that was Bob. Then recovery, and building up physically before starting chemotherapy and radiation treatments to ensure it was all gone. Bob and Jacqueline agreed to the treatment.

Jacqueline didn't pause long to wonder why this was happening to their family. There wasn't time to get philosophical. All she could do was go day to day and confront what needed to be done. Bob told some of the other guys the news up at a fishing cottage in Picton. Guys like his friend Rob Kimbell, who was shocked. Bob had always had this aura about him, always in such great shape, he was like a hero, Kimbell reflected. It didn't add up.

On June 18, Bob and Jacqueline met with the surgeon. Bob had had a CT scan. It appeared that the tumour could be cut out. The surgeon went over in detail what would happen. The surgery took place the next week at St. Joseph's Hospital, on June 24. They removed all of Bob's esophagus and half of his stomach. He was in the hospital for three weeks after that, recovering. On July 31, Bob and Jacqueline met with a new cancer specialist. The doctor laid out the next set of options for them. He said there was an over 80 percent chance of metastasis—that cancer would develop outside the original area. Esophageal cancer is a form of the disease that can spread quickly. A combination of radiation and chemotherapy treatments should get it. But the side-effects would be considerable. It was likely to make Bob very sick, but he could stop the treatments at any time he wished. When Bob left the hospital after recovering from the esophagectomy, it was time to get healthy, to build up his strength in preparation for the radiation and chemotherapy.

He had to learn to eat all over again with his stomach now partly gone. He progressed through liquids to puree. Loved eating so much, he would not stay on puree for long, he made sure of that. Bob worked his way back to regular foods, just not large amounts. Even the medical experts thought the solid food would go right through him, but it didn't. Bob's system rebounded remarkably. He could speak fine, his vocal cords had not been damaged by the esophagectomy. The doctors couldn't believe he recovered so fast. His determination was remarkable. His body had been such an advantage, but his positive outlook was just as important. He did it and Jacqueline was not surprised. It was what Bob had said would happen. The diagnosis had been a big blow to both of them, Jacqueline could tell he had been reeling from the news, but did not talk much about it. But she had remained optimistic. Because of him. The worst seemed over.

*****

So much time had passed since July 1997. So why had the arsonist started talking about it? Why was he now telling a couple of friends that he was the one responsible for the big one? Maybe it was an act of contrition, a confessional, his attempt to purge some guilt from his soul—to tell someone that not only had he set the fire, but he was sorry for doing it. Because it was true, he had regretted it even at the time, back in '97, from the moment he first saw it mushroom into the sky. And he still did. He didn't mean to do it.

On the other hand, the arsonist wasn't calling a press conference to announce he had set the Plastimet fire. He was not phoning the police to tell them, either. He was telling people who had no profile at all, just a couple of friends who themselves had fallen through the cracks at a young age. "Yeah, I lit the fire," he told one friend. "When I woke up that day, didn't expect I'd set Hamilton's biggest fire ever."

* * * * *

June 2003

The phone rang at Jeff Post's desk. Retirement from the police, and a new job opportunity, was just around the corner for him. He was leaving in October. He had been working with the intelligence section with Hamilton Police. But the next step was going to work for the Ontario Fire Marshal's Office, continuing in a line of work where he could use the expertise he had gained with the police investigating fires. He picked up the phone. At first he didn't recognize the voice of the woman on the line. Then she said her name. Now he remembered. She was an old contact from his days as arson investigator, someone who had her ear to the ground, heard things. A credible source.

"Hey, what can I do for you?"

"It's been a while, but I thought you should know. There was someone bragging the other day that he set the Plastimet fire."

Plastimet? A cold case. But even though Post was out of the fire business, the file sat in a brown box under his desk, a reminder of the big one he had not yet solved. There were still suspects listed in the file. But nothing solid. Post had cleared the owners of the business and property of any wrongdoing. There had been other rumours, stories floating around ever since the fire started. And now someone was confessing to lighting the fire? It wouldn't be the first time someone had talked like that. Post was skeptical.

"So who said it?" Post asked.

Post's ears perked up at the name. He hadn't heard it in years. He had crossed paths with the arsonist before. And at one time, the arsonist had lived a couple of blocks from the Plastimet site. Post wasn't anxious to go on a fishing expedition. But this had something to it.

"Do you want to talk to him?" she asked.

"Yes. I do."

* * * * *

The firefighters who spent time with Bob Shaw as the shadows lengthened on the summer of 2003 were, like the doctors and nurses, amazed by his progress. Bob had attacked his recovery from surgery fast and hard. He was determined to save Nathan and Jacqueline from worrying, determined to look and act like himself. But the surgery had been highly invasive, would have kept most people bed-ridden. He was still vulnerable. By the end of August, he had come back enough from the surgery. Now the chemotherapy and radiation would begin.

It was a great time in the city. The Canadian Open golf tournament had returned to Hamilton Golf and Country Club in Ancaster after an absence of more than seventy years. Bob was excited. He volunteered to work at the event as a marshal, operate a laser to track shot distances for the players. A great chance to get close to the stars of the PGA Tour. Beautiful. The morning rain stopped and the clouds broke soon after dawn on Tuesday, September 2. Bob got dressed, put on his special Canadian Open marshal's shirt. He was excited about what was to come in the afternoon. He was working the second practice day. He was ecstatic.

But he had a stop to make first on Concession Street. Today was also the day he would start his chemo, which would last for one week, prior to the radiation starting. Then he would finish with another round of chemo. That morning he got fitted for a chemo pump that he would wear on his hip, on his belt. The chemicals would enter his system through an IV line in his arm. It would run for five days. It sounded like a pretty aggressive attack. Bob had built up well, but his body had already been through so much.

"This will blow anything else out that might still be there," said the doctor to Bob and Jacqueline. "It should get it all." Bob nodded. Whatever it took, he would do. Just give it to him. Let's get it done.

THE BATTLE BEGINS

By 1:00 p.m. that day, the air was warm but the clouds had returned to cover the sky. Jacqueline dropped Bob off at the golf course. He was excited and determined to work at the Open, to rub elbows with the best in the world, in the natural beauty of the country club, even as the cancer-killing poison coursed through his body. But within an hour, he knew he couldn't do it. He felt a retching sensation. He went to a bathroom and vomited greenish fluid, his body heaving violently. He phoned Jacqueline. He needed to come home.

On September 10 he started a four-week radiation program, after they had mapped the spots on his body, made a special protective mask for him. Then the second round of chemo started.

By mid-September, he was constantly sick. His body, which had been a finely tuned instrument all his life, was breaking down. He couldn't swallow, lost his voice, the pain was incredible. He was advised to be admitted to the hospital to complete the treatments. No. He didn't want to go. But finally he gave in. Bob was admitted to Henderson on September 29 for nausea, vomiting and malnutrition. He had dropped ten kilograms in two weeks. And still, he finished the treatments, which lasted until October 9.

* * * * *

On October 2, firefighter Colin Grieve visited Bob in Ward 395, Room 14. Grieve was also the Workplace Safety and Insurance Board chair for the Hamilton Professional Fire Fighters Association. He had once been a police officer in Guelph, before being hired by Hamilton's fire department in 1987. Until the summer of 1997, Grieve had always had an interest in personal health issues, but had not got involved in claims. But then came Plastimet. He worked two nights there, got sick, and the experience led to directing claims for the union. And now he was the one the firefighters turned to when making a claim. He became a highly respected member of the union. Firefighters told their wives: If anything happens to me, this is the number you call. Colin Grieve. He'll take care of you.

Grieve's own Plastimet claim had been successful. He received wages for time lost due to illness suffered immediately after the fire. There

Firefighter Colin Grieve is the WSIB chair for the Hamilton Professional Fire Fighters Association. He helped Bob Shaw pursue his claim for compensation for his cancer.

were seventeen Plastimet claims similar to his, for acute illnesses and lost time, from Hamilton firefighters, and three claims for permanent illnesses. All but one of them were accepted by the WSIB. Had they all worn their masks enough for protection at the fire, taken precautions? That was a moot point for their claims. The WSIB system is a no-fault one. No matter how anyone performs their job, any job, if it can be proved you are injured on the job, your claim has merit.

There were other firefighters who made Plastimet claims, but were denied. The WSIB ruled that their symptoms were similar to those for the flu. They couldn't prove, to the board's satisfaction, that Plastimet caused their illness. Grieve had once worked with Bob Shaw. And now he organized his cancer claim. Grieve had first filed the claim in June. Now he was gathering more information to send to the board and its science branch for its deliberations. Bob was so weak he couldn't write out an official statement himself. He was being treated for dehydration and weight loss. Grieve did it for him, with Bob dictating: "I believe that my illness is 100 percent related to this fire. I was a perfectly healthy man before this fire. I left the job early because of the health effects."

On October 6, Bob's family doctor wrote a letter to Grieve. "Although I am not an expert in occupational health–related matters, I do have concern that Mr. Shaw was a very healthy nonsmoker who has worked as a firefighter and was involved in the Plastimet fire. This is an extremely aggressive tumour and his prognosis is quite poor." That same day Bob and Jacqueline met with an oncologist. They had the option of repeating the chemotherapy treatment, or reducing it, which could reduce its effectiveness. Bob wanted the best treatment. Get it done. The doctor ordered a four-day infusion.

He was back at home on October 10, confined to bed. After the intense radiation, Bob looked like he had been in an explosion. From his chest up to his throat, his skin was marked by thick black scabs. He could barely move, could hardly make it downstairs or to the bathroom. He had lost nearly twenty kilograms on his compact frame. Recovery this time was going to be even more painful. Jacqueline took a leave of absence from work to be with him. But they could no longer sleep in the same bed. He needed so many pillows to prop him up, for his aching back and other discomforts, there was no room, it didn't work.

When Bob was on the couch, their charcoal-grey cat, Buster, would always jump up and lie on his chest. The cat loved Bob. Buster lost his fur when Bob was sick, it was amazing. Took him to the vet, it was stress, the cat felt anxiety from Bob's illness. Their black and white Shih Tzu, Freckles, suffered too. Bob cared for his pets like he cared for everyone, full bore. He was their protector, too.

One day Bob looked at Jacqueline.

"Jac, I can't wait to do the things we used to do. Can't wait to meet you on your coffee break again."

Jacqueline laughed. "So you can't wait for me to get back to work then?"

"You know what I mean."

And she did. It was the little things. He just wanted his life back, do normal things again, do something as mundane and routine as meeting his wife for a coffee-just-milk and a butterscotch scone. Bob tackled his latest recovery as he had the others. He worked hard, like a boxer training for a fight. He was doing it, again. He started to feel some strength return. In November he started small, just trying to walk to the mailbox. Insisted on doing everything on his own. Nathan would drive him, park the car somewhere, he'd walk to a bench. Eventually, he tried a longer haul, walking up to the Tim Hortons on Mohawk.

The oncologist told him, be gentle, don't go too hard. But Bob, of all people, had to get outside, had to push the envelope. In late November, he had another CT scan. The results suggested he was free and clear of cancer. It seemed like Bob was winning the fight.

* * * * *

Thursday, June 12, 2003
The arsonist felt his stomach churn as he watched the tall detective stride into the room carrying a video camera. This was it. He was going to be arrested, cuffed, taken to jail. He thought he was prepared for that, though. He had admitted to a few other people he was the one who lit the fire. He had decided that he would be straight with the police. He was going to confess. This was the end of the line. Jeff Post introduced himself, set up the video equipment. Post had actually met the arsonist before, years earlier. He had a history, had set a couple of alley fires. He had even co-operated with Post back then, had provided him with a tip or two. Post turned on the camera.

"Now. Tell me what happened that day," he said.

"I did it," the arsonist said. "I set the fire."

He saw the look on the cop's face. He didn't believe him, he could tell. Post asked the arsonist to lay it out in detail, and he complied. The morning of Wednesday, July 9, he had watched *Backdraft,* alone—a movie about fire, he said. Loved that movie. In the afternoon he went for a walk into the North End. Hot day. Cooled off a bit down at Pier 4 Park. Then followed the train tracks back towards home when a guy appeared out of nowhere—guy named J-Dog—who asked him if he wanted to have some fun, wanted to light a fire. The arsonist agreed. They went to the factory. There was a gas can hid in some bushes by the building. The can was red, half-filled. They retrieved it, hopped the fence, got into the building through an unlocked door. Threw gas around. Lit it. And ran.

The story made some sense, apart from the inclusion of J-Dog, the mysterious partner in crime who had egged him on. Post had reviewed his old notes prior to the meeting. In his previous dealings with this guy, the arsonist had always made reference to a partner who urged him to set fires. It clearly sounded like the arsonist fabricated a second person to absolve himself of total blame. But for now, Post decided to let the story of the collaborator ride. Post felt there was something to the confession. The arsonist gave a detailed description of how he had got into the building. But Post needed to corroborate the facts. Could he be making it up? Post had just over four months before he retired to chase this new lead, the best one yet. It would take time. He had a lot of work ahead of him. But it was a start. The case was open again.

* * * * *

Bob's cancer diagnosis had hit all the firefighters hard, especially those who had been at Plastimet. Not only did they feel for Bob and his family, but they wondered about their own fates. What had the fire done to them? Bobby Shaw was as healthy as they came. If this happened to him, who was next? The fear never quite went away, was often stirred when the media revisited the Plastimet story, showed dramatic images of that massive plume again. Physically, years after the fire, many firefighters still had the wounds to show for their experience.

Bob Shaw's crewmate Matt Madjeruh had small bumps develop on the skin of his thick forearms. Looked like psoriasis. It didn't go away. Where did it come from? Mike Ernst worked the snorkel. A quiet, articulate man who got saddled with the nickname Sweetcheeks for his youthful looks, he saw that his mild seborrheic dermatitis—small red marks on his face—worsened after Plastimet, and did not get better. He lost sleep over the fire in the early days, but then it faded. But there was always something to bring it back, like media coverage, talk. Ernst remembered that at the time, in 1997, his doctor had said no one would know the long-term effects, if any, for another ten years. Well, the "long term" was just around the corner. In addition to Bob, three Plastimet firefighters were diagnosed with cancer in the years following the fire. Phil Orzel was one of them, diagnosed with first-stage colon cancer in December 2004. He had been on the job for twenty years. Was his cancer from a career of exposure? Did Plastimet play a special role? For firefighters' occupational health, the issue of cause and effect is a tricky one. It was only as recently as 1999 that substantial firefighter claims on cancer-related occupational illness were first paid out in Ontario. Prior to that, there had only been about twenty cancer claims filed in the province, ever. Since 1999, there have been about five hundred. It wasn't until fire departments started to have individuals dedicated to pursuing claims that the numbers increased. Moreover, a number of recent scientific studies were consolidated that suggested links between firefighting and cancer. Colin Grieve was one of the trailblazing claim chasers. To date, the WSIB in Ontario has recognized about ten cancers as firefighter diseases for which claims can be awarded, among them cancer of the brain (if the disease started there), kidney and bladder, and several types of leukemia. Prostate, lung and esophageal cancer are not yet on that list. The volume of cases that could be directly linked to firefighting was not considered large enough by the WSIB. Even so, there were five other cases in Hamilton alone of firefighters who had been diagnosed with esophageal cancer.

The claim for Bob Shaw's disease had first been filed in June 2003. In November the claim was denied. Grieve asked the board to review that decision. He did more homework, obtained doctors' letters, notes documenting that Bob had come down with symptoms at the Plastimet fire and that they had never let up. For some of the Plastimet veterans, there remained bitterness that never went away. Orzel thought back to the officer who seemed to make light of their concerns at the time, and afterwards. At the fire he had been told, "Suck it up, it's your job."

* * * * *

"It'll be a great time, Bobby, we'll get you up on an ATV up there, take it around the golf course, put a La-Z-Boy chair right on it, you can just ride around and get out every once in a while and hit a shot."

Mike (Bronco) Horvath could talk pretty much anyone into anything.

But he was meeting with resistance from Bob Shaw. It was the fall of 2003, Bob had been doing well, building up again from the cancer treatments. The guys came by the house to pick him up and take him to The Brassie in Ancaster, a bar that was totally smoke-free. Boyhood friend Paul Anderson had found the place with Bob in mind. New place, with clean carpet and nice wooden furniture. Not at all like the down-home charm of Doc's, it was in a strip mall. But it was clean and it was a bar. It felt good to be together again. And now Bronco wanted to get him up with the boys near Parry Sound, nothing strenuous, just out on the little par three golf course they had dubbed "Beerhurst."

"You have to come up, Bobby. You won't have to lift a finger."

"I don't know, Mike," he said.

"Bob, how are you feeling? Are you up to it?"

"I'm feeling better. Things are good."

"Well? We'll get you on the back of the boat, too, just ride around, drop the line here and there. Or just relax."

"I think I should probably stay around here."

Mike was disappointed. He was a relentlessly positive person. Why lie around in the city, when he could lie around with the boys? But maybe Bob just wanted to be with his family.

When the new year turned in January, Bob's back, which had given him trouble in the past, flared up again. He had had recurring back pain from a fall through a flaming floor on the job. And all the lying down for the treatments and recovery had not helped. He couldn't exercise to strengthen it, it drove him crazy. He was putting his feet up on pillows to watch TV. Jacqueline took him for acupuncture, tried everything for the pain. It provided some temporary relief. As for the cancer, one thing was certain. Bob was determined that, when he had beaten this once and for all, he was going to live in style. In early January he went with Jacqueline down to Poole's Cycle out on Parkdale. He had always wanted to own a Harley-Davidson. Black. It represented something magical to him, and never more so than now. The Harley was about roaring down the highway, open air, the power, the freedom. They checked out the bikes. Jacqueline suggested one of the larger bikes with built-in luggage containers.

"Give me a break," Bob cracked with a smile. He wanted more of the classic look, not the two-wheeled equivalent of a minivan. They talked about it some more at home. Jacqueline encouraged him to pull the trigger. Now was the time.

"You think so, Jac?"

"What are we waiting for?"

They bought the bike. Bob, Jacqueline and Nathan went down to get fitted for helmets. On February 1, 2004, he turned 55 and Jacqueline held a little Harley-themed party for him. He kept the purchase a secret from everyone but his family and his old friend Paul Anderson. Paul got him a Harley certificate, he got Harley-themed books, accessory catalogues. Bob didn't want to have it delivered to his house. No, he had a plan. In the spring he'd go down to Poole's, wheel it right out of the store. Hit the road right on the spot, feel the wind in his face, and take it up the Mountain, park it in front of Doc's for all the boys to see. Later that month, Bob was back in the hospital for another CT scan. The last one, three months earlier, in November, had showed he was clear of the cancer. The results came back. Bob and Jacqueline couldn't believe it. The cancer was back, and had spread to his liver. That was where the increased back pain lately had been coming from. It hadn't been from work, from humping hose, falling from a ladder. No, for that kind of pain he could get treatment, could work his muscles in the gym to compensate, will himself over the hurdles. No, this was the disease. Jacqueline felt almost like she was losing her mind. It was all surreal, beyond comprehension. The last CT scan had gone so well. He was on the way back. Bought the Harley. And now this. They had returned to the start of the cycle: Bad news, treatment, pain, recovery, hope—and now bad news again.

Bob was scheduled for more radiation and chemotherapy. He was a rock of a man, but how much more could he take? He hadn't even recovered from the last stage. The treatments started again. The oncologist thought Bob looked exhausted, spent. He suggested the treatment would go better in hospital. Bob was admitted on March 18 to Henderson, the hospital that once had the plume of the Plastimet fire float over it and had closed its air intake valves to keep the toxic smoke

THE BATTLE BEGINS

from seeping in. He was given two radiation treatments. Later, Bob looked at Jacqueline from his hospital bed. He looked so tired, and small. He took a deep breath.

"We can do this, Jac."

"I know."

He could do it again. Everything would be fine. Jacqueline left his room. A nurse stopped her in the halls. "You know, Jacqueline, your husband is the nicest man."

"Yes, he is."

"I mean, he says please and thank you for everything. You give him a shot, and he just says, 'Thank you.' Amazing. He is just a polite and decent man. I thought you should know that."

"Thank you."

Nathan, who had turned 19 in December, heard the things said about his father by the doctors and nurses. His dad was, he reflected, pretty much like Superman.

21

"I'M GOING TO MAKE IT"

As the weeks passed, the visitors who came to see Bob at the Henderson were fewer. Now it was just Bob's closest friends or family. It was the way he preferred it. He didn't want others seeing him in a weakened state, except for those closest to him. Ricky Morton, his old bowling buddy from Uncle Sam's, dropped by. Rick's daughter had once called Bob "Uncle Bob," and the two of them started a routine that never ended.

"Hey, Uncle Ricky," said Bob upon seeing his friend. They talked about old times. Inch Park, Mountain Lanes. The Pinery park up near Grand Bend. Remember? Bobby and Ricky are in front of the campfire, it's late, they're falling asleep. The wives are in the tents. So Bob gets up from the fire to use the outhouse. Meantime, Ricky wakes up, sees Bob is gone, assumes he's back in the tent with Jackie. So doesn't Ricky put out the fire, and the whole site is pitch dark. When Bob gets out of the outhouse and tries to return, he gets lost, ends up at some other campsite trying to find his way back to the tent.

"Geez, Ricky, why did you kick out the fire before I got back?" Bob said weakly from his bed, and Ricky smiled and laughed. Later, it was time to go.

"See ya, Uncle Ricky."

"You got it, Uncle Bobby."

Bob's recovery was not going well this time. His body, the temple he had built over the years, had taken too much. He continued to lose weight, he was shrinking, his skin tone appeared grey. But his hair and neatly trimmed moustache had somehow survived the chemo. Jacqueline had never seen Bob without a moustache, and never would. The hair was still as thick as ever, with just a few noticeable specks of grey. The nurses couldn't believe it. Mentally he was, still, positive, believing that somehow he'd pull it out. But the pain, it was incredible and constant. He was taking medication to manage it, but Bob wanted to keep his head clear, too, wanted to talk coherently with his family and friends. Paul Anderson was by to see him several times. He sensed how the battle was going to end. Paul worked in the health industry, had witnessed what cancer can do. It kills you slowly at first, breaks you down, then accelerates in the blink of an eye. And yet, remarkably, his friend never complained, not once. Not so much as a "Geez, I'm hurting today." Nothing. It was always "I'll get through it. I'll be fine."

Paul had believed for some time that Bob was not going to make it. Said nothing about his gut feeling on that, but he just knew. His job was to comfort Jacqueline and Nathan as much as he could, help them keep reinventing hope. Maybe he'll pull out of it. One of the doctors is still optimistic. You never know.

Saturday, March 20, was damp and mild, fog hanging over the city, rain falling off and on. Paul met Jacqueline in the hallway at Henderson. She was fighting back tears. Bob was fading before her eyes. "Paul. What am I going to do?" she said, her voice halting, choking on the words. "Bob is my breath."

Paul's chest tightened, he fought hard to keep it together. He hugged Jacqueline and walked down the hall and into Bob's room. He was out of bed, sitting in a regular chair. What? How could he even contemplate doing it? Somehow Bob had willed himself to use the bathroom by himself; this pale, thin shell of the strapping athlete Paul had known, had done it and made it back to a chair by the bed, where he sat, exhausted, spent, his chin in his chest, slumped over. Paul couldn't believe it. Incredible, the excruciating pain he was in. God, he is tough. Nobody else could do what Bob Shaw is doing, he thought. Nobody. He was doing it for Jacqueline and Nathan, willing himself through it. Trying to make them feel better. Incredible. It inspired Paul to suck up

Jacqueline's sister, Trish, second from left, along with her husband and Bob's boyhood friend Paul Anderson. Bob is at far right.

his own courage, to say what needed to be said, to put the message in Bob's head, his soul, while he could still hear. Paul kept his voice steady, fighting emotion.

"Bob, I want you to know that no matter what, Jackie and Nathan will be looked after."

Bob raised his head slightly, looked at Paul.

"I'm going to make it," he whispered. "We'll get a golf game. Beginning of June."

Bob paused.

"For sure," he said.

Paul said nothing, just looked at him, astounded, rendered speechless by the fight in the old Mountain boy. Bobby was a hero.

That same day, just up Concession Street, at Doc's, Bronco sat with a couple of the boys. Some of them had visited Bob already and could no longer take seeing him, it hurt too much to see the toughest guy they knew, the firefighter in the best shape of all of them, like that. Bronco? Perhaps somewhere inside, he knew that the end was near. But like Bob, his optimism knew no bounds, and he was going to buck up his buddy as much as possible. You don't give up, and you never stop drinking in life as best you can. It had been one day earlier that Bronco had visited, basically ordered Bob to get better, do the treatment, take the pills, whatever it takes, but the bastard would beat this cancer, and they'd be back fishing and golfing in no time. Bronco promised.

Today, he had a new idea. Yes. He went down the street to the Tim Hortons. Grabbed two empty brown coffee cups, with lids, and a cardboard tray. He returned to Doc's, told the boys he was going to see Bobby, then walked on the wet sidewalk along Concession Street to the Henderson. Took the elevator up to Bob's room. He walked in carrying the cardboard tray. Bob was in bed.

"Bobby, look what I got for ya." Bob looked back at him with that drained expression.

"Mike, I don't think I could take coffee right now."

"Coffee? Who said anything about coffee? Unless Labatt's makes coffee."

Bob felt a thin smile on his face. "You're kidding." Bronco opened a lid.

"Try this."

Bob put the cup to his mouth, felt the old cold friend on his lips, the tingling on his tongue, the liquid gold sliding down his raw throat, like a burst of sunlight entering his ravaged body. Had it ever felt so good? At that moment he was tipping back a draft in Doc's with the boys, or on a golf course in the heat of summer, sweat running down his strong, muscled back.

"Blue Lite, Bobby," Bronco said. "Cheers."

And Bronco took the lid off his Tim Hortons cup of Canadian, tapped it against Bob's. The firefighters sat there, drinking their beers.

* * * * *

The next morning, Sunday, it snowed, the wind was hard and bitter, the temperature dropped below zero. Bob had nothing left. Just a bit up the street from the hospital were his old stomping grounds, the Mountain show; around the corner, Mountain Lanes; and hard to the north, the brow, overlooking the lower city, North End, the steel-grey lake bleeding into the colourless sky.

That morning, he went into respiratory failure. Bob was taken to the intensive care unit and placed on life support. Jacqueline and Nathan stayed at his bed during the day, went home at night to lie awake in their beds. Maybe Bob would come out of it. Anything was possible. He had vowed to make it. Monday, Jacqueline and Nathan sat with him all day again. And on Tuesday. They went home again that night.

Though Jacqueline was raised a Roman Catholic, she was not a church-going person in her adult life, not especially religious. But back at home, in the bedroom where sleep did not visit her, she closed her eyes and prayed. For a miracle? No. She had a choice to make. Would she give her consent to have Bob taken off life support? Or would she decide that he continue to live, but only through a machine? Bob had always been the one to plan, look at the big picture for the two of them, make the decisions. But he wasn't with her now. Jacqueline asked God to give her the strength to make the right decision, to help her to do the thing that Bob would want her to do, that would save him from any more pain. At the hospital on Tuesday, Jacqueline and Nathan both spoke with a doctor.

"It is a very difficult decision, but it's your decision," he told her. "Bob has been so strong for you. Now you have to be strong for him."

Would Bob Shaw, of all people, ever want his life to be dependent on a machine? Jacqueline and Nathan made the decision. They had never had a chance to say goodbye before he slipped into respiratory failure. You don't think about that at the time. He was in so much pain, you just deal with the moment, you're not conscious of planning for the possibility of his death. And even with his body ravaged and weakened, Bob had still given them the sense that he could pull off a miracle. Maybe Bob had known his time was running out, but put on a brave face, figuring that it would have been unbearable for them to say goodbye while he was still conscious. Perhaps his last unselfish gift to them was protecting them from that. Always protecting. Jacqueline thought about that a lot. No one would ever know what Bob was thinking. In the end, she was convinced that he never lost hope.

It was time to say goodbye. Nathan opened the door to Bob's private ICU room and walked in. There was an interior window to the nurse's station. The nurse closed the blinds for privacy. Nathan spoke to his dad. He knew Bob could hear his voice, and not in some metaphysical way, either. No, you could see the heart rate and blood pressure go up on the computer monitor when he spoke, when he told his dad how much he loved him. Later, a nurse gave Nathan a computer printout of the heart monitor. It had been fluctuating as he talked. Bob was taking it all in. Dad never did throw in the towel.

Then it was Jacqueline's turn. She walked into the room. Her heart ached. Pain, fear over the finality of it all, that Bob was going away, forever, and this was the last chance she'd have to speak to him. She couldn't comprehend such a thing. She stood beside the bed, took his hand in hers. She started to cry. And then made herself stop. There were things she needed to say, had to make sure she said them clearly, so he could hear, take the message with him. Jacqueline found the strength to say her piece. She never told a soul what words came to her at that moment.

How long was she at his bedside? She never could be sure. Time did not exist, she was in a different world, could it all be happening? She did not want him to go, and she did not want to leave his side. She put her slender arms around his head that still had the thick hair, the moustache, and she cuddled him, their faces coming together for the last time. The next day, Wednesday, March 24, at 10:00 a.m., after Bob had been removed from life support, he died. The celebration of his life, his meaning and legacy, was just beginning.

*****

Bob Shaw did not die at the Plastimet fire. But symptoms that developed inside him at the fire never abated. Common sense, and expert medical opinion, said the fire either killed him or contributed to his death. In a sense, it didn't matter if it was Plastimet or not. He had been a firefighter, had worked and risked his life for the community, and had died a tragic, courageous death, a hero to the end to his friends and family and colleagues. The firefighters' association decided that a death-in-the-line-of-duty funeral was appropriate, just like the ones so many of them had gone to in other cities, often in the United States. It was the first one ever in Hamilton.

Before the funeral, at the visitation, Jacqueline and Nathan saw all Bob's old friends, colleagues. She stood there, greeting, talking, all afternoon, all evening, barely pausing to have a drink. It was exhausting, but she kept smiling, chatting, appreciating the kind words.

The firefighters marvelled at her strength. Jackie was such a classy woman. That was the way she had, this natural dignity and grace that put anyone at ease. But she didn't feel strong. Inside, she was crumbling. She had faced such tragedy in her life, but this was the worst of all. She was so tired. Part of her just wanted to lie down somewhere and let someone take care of her. But that's what Bob had always done. A reporter and photographer from the *Hamilton Spectator* had come by her house, spoken to Jacqueline and Nathan. The journalists were nice, thoughtful. But Jacqueline never could remember anything she told them, it was a complete blank, she was on a separate emotional plane, she just wasn't there.

The funeral would bring all the chapters of Bob's life together. His first fire chief, Len Saltmarsh, was at the visitation, old friends. It was incredible the number of people he touched. Jacqueline wasn't surprised by that. It was the story of his life, frames from a movie clicking by, boyhood buddies, the Mountain brow, the playground, dances, bowling, pool, cards, fitness, fishing, golf, beers, firefighting. Family, friends, duty, honour.

Mike Horvath talked with Jacqueline off to the side at the visitation.

"You know what I regret, Mike?" she told him with a smile. "Bob always wanted a beer when he was in hospital. And he never had one."

Bronco looked at her and grinned.

"Jackie, have I got a story for you."

22

PRAYERS FOR A FIREFIGHTER

Saturday, March 27, 2004

Firefighters came for the funeral from all over, southern Ontario, the United States, Manitoba. It was a cold, grey day. The firefighters all wore their formal dark uniforms, packed in Regina Mundi Church on the west Mountain. Some had to listen from the lobby. During the service Paul Anderson read a prayer. Nathan was due to read as well. The priest kept looking at Bob Shaw's 19-year-old son, as though gauging his state of mind. And then he stepped down and walked towards him. The priest had seen the hardened firefighters openly weeping. He leaned over and whispered, "You don't need to do this." Nathan said no, he wanted to do it. He had selected the passage from the *Apocrypha* himself. He thought it fit perfectly. Wisdom 3: 1–9, called "The Destiny of the Righteous." Nathan stood before the congregation and began.

> But the souls of the righteous are in the hand of God, and no torment will ever touch them.
> In the eyes of the foolish they seemed to have died, and their departure was thought to be a disaster, and their going from us to be their destruction; but they are at peace.
> For though in the sight of others they were pun-

> ished, their hope is full of immortality.
>
> Having been disciplined a little, they will receive great good, because God tested them and found them worthy of himself; like gold in the furnace he tried them, and like a sacrificial burnt offering he accepted them.
>
> In the time of their visitation they will shine forth, and will run like sparks through the stubble. They will govern nations and rule over peoples, and the Lord will reign over them forever. . . .

He read it all without a hitch. Everyone stared in disbelief. Nathan was so composed. Where did he find the strength? He sat back down in his pew and Jacqueline put her arm around him. Firefighter Rob Kimbell was next. He was a member of the honour guard, was dressed immaculately in the dark uniform with a light-blue stripe down the pants, white gloves, white belt, white hat. Every year Kimbell read the *Fireman's Prayer* at the pensioners' dinner. Always choked him up a bit, especially the last line. He had sat in his pew, reading the words over and over to himself. This was going to be difficult. Focus. Just read the words. Don't think about why you're here. He rose, stood behind the lectern, and began.

> When I'm called to duty, God,
> Wherever flames may rage
> Give me strength to save a life
> Whatever be its age.

Kimbell was dressed like a marine, had a role in which he was expected to be stoic, grim-faced. But he couldn't pretend any longer. He was a buddy, had gone on the fishing trips, admired his friend, was shocked that someone like Bob had been taken like that.

> Help me to embrace a little child
> Before it is too late

> Or save an older person from
> The horror of that fate.

Now he started to lose it, his voice cracked, he started to cry, wept through the rest of the reading. Just keep going, make it to the end, he thought.

> Enable me to be alert
> To hear the weakest shout
> And quickly and efficiently
> To put the fire out.
> I want to fill my calling and
> To give the best in me,
> To guard my every neighbour
> And protect their property.
> And if according to Your will
> I have to lose my life,
> Please bless with Your protecting hand
> My children and my wife.

The last line always got to him, and this time, especially. He thought of his own wife, his two girls, and then Jackie, Nathan. Kimbell was a mess. But he made it through, he read it all. Before leaving the church, Jacqueline and Nathan were presented with the International Association of Fire Fighters' line-of-duty-death medal. Then the honour guard paraded out of the church and down to the street. At that moment, Ricky Morton, Bob's old bowling buddy, stayed back in the church, watching out the window. He didn't know why. He was not a firefighter. He just stared at the procession from afar, just as he used to look in on Bob and the Continentals gang through the fence at summer dances at Inch Park. The coolest thing going.

The procession was formal and dramatic. Few dry eyes among the firefighters. After the procession, Bob's old station truck drove past the hearse and gave two honks of the horn. Hadn't been part of the plan. But it felt good. Bobby would like that. Then, it was back to the station. There was, among more than a few of the boys, an unspoken

Line-of-duty firefighter funeral procession for Bob Shaw.

feeling: It could have been me—still might be, one day. His death hit hard for all sorts of reasons. Plastimet was the worst kind of killer, the one you can't see coming, attacks even the strongest among us with no rhyme or reason to it.

Ticker Blythe was there. It was so emotional, he reflected that, if he died in the line of duty, he wouldn't want to put his family through it. Kimbell thought otherwise. It would be an honour to have the guys pay their respects like that. If he died young, though, would Kimbell prefer to die in the line of duty? He thought about that one. It was a tough question.

And what would Bob have wanted? No one knew for certain. It had not been planned, and no one talked to Bob about "what if" he died, because he believed to the end that he could pull it out, somehow. But Bob appreciated the pageantry of the line-of-duty funerals he attended, appreciated the respect that they were all about, about how they trumpeted the brotherhood, brought everyone together, reminded them of their common bond.

At the reception, the firefighters presented Jacqueline and Nathan with Bob's helmet. There was a rough road ahead for both of them. The funeral had been a wonderful tribute, but also so difficult to take. Not long afterwards, she got the phone call. There was another tribute in the works, this time out of town, scheduled for September. It would mean that she and Nathan would have to get on a plane and travel for the first time without Bob. Jacqueline dreaded the very thought of it.

* * * * *

Uhhh-shhh, uhhh-shhh, uhhh-shhh.

"Dickie—Dickie? The conditions are deteriorating." Captain Dickie Sherwood heard the chief on his radio. Dickie was inside the burning building, the heat wrapped around him like a blanket. It was a duplex. He was on the nozzle with another firefighter. Most of the others had left the building. But Dickie was not finished with the fire yet. The place was falling apart, flames were blowing up through the floor, knifing through the wall.

"The fire's venting out the second-floor windows, Dickie. Heavy black smoke."

Dickie shook his head. No doubt Chief is getting nervous. Probably thinking, Christ, what's he doing in there, he still hasn't come out? But I'm the one in the damn fire to start with. I know how bad it is. And when you're up to your eyeballs in fire you don't have time to find your radio.

Uhhh-shhh, uhhh-shhh, uhhh-shhh.

"It's really bad, Dickie—"

He took one gloved hand off the hose and fumbled to find the radio button.

"Dickie—"

"I know, I know—I'm well aware of the conditions, thank you very much," Dickie snapped in his southern English accent. "We're going to put the fire out now."

A few of the firefighters outside the building heard the exchange over the radios and grinned. Dickie and his second on the hose knocked the fire down. In 2005 he began his twenty-fifth year as a firefighter. Dickie had seen plenty of fires. Planned to see plenty more, too. He lived in relatively quiet Burlington, but had never wanted to work there. More action in Hamilton. He was at Station 6, at Barton and Wentworth, the lower city, the industrial end of town. A busy station. He was senior enough to entertain thoughts of becoming a chief, somewhere. But he didn't want that. No management for him. Nothing worse than just giving orders. Some want to be chief for prestige. Money. But there is also tremendous responsibility. No, he'd rather be on the nozzle, doing something.

Dickie had been on more than a few of the close calls, had personally pushed the envelope—you must ensure you keep your crew safe. As an officer, the safety of your crew is paramount. But what was it about Dickie? Firefighters take risks. Why did he push it more than others? Damned if he knew. He could joke that maybe he wasn't as smart as he thought he was. But in the end he had not miscalculated. He knew fire, knew its limitations, knew his as well. And so far, well, so good. Several people in his family tree had served in the British military. Some of them died fighting for King or Queen and Country, too. Both his mum and his dad had served in the air force. He had relatives who had fought in India, and in the Boer War, and the First World War.

He never much thought of it that way, but how could he do otherwise? Born into a later era, Dickie was not asked to put his life on the line for a great cause. No, he would do it another way. His mother visited him from England. She brought the box of family medals with her. They were Richard's now. Now they sit in his house, a reminder of what has come before him, of what service is all about.

Dickie had to work the day of Bob Shaw's funeral. He was thinking about the boys all day, though. He loved the people he worked with. A great group. Dickie figured there would be a big crowd at the funeral. Bob was a well-liked firefighter. A good man. As it happened, that Saturday was an uncommonly quiet day for Dickie, he had nothing to write in his daily journal. The day before had been busy, though, a chimney fire, a car fire. Dickie had been to firefighter funerals. He thought about one he attended in London, for the men killed in a subway fire. An awful thing. The wives and children were at the front of the church, sobbing loudly. They look right into your eyes, and pretty soon you feel yourself losing it, too.

Dickie heard there was going to be a gathering the evening of Bob's funeral. He did not normally frequent "the office." But at the end of his shift, he changed into his civilian clothes, drove up the Mountain to Concession Street, parked, and walked through the doors of Doc's Tap and Grill. It was packed with firefighters, most of them in their formal wear, having been at the funeral. They told stories, Dickie joined in. It was nice. The next afternoon, Sunday, Dickie was back at it, at a fire in a castings plant down on Hillyard Street. They hit it hard and early, had it under control within an hour.

And then, several weeks later, he was at a fire in part of Stelco's old Canada Works—a common port of call for the firefighters. It had been vacant for years. But vandals and arsonists got into it every once and a while, lit something up. The building was on Wellington North, immediately south of the Plastimet site. The heat was terrific, the fire was going pretty good. Dickie had his men stand just outside a doorway. He crawled deeper inside to take a look, watched the smoke build, bank down the walls, listened to the structure strain under the force of the heat. He was mostly just nosy. Fire is so interesting to watch, to study, watch it move, react. Know it well enough, it won't get you.

A loud creak. A crack. The ceiling gave way, dropped in, just like that. A huge black pipe, probably 2.5 metres long, 30 centimetres in diameter, fell, Dickie moved and it landed right beside him, missed his leg by a hair. Close call. A thought crossed his mind: My God, what am I doing here? There's no need to be anywhere near this damn place. I'm not saving anything. Then he just felt thankful the pipe didn't hit him, and got out. No firefighter has ever died at a fire in Hamilton, ever. Dickie considered that fact. There had been a guy in the nineteenth century who died in a horse-cart accident. But no one had ever died at a fire. Lots of close calls. We've been lucky, he thought. Very lucky. Unfortunately, though, it's just a matter of time.

Dickie had no intention of dying young. He took risks but he did not have a death wish. He loved his family too much for that. If it happened, though, God forbid, would he want a line-of-duty funeral? It would, of course, be an honour. But in his mind's eye, he could see his wife and kids watching the procession, faces racked with grief, crying. He didn't care to think about it.

23

THE LAST FISHING TRIP

All Bob's old friends were at Doc's for the reception, Bronco, Pepe, Ticker, plus firefighters who were not among the inner circle but who worked with him over the years. And there were still others from out of town who attended the funeral to show their respect and support. They all talked about the nicest guy around, the fittest, too, and the extreme unfairness of it all. Maybe that's why it shocked and hurt. Bobby was truly a genuine guy. Why him? Why take one of the good guys? Why not me? And they did what they always do when looking the arbitrariness of death square in the face; Told old stories, mixed jokes with their grief.

"My favourite," said Jeff Wheaton, one of the best firefighters for one-liners, "was one time when Bobby went to Florida and we met him down there. And we're going out, having some beers, and Bobby's out late with us. But who do we see every morning, whipping by on his Rollerblades on the boardwalk, sweatin'? Bobby! You know, something's wrong here. Why am I still here and Bobby's not?"

Pepe Villeneuve listened to the stories, chipped in with a couple of his own. But it had been a rough day. Bob's pallbearers had been family members, all except for Pepe, the lone firefighter who helped carry Bob's casket. Jacqueline had asked him to. Pepe would never get over it all. It was just hard to believe he was gone. Of all the guys to go like that. Like some of the others, Pepe played Monday-morning quarterback. He was still trying to solve the problem, vainly trying to put out this fire that could not be extinguished. Did Bob need to go for the invasive surgery he did as soon as he was diagnosed with cancer? He had the cough, yes, but he wasn't doing bad otherwise, not until they started ripping his insides out, cooking him with radiation, running poison through his veins. Maybe if they had just let the cancer run its course, hell, at least Bobby would have got one last good summer of golf under his belt.

After the cancer diagnosis, Bob had options. Should he have waited it out, said no to the ravages of the chemotherapy and radiation, hoped for the best, maybe had a better quality of life in the final weeks and months? That wasn't Bob's style. Refusing treatment might have fit with his inclination to swim against the tide, but he also had a deep belief in himself, his body, his will. In this, he was a firefighter through and through. And the firefighter's instinct is to fight the fire, not let it burn, not leave it to fate. Control it, beat it. To the end, everyone agreed, Bob felt he would pull it off, somehow.

As for Pepe, he carried on, worked towards retirement. Planned some trips, had beers at Doc's, his round face still broke easily into the broad grin. But there were times when he'd get talking about Bob, he'd be laughing, old times, but then it would hit him, like an emotional dam bursting inside, the damn tragedy of it all, Bobby was gone, and he broke down and sobbed, try as the burly old hunter might to stop it.

Two months after the funeral, about a dozen of the boys went on their annual spring fishing trip near Picton. As it happened, the trips where the whole gang headed to the lake were about to end. It was getting tough to get everyone together. It was the end of an era, after twenty-two years of fishing junkets. Didn't seem right not having Bob there to take their money at the poker table. Bronco Horvath smiled. Bobby's probably up there somewhere, taking money from the angels.

The cottage was right on the water. Rob Kimbell had brought a twelve pack of Blue Lite. Bob's brand. Inside, they each had one. Ticker Blythe dug his hand in and pulled the last can out. Tick had been one of the lucky ones, had not been at Plastimet, had been on vacation at a place on Lake Huron when it hit. He placed the can on a table and stared at it.

"That's Bob's," said Tick. Silent nods all around. They stood up from the table, left the cottage, walked down to the dock, and slowly poured the contents into the cold spring water.

*****

Detective Jeff Post had left his interview with the one who claimed to have set the Plastimet fire, feeling optimistic. He had listened to the arsonist's story, the blow-by-blow account of what the arsonist said he did the day of the fire, how he got into the Plastimet building, set the fire, ran away. The arsonist had provided details from that day that Post had heard from other interviews. And he had been very specific about how he lit the fire.

If the arsonist was making up the story, he could simply have said that he threw a match into a trash can in the building. But no, he had said he used a gas can—a red gas can, half-full. The building had gone up so fast, an accelerant was almost certainly used—although no direct evidence of that had been found at the scene. Post thought the confession sounded convincing. But there was much work to do to determine whether the confession was legitimate.

In his final months as a police officer before retiring, he needed to backtrack over all of it, see if it added up. Needed to phone Jack Lieberman, find out if the access points to the Plastimet building that the arsonist described rang true with him. That would be the key.

A confession means little. Many times before, Post had heard suspects confess to all sorts of weird and wonderful crimes, tell beautiful yarns. And then when he checked out the details, he discovered it was all made up. In the case of the Plastimet fire, there was no evidence recovered. There was no smoking gun. If this arsonist had done it, the proof rested entirely on the veracity of the confession. How believable was it? He had set fires before. When Post listened to the arsonist tell his story, he had not only noted the details, but he watched, very carefully. Studied the arsonist's body language, listened to the tone of his voice. The arsonist was not searching for answers, not contradicting himself. At least that was Post's opinion. He needed to get an expert's take on it, though. He needed to run the tape by behavioural-science experts with the OPP. They could provide an opinion on whether the arsonist was lying or not.

In addition, the arsonist should be asked to write out his confession in his own hand. The behavioural-science people could study his writing and draw some conclusions from that, as well. The arsonist was not a highly educated person. If he's making it up, he might not be able to camouflage it on paper. Now, behavioural-science people are like politicians, mused Post. You never get a straight answer from them. But they would help him complete the puzzle. It would take time for the arsonist to sit down and write out his confession. It would take several weeks at least beyond that for the behavioural scientists to complete their analysis. In the end, Post hoped the analysis would help determine whether the arsonist was a convincing storyteller and an excellent liar—or the one who set the fire.

*****

On a crisp fall day, the only sound at the old Plastimet site is of basketballs bouncing off clean new pavement, the only smell that of asphalt baking in an Indian summer sun. It is a park now, the site completely rehabilitated. Green grass, sparkling water fountain. It is called Jackie Washington Rotary Park, named for the legendary Hamilton-born jazz- and bluesman. In the aftermath of the fire, a small group of North End residents led by Anne Gallagher had doggedly kept on the Ministry of the Environment, and the City, to rehabilitate the property. The MOE spent $5.5 million in public money to clean it up. The City had then put the lot up for sale but there were no bidders. The City took control of the land, which had more than $6 million in back taxes owing on it that would never be paid.

There had been a push to call it Firefighters' Park, to honour the ones who battled the blaze. But some firefighters didn't want their name associated with it. A vote was taken at a union meeting and a majority of those in attendance rejected the idea. Why? Some did not see the value in the symbolism of it—that new life had sprung from that once-ugly place, that they had performed heroically at that battleground. To some, Plastimet was simply a bad memory they wanted to erase. Many of the firefighters were frightened at how Plastimet had affected them physically and mentally. The media attention around the fire had been relentless. It heightened their anxiety. For years, most firefighters wouldn't talk about it. But when a reporter for the *Hamilton Spectator* researched a big series on the Plastimet fire, they started to come forward. It started slowly at first, a few guys gathered to talk over eggs, hash browns and bacon at Rankin's on Main East. Turns out they wanted to talk about it, air out their fears, their experiences, the defeat and victory that was Plastimet, some bitter, some just reminiscing.

Plastimet led directly to a new health-testing program for the fire department. Called the Occupational Health and Exposure program, it began back in April 1999. The firefighters' union president, Henry Watson, pushed to have the program, and firefighters Walt Baumann and Ken Phillips got it off the ground. It is a unique twenty-five year project tracking health impacts of the job on Hamilton firefighters. Firefighters are given tests once a year—blood samples, lung capacity measurements. Prior to the program's launch, a handful of firefighters had been referred by family doctors to Dr. David Muir, the director of McMaster University's occupational health program. They needed to know if they would be OK. Most felt better just being able to talk about it. Once the program started, all participating firefighters had an annual consultation in addition to the tests. Firefighters are an atypical study group because they are much fitter than the average person, but their work takes place in far more dangerous environments than average. When long-term health problems do show up in firefighters, the effects may be far more advanced than with the average worker. A specialized program helps with early detection specific to firefighters.

All those who were at Plastimet are monitored as a distinct group within the study. They filled out forms describing the work they did and their health concerns. Bob Shaw had been one of the first participants. It is still very early in the program. The good news is that, while there had been a long list of short-term symptoms suffered by firefighters at Plastimet, the study to date gives no indication that Plastimet firefighters are experiencing long-term health effects distinct from other firefighters. The study has shown that some firefighters are experiencing health problems, certainly—respiratory issues, sleep disorders—but these symptoms were not confined to the Plastimet cohort. The program has an 88 percent participation rate among active firefighters, and most of those members were at Plastimet.

Bottom line: Nothing is conclusive this early in the study. But for the Plastimet veterans, "So far, so good" isn't too bad.

Firefighter Dale Burrows, who took it in the face at Plastimet atop the snorkel rig, started to suffer from serious headaches immediately after the fire, and they never stopped on most days in the years that followed. Still has to plan his life around the headaches today. Can't have a drink any more, for one thing. If he just starts in on a beer, the migraine begins before he finishes. Might not seem like a big deal, but it's to the point where he doesn't even toast the bride and groom at a wedding. Other Plastimet firefighters still have the headaches, too. You just take your medication and learn to live with it. Burrows had felt anxiety early in the testing program, was curious about what the blood tests would show. But so far he's done OK. The annual blood tests and lung capacity tests keep coming back with no problems. Is he still nervous about being tested each year, this annual figurative return to Plastimet? No. Not that he was admitting to, anyway, he said with a smile.

* * * * *

The battle over the claim on Bob Shaw's life continued with the Workplace Safety and Insurance Board. Colin Grieve was still handling it. When Bob was alive, the board had ruled that his cancer could not be related to Plastimet. They turned down the claim. The fact that Bob's father, Harry, had died from cancer was not an issue in that claim. Harry died from cancer that started in the prostate, and there is no proven genetic link between prostate cancer and esophageal cancer. The WSIB's position was that a link between Plastimet and Bob's cancer had not been proved. In a letter the board told him that it was "unable to establish a causal relationship between the disease" and Bob's career as a firefighter; that esophageal cancer takes so long to develop—it is a "long latency cancer"—that it was "unlikely that exposure at the Plastimet fire caused the squamous cell carcinoma of the esophagus diagnosed in 2003."

There were experts in the field who took a much different view, opining that Plastimet may well have been, if not the only thing that killed Bob Shaw, then probably the decisive blow that shortened his life dramatically. In a letter dated January 26, 2004, Dr. Raimond Wong, a radiation oncologist at the Juravinski Cancer Centre who knew Bob's case well, dissented from the WSIB view. He wrote that the board's case was biased against Bob Shaw: "The statement that the latency period of esophageal cancer is greater than 15 years is not valid. There is still no concrete evidence that all solid cancers involve a multistage gene mutation process. The (Plastimet) fire may well be one of the last inductions of gene mutation in the multistage process of his esophageal cancer."

Dr. James Melius, a renowned American occupational physician and epidemiologist, wrote in a letter dated February 16, 2004: "I believe with a reasonable degree of medical certainty that Mr. Shaw's cancer was caused by his exposures as a Hamilton firefighter. Exposures at the Plastimet fire are most likely responsible for the cancer although I cannot rule out exposures at an earlier fire as the cause. It is very possible that Mr. Shaw's exposure at Plastimet 'promoted' the development of an 'initiated' esophageal tumour."

Both letters were filed with the board before Bob died. In August 2004, five months after his death, the review of Bob's cancer claim again resulted in denial. Grieve prepared to file a formal appeal. He expected it would end up at a tribunal, in which he would call experts to testify that Bob's exposure as a firefighter led directly to his illness. Melius would almost certainly be one of those called. He remained surprised that Bob Shaw's claim had been denied, and the doctor still believed that Plastimet alone may have killed him, or that at the very least it was a combination of Plastimet and Bob's other exposures during his career as a firefighter. Bob Shaw had been exposed to toxic chemicals at Plastimet, said Melius, and because he continued to work right after the fire, his body never had a chance to recover and cleanse itself of the poisons it had absorbed.

24

"YOU'RE DONE, BUDDY"

"You're from Hamilton?" The firefighter dressed in his dark uniform fatigues nodded yes. Whenever Hamilton firefighters attended conferences or training sessions out of town, they were always in demand to tell stories. Most newer cities don't have the variety of structure fires that Hamilton has. But there was one thing everyone wanted to hear about: Plastimet.

"Were you there? At the big plastics fire a few years back?"

The firefighter heard the question. "Me? No, I wasn't there. But he was." He pointed his finger across the room at Paul Croonen, who had, as usual, tried to stay out of any discussion that involved Plastimet. With most fires, you're happy to tell war stories. But the thing was, with this fire, even go-getters like Croonen wished they hadn't been there. The other firefighters gathered around him, wide-eyed, maybe a dozen of them. What was it like? He talked a little. One of them cut him off. Firefighter humour can be darkly blunt.

"Sorry, buddy, but you're screwed, man," he told Croonen. "You're done, buddy."

"Thanks."

Like the other firefighters, Croonen is mentally tough, competitive, has sublime faith in training, teamwork. But there was something about Plastimet that stayed with him. At a typical structure fire, there is the immediate risk involved, but then it's over. And injury or death is preventable if you use your training, your head. Plastimet was all about the unknown, about not knowing what the future held, no matter what you did. Croonen had always leaned on his wife, Kim, for support. She was relentlessly optimistic. But there were those moments, in bed in the middle of the night, when a vision from an incident on the job from years before might creep into Croonen's consciousness, and he'd wake up, the muscles in his stomach constricting, a band of pressure wrapped around his head. And Kim would ask what was wrong, and they'd talk about it. And everything would be OK.

Kim, Paul and their family had had a cancer scare. Kim's father, Garry Smith, the former Hamilton fire chief, was diagnosed with colon cancer. He had no symptoms, but had heard about colleagues being diagnosed with cancer, so he had a colonoscopy done. When the test results came back, Garry was down in Florida, his doctor couldn't get in touch with him. The colonoscopy had detected a huge tumour, fifteen centimetres up, they couldn't detect it with a regular colon exam. It was malignant. They opened him up, took it out. The operation was a success. He's a cancer survivor.

Perhaps the cancer had come from Garry's chosen occupation. In the old days he had never worn a mask, had eaten his share of smoke. That's how it was with all firefighters. Even when masks started to be used in the early 1970s, they often stayed in a box at a fire scene. The old-school mentality never entirely left the department, either. Croonen noticed a change in his father-in-law after the cancer scare, he seemed to worry about stuff more. And Croonen? He became obsessed with Plastimet. He started doing better, but the death of Bob Shaw, a firefighter he knew, but not well, brought it back. Nearly a year after Bob's funeral, Croonen had mentally blocked out even attending the visitation, could remember little about it unless prodded. Then it came to him. Yes, he could see it now: There was Bob's wife, son. Pictures on display. Bob was such a good-looking guy, young guy. Oh my God, Croonen thought at the time. Did Plastimet kill him?

Some of the guys who were at the fire were telling their wives: If I die, you make sure they do an autopsy. Make sure they study the cause of death carefully, because it might be cancer, and it might be because of Plastimet.

"YOU'RE DONE, BUDDY"

If compensation is a possibility, make sure you and the kids get the benefits. Even Croonen's young sons were affected by the dark celebrity their father had attained. One of the boys came home from school one day upset. There had been stories and pictures in the *Hamilton Spectator* of Bob Shaw's funeral. At the boy's school, kids were talking about it, firefighters, Plastimet.

"My dad was there," said Paul and Kim's son.

"Your dad's going to die," said another boy.

Firefighter Paul Croonen, right, and his father-in-law, Garry Smith, who was Hamilton's fire chief in the mid-1990s.

Any talk about Plastimet got Croonen's stomach going. He took medication for it. The first three or four years after the fire it was always there, it was getting to the point where he couldn't sleep at night, had the shakes, twitches. One day, one of the firefighters who had a job on the side came over to give Paul and Kim a quote on new windows. They spent a few minutes talking about the windows, and then an hour on Plastimet. When his friend left, Croonen was cracking open medication. A couple of years ago, he was still based at Station 1, driving Pump 1. It was always out of service. Croonen told the guys, this is one of the last rigs that was at Plastimet. He asked them: Why do you think it's breaking down? It's rusting from the inside out, falling apart, paint coming off. Pump rigs are supposed to have a stainless steel body, so why's the paint coming off? The rig was relatively new. Croonen hated that rig, just because of that. Hated it.

The doctors told him that the stress from worrying was not doing him any good. You're just getting yourself so worked up for nothing. It just did not fit with his gung-ho personality. That talk wasn't good enough for him a few years back. But eventually it hit him: *I got to let go of this or it's going to drive me crazy.* The department's occupational health testing program helped. Croonen looked forward to the annual blood tests, lung capacity tests. Bring it on. The fear had all been about not knowing. His was scoring above average on the lung test. The vote of confidence helped. Today, even media coverage of Plastimet anniversaries doesn't faze him like it once did. You move on, you live. During his off time he worked a bit on his golf game, and took up hockey for the first time, plunging into it with the same passion he had for firefighting.

* * * * *

Paul Croonen's fire rig pulled in front of a house. Croonen was in the passenger seat. He's an officer now, a captain. Still knows every street in the lower city, but no longer drives. The call was a VSA: Vital signs absent. The house was two and a half storeys, had four apartment units in it, ground floor commercial. The call over the radio said the landlord phoned it in. He hadn't seen this particular resident in a couple of weeks. But he could smell something odd coming from the man's unit upstairs. The firefighters got there before the ambulance or police. That is usually the case, and when they arrive, firefighters don't wait for the others. Croonen certainly never did. You go right in. Someone needs help, we're not slowing down just for the ambulance. And the paramedics take time to get their stretcher out and so on. Sometimes Croonen would take the first elevator available and leave a firefighter to wait for the ambulance. Every second counts.

At this call, you could smell it even downstairs. As Croonen and his senior man, Phil Orzel, climbed the stairs, the stench made their eyes water. Orzel was going full tilt, was ready to go up the final flight and in the door. Croonen sent him up with orders to just take a quick peek to see if it was obviously a VSA. It might be a crime scene, they had to be careful not to mess it up for the police. Orzel checked it out, came back downstairs. Yes, he said, it's obvious all right. Two paramedics arrived. Croonen escorted both of them up the stairs, and inside. One of the paramedics bolted back down the stairs.

The body lay on a pullout bed. It had been there two weeks at least. You couldn't even recognize if it was male or female. Only by the style of plaid shirt and jeans could Croonen guess that he was a man. The skull had inflated, the skin black and cracking against the bone, looked like a black bowling ball ready to pop. The smell was beyond the pale. Worse than rotting sewage. More like burnt flesh, or when you burn a pot on the stove, that burnt metal scent that rips your nostrils. You never forget it once you smell it. It was one of those calls where you throw out your clothes when you get home, shave off your moustache and scrub yourself in the shower repeatedly to remove the odour, which burrows into your skin. Croonen got home from work that day.

"How was your day, sweetie?" Kim asked, as always.

As usual, out of earshot of the kids, Croonen gave her the play-by-play. The VSA call. The smell. The bowling ball.

"Gross!" Kim said. And then she smiled and returned to making dinner for Paul and the boys.

* * * * *

Former fire marshal Bill Osborne had long been off the Plastimet case. In his final report, he had written that the cause of the fire was undetermined. There was not even a conclusion about whether arson had been the cause. But Osborne knew better. He knew in his bones that it had to have been set on purpose, it couldn't have gone up by itself. But he was done with it. Osborne continued to investigate fires in Hamilton for an insurance company, hit the gym, occasionally could be seen off the job stopping by Ray's Place on Dundurn Street for a pint of Guinness. One day, he was in Fortinos at the Dundurn plaza, within walking distance of where he lived. He heard someone call over to him.

"Bill!"

It was Jack Lieberman. Osborne had always felt for the man. His business had burned down. But today, he looked pleased. Why? Lieberman had paid for the Plastimet fire in more ways than one. His wife, Lynne, had felt haunted by it. She had felt scorn from the community about it, believed the media had harassed them, then unfairly tarred and feathered them for being responsible for the fire. Inevitably, the Plastimet fire had been the stuff of legal action. Class-action lawsuits are far less common in Canada than in the States, but Plastimet spawned one. The fire had spewed massive amounts of toxic smoke into the air, polluted water. Someone was going to pay for that.

The suit, the first of its kind in Hamilton, was filed by North End resident Jay Cotter on behalf of his family and his neighbours. The claim was steered by lawyer Gerry Swaye. Among the defendants named were the Province of Ontario, the former Regional Municipality of Hamilton-Wentworth, the City of Hamilton, Plastimet property-owner Frank Levy, Lieberman, and various tenants and former tenants of the Usarco plant site. In the statement of claim, the plaintiff alleged, among other things, failure to install a sprinkler system, failure to provide proper security, and unsafe storage of plastics in a manner that increased the risk of fire. Eventually, after some difficulty getting the lawsuit certified, it was settled through alternative dispute resolution. In the spring of 2001, after several months of negotiations, Superior Court Justice David Crane approved a settlement of up to $3.9 million. Plastimet's insurer put up $1 million and the City of Hamilton $250,000. The City's lawyer said the Province's insurers also contributed to the settlement fund.

About 9,400 people who lived in the area of the fire were eligible to apply for money from the fund. Almost a year later, 3,046 of more than 4,000 individuals who had applied were paid $175 each to compensate for evacuation costs, short-term health effects, minor property damage, cleaning expenses and loss of enjoyment of property. Ball Packaging Products, which manufactured cans in a plant just across Wellington Street from Plastimet, received about $525,000. Nine other businesses got about $20,000 between them. A few people and businesses successfully claimed a total of $4,100 in extra costs from a contingency fund included in the settlement. In the end, $2.1 million was paid out, about $1 million of it to the plaintiff's lawyers.

Prior to that lawsuit, Levy and Lieberman had already been convicted under Ontario's *Environmental Protection Act* for permitting smoke and chemicals to be discharged into the environment. The two men had pleaded not guilty, but did not contest the facts. The maximum penalty could have been a year in jail. They received suspended sentences, probation and fifty hours each of community service. They were also required to pay $270,000 towards cleaning up the site.

On August 27, 1997, forty-nine days after Plastimet went up in flames, a new company run by Lieberman was incorporated in the North End. The company is still there in the North End, at Princess Street and Sherman Avenue North, called Diversified Polymers. It is a plastics recycling company. Today, a Hamilton fire prevention official says the plant "is fully sprinklered and the sprinkler system is monitored."

That one day in Fortinos, having heard the friendly greeting from across the aisle, Bill Osborne walked over to Jack Lieberman.

"Did you hear they solved the case?" Lieberman said.

"What? No, no, I didn't."

It was true, said Lieberman. The police had found the arsonist. They told him so. Osborne made a phone call. Was it true?

25

TRAGEDY AND HONOUR

The arsonist walked along Main Street East. It was just after 5:00 p.m., a brisk winter day in 2005. In his soft hands he carried a large cup of tea with four sugars, four creams. The arsonist is five-seven, maybe, thick black wavy hair, a slight olive cast to his skin. Wears glasses on occasion. The black eye was nearly faded now, the one he got in jail recently. Got thrown into an overnight cell, got into a fight. There had been some other incidents recently, too. Got into a fight on New Year's Eve, threw a guy through a display window. Cops picked him up for that one. As he walked along Main East, his eyes wandered, he looked up into the sky to the north. In the distance there was a large white cloud of industrial smoke frozen in the crisp air. That's what it looked like years ago, he thought, just like that, the big fire he had set. A cloud like that, except it was black. He continued along the sidewalk, his hands holding the paper cup shaking with more vigour than the cold suggested.

* * * * *

Jeff Post was no longer with Hamilton police, he now had a job with the Fire Marshal's Office. He had moved out of Hamilton, handed the Plastimet case over to Sid Millin, Hamilton's arson investigator. But before Post retired from the police, he had retraced details of the arsonist's confession to see if it stood up. The key had been the arsonist's access to the building. He did not say he entered through the broken-down north section of the complex, rather, he claimed to have entered through a working door.

After Post heard the confession, he interviewed Jack Lieberman, who corroborated elements of the arsonist's account: There had indeed been a couple of doors in the building's operational south end that offered access, that were not always locked. Also, the arsonist had provided a description of some of the garbage in the part of the building where he set the fire. For example, he had seen mounds of tangled videotape strands. That, too, was true.

There was a chance that the arsonist knew of details like this from previous visits to the building. But still, it did lend credence to his confession.

The arsonist had opportunity, and his play-by-play account of how he got in, how he got away, and what the fire did when he lit it added up. He had a previous history of fire setting.

Post had sent the arsonist's videotaped confession to the OPP's behavioural sciences division. Sid Millin ensured that the arsonist completed a written confession, which was also passed along. Post did not expect behavioural sciences to come back with a categorical decision, and they did not. But the important thing was, the experts believed the confession.

Just as Post had intuited, the arsonist's body language on videotape, his cadences, were natural. And to the experts, the handwritten confession also looked to be the real thing.

It all suggested he was not making it up. The analysts also agreed with Post that the arsonist's partner in crime, J-Dog, had been a fabrication. Other than that, they felt the arsonist was telling the truth. While Post could never be 100 percent sure—not without direct physical evidence at the fire scene, of which there was none—he was convinced. The detective had his Plastimet fire setter.

Why did he do it—why did he set the fire? The arsonist didn't have an answer to that one. Experts say that some pyromania is motivated by thrill seeking. The arsonist mulled over that theory. That might be it. Yeah, probably thrill seeking. He liked fire. Liked to see the flames. So much damage, pain, anxiety and even death, sparked by someone who had images of orange and black explosions from *Backdraft* reeling through his mind's eye. *Burn it all*. He could never really be sure if he had run into someone who egged him on to do it that day. Maybe it was just a voice he imagined. What he did remember was swimming in the harbour not long before the fire, his white shorts and white T-shirt were still damp when he made it to Plastimet. He had psychological problems. There was deep-rooted anger, a rage that found an outlet in a match or a lighter, solace in seeing flames he had created grasp at the air for purchase. He told friends that when he was young he saw visions. It was all because of a near-death experience as a newborn. "I used to see strange things," he said. "I used to see dead people." Was that a symptom of mental illness, or just a reflection of his obsession with Hollywood horror and mayhem in movies like *Backdraft* or, in this case, *The Sixth Sense*, whose catchphrase is "I see dead people"?

One thing he stuck to was his story that he hadn't meant to light up the whole Plastimet building. Didn't want to hurt anyone. He wasn't trying to make money, kill, wreak revenge. He didn't mean to: It was an appropriate end to the senseless Plastimet disaster. There was no malicious or greedy mind behind it. Flames grow anywhere and everywhere the three points of the fire triangle are met: Oxygen, fuel and a spark. The decrepit Plastimet building was broken down, plenty of oxygen available. And with the massive overstock of PVC plastic, the lack of a sprinkler system, the spotty security, there was plenty of accessible fuel that, when ignited, would go up quickly. All that was needed was a spark. That spark was the arsonist. He simply existed, the third part of the triangle, living right there on the edge of the North End, wandering the streets, whatever snakes from his past wrapped around his head, also a fire waiting to happen. In a sense, he represented the arbitrary nature of life and death itself.

In the winter of 2005, seven and a half years after the fire, when the arsonist talked, he could sound relatively coherent. But at times there seemed to be something not quite right, either.

His recollection was that he had a normal family upbringing. He drank that forty-ouncer when he was a child. But he learned his lesson with that one. His parents? Mom drank a bit when he was little, but not too much. That was how he remembered it, anyway. Alcoholism? No, no, nothing like that. Just a few drinks a day. Dad was a long-haul trucker. Didn't see him much. Brothers and sisters? Three biological ones. Twenty-one steps. Twenty-one? Hey, my dad was a busy man! He got into some trouble as a kid. Set fires. The experts say that some adolescent fire setting comes from curiosity or experimentation, but most of it derives from psychosocial conflict. It can often be traced to family dysfunction: Violence between a child's parents, or alcohol abuse by a parent. The Plastimet arsonist figured that sometimes he was simply in the wrong place at the wrong time, flicked a match in the wrong direction. Really, that's all it was, he was sure of that. He was young, didn't know what he was doing.

The one time, he was out in a forest aping another guy who was spraying a can of WD-40 solvent and using a lighter to turn the spray into a torch—but his happened to light up a large tree.

Or the other time when he flicked his cigarette and it happened to set his sister's garbage can on fire, then before he knew it the side of the house was going up in flames. Didn't mean to. Just like Plastimet. It wasn't always like that, though. He lived for a time in Thunder Bay. Both of his parents were with him then. He never lit any fires up there. The place just seemed too peaceful, life was too calm, for that. As a teenager, he got in more trouble. Fights. Drug abuse. His mother tried hiding the matches and lighters, the copy of *Backdraft* he watched religiously late into the night. His dad was always on the road.

As a teenager he became a ward of the Children's Aid Society, lived in a group home with other youths. Other boys were there for breaking and entering, pulling knives on family members. Got in more trouble, was picked up from the home by police for being high as a kite. Shitty buzz, man. The arsonist felt bad about the big fire. Regretted it. Was glad he came clean and confessed. And yet still felt some pride. Hamilton's biggest fire. He had followed media coverage at the time of the fire, but had not saved anything. Now he wanted to find some of the newspaper articles on the fire. Maybe put a photo up on his wall.

Jeff Post could only shake his head. A terrible thing, the fire. For some people around the world, he reflected, Plastimet remained the defining moment that was Hamilton. As for what drove the arsonist, well, the former detective wasn't going there. He stopped trying to figure these people out a long time ago. He simply hoped the arsonist would not light up anything again. In February 2005, Post submitted his final report to the Ontario Fire Marshal's Office. It mirrored the conclusions of a final report filed with Hamilton police by Sid Millin. The reports said the two investigators had concluded that the Plastimet fire had been deliberately set, and that there was no evidence to suggest a second individual was involved. The arsonist acted alone. Plastimet was no longer a cold case, it was a closed case. You could add one intentional fire to Hamilton's and Ontario's statistics for the year 1997.

Would the arsonist be charged, go to jail? Post knew that, based on what they had, in theory, there was plenty to get charges laid, get the arsonist before a judge and jury to decide his fate. But it didn't matter. There would be no charges. No jail. Never. Not for this fire. Not only could the arsonist never be charged for setting the Plastimet fire, he could not have his name published in the newspaper, not even eight years after the big fire. The reason? He didn't even qualify to be charged under the controversial *Young Offenders Act*. On that perfectly clear July evening in 1997, the one holding the match in the Plastimet building was a child. The arsonist had been 8 years old.

* * * * *

Colorado Springs
Wednesday, September 15, 2004
Sunlight burst off the chrome of the black Harley-Davidson, its engine rumbling rudely, the low-slung rider's greying hair blowing in the wind. The rider wore no helmet. A risk, certainly. But that was his choice. Colorado state law. He passed on the highway, whipping by dry scrub and dirt off to the side, mountains in the distance, like a ghost

from another time, riding free on the road to—to anywhere he pleased. The widow rode in the shuttle van. She was from Hamilton, golden hair, slim figure, bright face. Even now, at 51, Jacqueline at times looked like she might never stop resembling a teenage girl. Beside her, always beside her now, every possible moment, was Nathan, who was three months away from his twentieth birthday, and a student at McMaster University taking a double major in communications studies and political science. Jacqueline never imagined that the roar of a Harley would make her jaw tighten, her eyes go raw. It was to have been the symbol of his comeback, riding into the rest of his life.

The volunteer driver of the shuttle was a firefighter from Colorado Springs, Local No. 5. He knew she was family attending the ceremony Saturday at the Fallen Fire Fighter Memorial, where 106 firefighters would be remembered in the pre-eminent memorial to firefighters, an event held each fall to honour those in the United States and Canada who die from their work.

"Have you been to the Springs before, ma'am?" he asked.

"No. No, I haven't," Jacqueline said politely, forcing a smile, trying her best to put him at ease. "It's beautiful." He spoke quietly to her, deferentially. He did not ask for her own story. Did not hear that Jacqueline's husband had been at the centre of her life since she met him thirty years ago. Did not hear that he was a Hamilton firefighter who had died just six months earlier in her hometown, way up there in Canada, that he had been killed, slowly, by the big toxic fire.

On the drive into the city, soaring mountains framed the view, shaded with dark trees, Pikes Peak standing up highest of all, its tanned bare tip lit by the sun. Paul Anderson was also coming to the event, arriving just in time for the ceremony. He smiled to himself when he saw the mountains. Many years ago, when he and Bob were kids, for some reason they had heard about it. Bob used to talk about seeing Pikes Peak someday. Never did. Bob would have loved this place, the mountains, desert scrub, infinite mile-high sky so flawlessly blue, and the spiritual experience it all seemed to represent.

Everyone told Jacqueline it would be lovely. And it was. She gamely took Nathan to the top of Pikes Peak, even though she hated heights.

Did some shopping, a little touring. They tried to make the best of it. It was surreal being away without Bob. He had never felt right unless they were all together. They say it gets easier, the more time passes after losing someone. But Jacqueline knew better. Some days were better than others, but it did not get easier. If anything it got worse, she just missed him more, every day. She was dreading Thanksgiving already. Couldn't even let the thought of Christmas enter her mind, or his February birthday. The Colorado Springs volunteers and organizers and firefighters were all so nice at the hotel. Jacqueline did all the right things, smiled the way she always did, lighting up the room, elegant and pretty and warm. She really did appreciate what they were doing. But she could never tell anyone what she was really feeling. She did not want to be there. Couldn't they sense it? Her husband should not be honoured here, he should *be* here, in his dark formal uniform, spartan white gloves, chin held high, should be here to kick back and enjoy a beer with the boys after the ceremony. He should not be a name on a wall.

That afternoon she and Nathan stayed away from the crowds and rested in their room, Nathan watching TV on his bed, Jacqueline's thin figure occupying a sliver of space on hers. Strains of bagpipe music floated through the window like a dream:

> Amazing grace, how sweet the sound
> That saved a wretch like me.
> I once was lost, but now am found,
> Was blind, but now I see.

The band was practising in the parking lot behind the hotel. "You've got to be kidding me," Jacqueline said to Nathan, and they could almost chuckle at the emotional torture.

> Through many dangers, toils and snares
> I have already come.
> 'Tis grace hath brought me safe thus far
> And grace will lead me home.

Home—that was how the minister at the memorial ceremony would describe the place the dead firefighters had travelled in spirit, to the afterworld, heaven. But Jacqueline yearned to be with Bob in their real home, wrapped in his strong arms. Early that evening, Thursday, she got a ride to the wall of honour. It was a chance to see it before the crowds packed the park on the day of the ceremony. She crouched down, her small fingers touched the cool smoothness of the dark granite, and then the rough letters of Robert M. Shaw's name engraved in place. Her eyes glassy, she stood and turned her back to the wall of honour and walked away, towards the lowering orange sun that was still throwing heat, now a perfect round ball of fire.

Bob visited Jacqueline in her dreams. He always would. The backdrop varies, she can't place it. But the figure is Bob's, right there in front of her. He turns towards her, but try as she might, she cannot see his face, that beautiful smiling face, ever. But she knows it's him.

Early Friday, must have been 4:00 a.m., she lay awake, unable to sleep. She heard Nathan shuffling in his bed, too.

"Nate?"

"Yeah, Mom?"

"You can't sleep, either?"

"No."

"What do you want to do?" On went the TV.

Friday night, a reception, Jacqueline dressed in black pants and black tank top, under a green jacket, hoop earrings, greeting everyone with warmth and a smile. Ed Stanisz was there representing the Hamilton Fire Department. Stanisz had been on the snorkel crew at Plastimet from the start. It was a festive reception, but it never lost the respectful tone of the week. Firefighters from all over the States and Canada were there, most dressed casual, some in their jeans and snug T-shirts or golf-style shirts, with things like "Houston's Bravest" written on them. Bob would have loved it.

The next morning, Jacqueline, Nathan and Paul Anderson rode a tour bus to the ceremony. Nathan kept busy pointing out landmarks, reciting facts about Pikes Peak. And Jacqueline stared out the window, her face empty, wishing it wasn't even happening. At the memorial site: Flags, a

The name Robert M. Shaw is among those cut into the wall of honour at the Fallen Fire Fighter Memorial in Colorado Springs.

long line of fire rigs, two ladders stretching into the heavens, and many firefighters in their formal dress, bright patches, hats. By 11:00 a.m., the heat was dry and oppressive. There were no clouds to block the beating sun which, at that altitude, was intense, burning right through pant legs, enough to make you pass out. Some family members carried umbrellas to block the rays. There was no breeze, it seemed like there was no air to breathe. Jacqueline sat in her chair on the lawn among hundreds of others, holding a program over her head like a shield. Nathan kept himself occupied. The firefighters had marvelled at his composure at the funeral in Hamilton. And now, as everyone milled around prior to the ceremony, he gravitated towards his journalism career path, took photos, looked at the flags, the pomp, commenting on it as though he were not actually involved in what was taking place, like he was outside it, distracting himself by assuming the position of observer.

The ceremony itself was like a lead weight placed on Jacqueline's chest. She sat with her eyes alternately welling with tears and drying up. She looked small sitting in her chair. This was why she hadn't wanted to come. It was the funeral all over again. It had a military flavour, the pageantry, drums rat-tat-tatting, bagpipes bringing in the honour guard, a bugle played taps. The city's vice-mayor spoke, closed his address observing that if Jesus Christ chose an occupation today, it might well be firefighting, the job was that righteous a calling.

The International Association of Fire Fighters' president, Harold Schaitberger, spoke. "When sudden danger arises they answer the call," he said. "Why do firefighters do what they do? Reasons come to mind like duty, commitment, courage, sacrifice. Those are concepts our profession lives by, and sadly, they are also the reasons by which our own die. But these are things that also bring us together, as a family." The words stuck in Jacqueline's mind. She thought about that some more.

The names of the firefighters were read, a silver bell clanging with each, a stab to the heart over and over again. Grim-faced firefighters dressed in their formal darks from across Canada and the United States were each assigned one family to present to. In dead silence, broken only by the rustling of leaves, a firefighter named Dareek, from the Las Vegas fire department, a tall, muscular African-American man, carried the triangular dark wood and glass case containing the folded firefighter flag to the seats in the grass where Jacqueline and Nathan sat with Paul. Jacqueline and Nathan, their heads light from the heat, the altitude, the emotion, stood. Dareek had met them before the ceremony, was struck by how young Nathan looked. Although Nathan was nearly 20, Dareek thought he looked 14.

Jacqueline had already cried that day, and stopped, and cried again, she was spent. Nathan had been a rock. The silver bell rang once. His name was read. "Robert M. Shaw." Dareek had wanted to present the flag to Jacqueline. She told him before the ceremony, no, it would be Nathan. He told her it was usually the widow. No, she insisted. Nathan. Bob would be so proud of that. And so Dareek had walked to their spot in the crowd, stood and handed the heavy wooden case to Nathan. He held it, standing bravely, a serious look on his face. Dareek's big white-gloved hand was clenched. The fist rose slowly upward, changing into a stiff salute as it reached his brow. He held the salute, staring at Nathan, stone-faced.

"A grateful nation salutes you," he said in an even voice just above a whisper.

The words hit Nathan like a hammer. "Thank you—," he barely managed, and his face broke, and, finally, he sobbed.

*****

Early that evening, as the sun dropped, Jacqueline, Paul and Nathan had dinner at a steakhouse not far from the hotel. Paul's treat. Bob would have loved the place. He loved a big meal. Would have ordered a huge slab of ribs, for sure. And then risen early the next morning to work it off on Rollerblades, running, biking. While they waited at the bar for their table, Nathan sipped on an ice water, Jacqueline allowed herself a glass of the house red. Nathan noticed a yellow bracelet on a woman sitting at the bar. It was the popular bracelet celebrating those who fight cancer, with the inscription "Livestrong," popularized by cyclist Lance Armstrong. The woman had no idea who Nathan was, or why he was in Colorado Springs. Did not know that his father had fought the disease himself to the end.

"Is that one of those Lance Armstrong bracelets?" Nathan asked.

"Yes, it is," she said. "You can have it."

"No, no, that's fine, I just hadn't seen one before," he said.

"No," she said, taking it off and sliding it over his hand and around his wrist. "I want you to have it."

They left the restaurant after dinner. The hotel was within walking distance. For the first time on the trip, that evening Jacqueline had started to feel a bit better. At least she no longer regretted coming to the Springs. Somewhere, she thought, Bob was so proud. Proud that his son had been there to accept the flag. Proud that his name was part of such a moving celebration of the work firefighters do. And she reflected that wherever Bob was now, he was in good company. The way Bob used to talk, with an eye always to the distant future, always planning, it was like he expected to live forever. Probably never thought of it this way, but he followed the saying that the best life is the one where you treat your body as though you'll live forever, and your soul like you'll die tomorrow. The meaning of his story in the end was simple and profound. It was about love—of family, friends, honour, duty. In all of this he didn't talk a good game. He just lived it.

Turned out that in death his name would go on forever, linked with others like him, on a granite-faced stone at the base of Pikes Peak. And his reputation and legacy would be lionized in Hamilton. Bob used to joke that when he died, Jac should sprinkle his ashes over St. Andrews in Scotland, the cradle of golf, the place he had never gotten to visit.

"Maybe he's there now in spirit, eh, Nate?" Jacqueline said with a fragile smile. There today and every day, riding in on the early morning wind whipping off the North Sea as it brushes the faded grass on the first tee.

She kept thinking about the words from the keynote speech, and the feeling she had near the end of the ceremony: "These are things that bring us together, as a family." Jacqueline had known such tragedy. Her mother. Her sister. Most agonizing of all, Bob. She had never got much involved in firefighter functions. And now, first with the funeral back home, and now in Colorado Springs, it was the first time in her life, really, she actually felt what Bob had talked about, had sensed the brotherhood, what it was like to be a part of it, this collective embrace.

For the first time since Bob had died, she felt protected again. In the months to come, there would be many difficult moments. But at that time and place, she felt part of a new family, felt stronger knowing that she was one of those who lost loved ones, lost heroes, to the fires. Bobby Shaw's wife, son and boyhood friend walked from the restaurant. Now Pikes Peak was just a shadow, the air was cool and dry, the heat put to bed, for now. They walked back to the hotel under a blue-black sky dotted with silver.

EPILOGUE

Historians have written that the prolonged trench warfare battles of the First World War shattered illusions widely shared at the turn of the century, that warfare was a glamorous undertaking. The start of the war had been welcomed as a glorious event, one that would be both quick and exciting, but it turned out to be the opposite. In this sense, in its own way, the Plastimet fire turned on its head some of the romanticism associated with firefighting. On the day the big one went up in the North End, a man named Jim Kay had been at Hamilton General Hospital. Along with his two young daughters he visited his father, who was being treated for cancer. The General was just about next door to the fire, so when Kay walked out the door he saw the plume blasting into the sky. At that time, Kay was deputy chief with Burlington's fire department, but was just in jeans on a day off. He got the girls in the car and drove a couple of blocks along Barton Street past Wellington, closer towards the scene like a moth attracted to a flame. It was hot that afternoon, he left the air conditioner running in the car for the girls and stepped out to look. Couldn't believe the fury and intensity of the fire, even from a safe distance, how rapidly it grew. He wasn't about to hang around, not with his kids there. And in any case, he couldn't get closer, there were too many people flocking to it. The saying is that firefighters race to the fire while others run away. Not this time. Adults were running down the street towards the scene, some were carrying their kids on their shoulders like they were in a race at a family picnic.

"What are you doing?" Kay asked a couple of parents as they ran past him. "Leave your kids with me." And then, he thought, what would he do with all the kids anyway? He got back in the car. His daughters were tired of it all. He drove home.

Eventually the firefighters dug in at Plastimet, mired in the toxic runoff and the acrid air. For the firefighters, and residents in the North End, the excitement would be replaced by dread and fear. And seven years after Plastimet, Kay was named to head Hamilton's new emergency services department. That made him fire chief, although in amalgamation-speak those words were not included in his official title. Looking back on Plastimet, like many firefighters, he was not one to engage in second guessing everything that happened. Senior commanders made decisions at the scene that needed to be made. No one at that time could have known how intense it would get, how the weather inversion would impact the conditions. But Kay does feel that if there is a future Plastimet under his watch, some things would be managed differently. Mostly it would mean more emphasis placed on the health and safety of the firefighters: Rotation of the crews, ensure everyone is wearing masks and proper equipment at all times, use more unmanned hose lines, and minimize the number of people that absolutely have to be in the hot zone. The exposure issue goes for all emergency personnel, paramedics, police. The incident commanders have to be aware of the working environment for everyone.

The long-term impact of Plastimet on firefighters was felt not just in Hamilton, but across Canada. Lorne West, a firefighter captain in Surrey, B.C., felt it was a wake-up call, an event so powerful that over time it has tangibly altered the risk-taking culture of the firefighter. Owing to this culture, even after Plastimet, he said firefighters out west continued to resist suggestions from their union representatives to take more precautions with their gear after a fire, to wash it, leave it in the truck bay after a call where there may have been contamination. The tradition is that when you return from a fire, you leave the gear on half-off, a warrior returned from battle, buckles undone, walking into the station, the more

EPILOGUE

black soot on your face the better. It was all about showing off your pride in the fight.

"It used to be a sign of valour to have the darkest, blackest or smoke-filled gear, but today it is regarded as sheer stupidity," said West. "And today stations are built with a washing machine and all gear is washed after every single fire."

Two issues that Plastimet brought into focus were how to prevent a future toxic blaze of that magnitude, and also which tactics to use the next time to fight the fire. The plastics industry itself became involved. As a result of the fire, the Canadian Plastics Industry Association released a new "Emergency Action Guide for Fires in Plastic Storage." The report was reviewed and commented upon by Ontario's Office of the Fire Marshal, Toronto Fire Academy, and Emergency Response Department in Edmonton. It detailed thirteen types of plastics and their products of combustion and recommended fire-suppression strategies. For all thirteen plastics fires cited—including polyvinyl chloride that burned at Plastimet—it called for using master streams and also "foam as a suppression agent." As for safety precautions, the report said firefighters should stay upwind in full bunker gear and masks, and officials should consider evacuation of the local area "and maintain until overhaul is complete."

The Office of the Fire Marshal released two reports, one in the weeks after the fire, and another a year later. The OFM called for a new strategy to prevent another recycling or waste-handling facility from being such a potential fire hazard to the public. It identified 30 large-scale plastic recycling sites across the province, and 450 facilities recycling other materials that required closer inspection and monitoring by local fire departments. The OFM found that the majority of danger spots were not, in fact, larger industrial cities like Hamilton, but instead smaller communities that lack the resources to adequately patrol and police these sites. In many cases, these smaller towns and cities had not even known these problem sites existed. The OFM has advised municipalities on how to clean up abandoned sites, and how to enforce safety at those facilities that are still operational. Today, the OFM offers a three-day course at its fire college to teach fire officials how to police and enforce fire safety at these sites. In cases where an owner of a recycling facility is dragging his feet on compliance, the OFM involves other government agencies to do some arm-twisting, such as the Ministry of the Environment and the Ministry of Labour.

The OFM's course also offers instruction on how to fight large-scale toxic fires once they start, using Plastimet as a key teaching point. It advises that the option of letting a plastics fire burn for a time is one that should be considered. At Plastimet, attacking the blaze with master streams from the start contributed towards cooling the plume and sending contaminants plunging down to ground level rather than dispersing them high in the atmosphere—a problem that was later exacerbated by the weather.

"Do we keep pouring water on it and make it worse?" asked Ed Gulbinas, the OFM's applied research manager. "Or do we protect our exposures and have a hot, fast fire? Firefighting is an evolutionary thing; tactics change over the years. Would another Plastimet be fought the same way today? Probably not. But you do your best with the technology you have at the time."

Lorne West thinks Plastimet has influenced a dramatic change in tactics. He thinks incident commanders are more inclined to strike a defensive posture at fires where there is the potential for toxic contamination. "Essentially we deploy and utilize the least exposure-based tactics possible," West said. "We are action-oriented people trained to go in when everyone else is getting out, but now we try to go slow enough to make reconnaissance-based decisions."

Apart from safety and exposure issues, however, the question of tactics to fight another Plastimet—"fire suppression"—is one where there is still debate. Regardless of advances in technology and changes in the firefighter culture, a basic fact of fighting fires remains unpredictability. While individual opinions are strongly held, there remains no agreed-upon template on precisely how a large-scale toxic fire should be fought in every case—and that goes for looking back at Plastimet itself. Free burning? Had Hamilton's firefighters not attacked and allowed Plastimet to burn, who knows how many days it would have lasted, with more than four hundred tonnes in bales of self-igniting

EPILOGUE

plastic on site. A hotter plume would have spared the North End from the smoke for a time longer, but what about the contaminants polluting the atmosphere, and downwind? In the end, there were many tonnes of plastic bales that remained unburned, thanks to the attack strategy. Had it all burned, perhaps the fire would have lasted several more days, further damaging the broader environment.

In Hamilton, while Plastimet provides the context for any future big toxic fire, there is no formal code that will go into effect should another one strike. The next time, as with all fires, it will again be up to the chiefs at the scene to make decisions on the spot in terms of how to put the blaze out. While safety precautions for emergency personnel will be stressed, Jim Kay said that suppression tactics for fighting a big fire, any big fire, don't change all that much. Get there as soon as you can. Surround the fire with large quantities of water. Protect exposures. Consider all suppression alternatives. Will the wind blow in a favourable direction? How will the material burn? As for free burning, Kay said it is not a panacea, because not all fires are guaranteed to burn hot enough to destroy the harmful by-products of combustion, which is how it's supposed to work in theory. Free burning is a tool available, but must be used only when the circumstances surrounding the fire are right, and the judgment of experts is consulted.

"This is not a exact science, and as such each fire and the ramifications of the tactics deployed must be judged on their own merit. Prejudging a strategy for fire tactics is somewhat dangerous," he said.

* * * * *

Just after 2:00 p.m. on April 25, 2005, a cool, windy afternoon, thick black smoke churned into a grey sky in Cobourg, a town on Lake Ontario an hour east of Toronto. The fire raged at a plastics manufacturing company just south of the 401 highway. It had been nearly eight years since the big one in Hamilton, and yet the word instantly jumped into the mind of Cobourg Fire Chief Al Mann: Plastimet.

The fire at Horizon Plastics bore some of the same characteristics as Hamilton's. The material burning—piles of plastic lattice—was toxic, the fire was running very hot, the acrid plume shooting high into the sky. The fire burned so hot, there were reports of heat shattering the windows of some firetrucks. The mayor declared a state of emergency in the town of 17,000. More than 300 people from the immediate area were evacuated. But the fire went much differently than Plastimet. While water was put on the blaze, for the most part it free-burned, very hot, the contaminants sent high into the atmosphere. A foam truck was brought in from CFB Trenton, and foam applied in an effort to suffocate the flames. In the end, the fire was out in about six hours. Residents returned to their homes by 9:00 p.m., and Horizon Plastics—having experienced no structural damage to its building—was operational within thirty hours.

The fact was, however, that the Cobourg fire was not "another Plastimet." The chemical properties of the plastic burning were polyethylene and polypropylene—not as toxic as the PVC (polyvinyl chloride) plastic at Plastimet. The fire did not rage inside an old building, but entirely outside in a storage yard, which is why it burned so fast and hot. There was no weather inversion blowing the contaminants back to the ground level. And the immediate area of the fire did not feature a regional hospital and jail among a dense residential population. As for suppression tactics, Al Mann said the fire did indeed free-burn—but as a matter of necessity, not choice. The Cobourg Fire Department has just twenty-seven total firefighters, fifteen full time including the chief and his deputy, and twelve volunteers. They couldn't get a jump on the attack like Hamilton had, they had to call in help from thirteen different area fire departments. They did not let it burn, the 138 firefighters working the job threw all the water they could at the fire, but it was so intense, with such a steady oxygen supply from a 30 km/hr wind, that it kept burning hot. As for the foam, the truck arrived about three hours into the fire, but Mann said the treatment had little impact. If not applied at the right application rate, foam is ineffective. There wasn't enough of it applied fast enough. It did hold the fire somewhat, and when they ran out, they switched to straight water.

One lesson from Plastimet that was heeded was ensuring that firefighters who were close to the blaze and the toxins got themselves

EPILOGUE

checked out. That included a couple of guys who got caught in smoke towards the end of the fire when the plume cooled. They didn't have their masks on when the smoke had banked down and caught them by surprise. Two days after the fire, two occupational disease representatives from the Ontario Professional Fire Fighters Association were on the scene: Toronto's Paul Atkinson and Hamilton's Colin Grieve—the firefighter who continued to handle the cancer claim for Bob Shaw's family. They advised firefighters to record everything they had done fighting the Horizon Plastics fire, and to get their health checked.

There weren't many similarities between Plastimet and the Cobourg fire, but one was the general cause of the blaze. Both had been arson. An investigation determined that the Cobourg fire was set in a storage shed on the property, and quickly spread to the plastic products. Two boys, ages 15 and 12, were charged with endangering life and mischief to property.

*****

Is Plastimet still on the mental radar for firefighters in Hamilton? For the new breed it's not. Some of the older guys sometimes bring it up, but it is no longer talked about much among most of them. It was a long time ago. But still, when the fire is mentioned in the media, when a newspaper prints a retrospective photo of the plume blasting into the air that summer night, it still brings back the ghosts for those who were in the thick of it and will never quite feel safe. A lingering question for those who were there, or know the stories well, is: When the next big one hits—and everyone feels it's just a matter of time—will they take it on the chin again? How will they respond to the alarm knowing what might await them? One of the firefighters who was at Plastimet put it bluntly: "I'm running the other way." But that was probably a minority view. The firefighter culture led to some unsafe practices over the years, but as with the soldier, the essential core of that ethos will always be necessary. Technology or not, culture change or not, the fact remains that firefighting is a courageous act, perhaps a reckless one. We still need people willing—anxious—to run to the fires. Matt Madjeruh worked alongside Bob Shaw at Plastimet. He has a family now, three kids he didn't have when the big one hit. Still hits the gym hard, has the chiselled calendar-worthy physique. He knows what he'll do the next time that alarm sounds. Knows what all the boys will do.

"I'll go. We'll all go."

* * * * *

The present
Doc's Tap and Grill
Bronco, Ticker, and Pepe still meet at Doc's for beers, and when they do, Bob's image, and the event that killed him, is right in front of them. Behind the bar, pretty much across from the stool where Shawzie used to sit, hangs a watercolour painting. It is of Bob in his bunker suit looking spent after a day at Plastimet. Bob's friend Garth Turpin, the owner of Doc's, commissioned the portrait by William Biddle, an artist in neighbouring Dundas. Several of the firefighters got a copy and hung it in their homes. Yes, they can still toast Bobby at the office, reflected Bronco. As for the big fishing trips with all the guys, those stopped after Bob died, but the inner circle still got together, still went away on fishing and golfing jaunts, just the three of them. And that included pilgrimages in the fall up north to "Beerhurst." Life goes on. But Bobby's name comes up on the trips, they think about him all the time, mostly because they are still doing the things they did when he was alive. Bob would have been up for the trip. Could've used a fourth, too.

Pepe stays in touch with Jackie, checks in on her occasionally, just to chat and offer to help around the house in any way he can. Was up on her roof doing some work on the eavestroughs recently. Don't call anyone else, he said. Just give him a shout, any time. As for their careers, Ticker Blythe is retired and Pepe Villeneuve and Mike Horvath are not far behind. Pepe turned 57 in June 2006, and the year had been a pretty busy one. Back in the winter had a couple of good house fires that were well-involved when they arrived. And there was a factory fire in Hamilton's east end, where some containers caught fire, big vats that contained hydrochloric acid. Pepe was on the hose, deep into the

EPILOGUE

building. Lots of smoke. Nobody knew what was burning, so it wasn't declared a haz-mat fire at first. Couldn't smell the acid burning because they had their gas masks on. The firefighters contained the blaze, ultimately it was declared a haz-mat fire and a special team was called in. Could have ended up a lot worse for them.

Pepe didn't spread the word, but he expected to retire in September 2006. Ninety percent sure, anyway. That would mean ending his career thirty-one years to the month when he first left Stelco and started with the fire department. He's seen enough. And you know, you keep hearing about guys who don't live that long after they hang it up, whether they are firefighters or not.

As for Bronco, he turned 53 in the spring of 2006. He's now an acting district chief and expects the formal promotion to come in about a year or so when a couple of the senior guys retire. His health is good, he never suffered serious effects from Plastimet. He shared the concerns everyone had, and for a time he had headaches, a hacking cough, but nothing that he was too concerned about. He never really allowed himself to live with fear. Doesn't think that way. Whatever happens, happens. On the job the fires still follow him, as do the unusual calls, which included being the incident commander for a tornado strike back in November 2005 that hit along a six-to-seven-kilometre track across the east Mountain and the lower city. Hit an occupied elementary school gym, another school, took the roofs off two houses, damaged seven others, snapped hydro poles. A hectic day. Nobody seriously injured, though.

He still loves the action, but sometimes you just feel like you've had about enough. It's not necessarily the fires. Bronco enjoyed fighting fires. He still had the positive attitude, but some of the experiences wore on him no matter how he looked at it. He thought about the one crib death call he had. The kind of thing affects you, when kids are involved. So innocent, carefree. Or there was a burn call that was really bad. Young boy playing with his buddies and some lighter fluid, lighting stuff on fire. Kid caught fire accidentally, then was completely engulfed in flames. When Bronco got there, the fire was out and the boy was on the ground screaming in pain. When he was turned over, there was no skin left on his back. Burns on 97 percent of his body. Later he died. You have a long chat with the peer counsellors after that. But you never forget. Yes, Bronco looked forward to his promotion, and the next adventure, but also retiring up on a lake somewhere up north. Doesn't need much, just wants to able to hunt and fish and enjoy the view.

* * * * *

March 2005

Jacqueline Shaw was in Zellers one day when she walked past a few people who were gathered around a newsstand. They were talking about a popular series that was running daily in the *Hamilton Spectator* newspaper. The series was called *Heat: A Firefighter's Story*—Bob's story. It was halfway through the four-week series at that time. Jacqueline paused at the newsstand, and a woman said to her, out of the blue, "Have you seen the series?" Jacqueline was a private person. But she heard the words coming out of her mouth, she couldn't help it.

"Actually I'm—I'm Jacqueline Shaw, from the story," she said. And the woman greeted her like a celebrity, the wife of firefighter Bob Shaw. She shook her hand. She loved the story—just wonderful.

"And what does your husband think of the story?" the woman asked pleasantly. Jacqueline felt the blood drain from her face. Then it hit her. In the series, Bob was still alive, had not yet been diagnosed with cancer. The woman assumed the story had a happy ending.

"My husband passed away."

"I'm so sorry," the woman said.

It was not always easy seeing their family's story unfolding like that in the newspaper, see it getting so much attention. One day she had nearly swerved off the road in her car when she came face to face with a larger-than-life picture of Bob on a red marketing poster in a transit shelter. But eventually the attention that Bob was receiving felt good, felt right. In the case of Bob's mother, Lily Shaw, the impact was an amazing thing to see. Lily had not been well for a long time. It seemed to start soon after Bob had been diagnosed with cancer, her health deteriorated. The thing was, she was not diagnosed with any disease. Just seemed like she was losing her will to live, she couldn't get enough

EPILOGUE

oxygen. When the *Heat* series started in the newspaper in March, Lily was near the end, in her late eighties, in a nursing home. But then she became something of a celebrity in the home. The nurses hung a *Heat* advertisement on her door. She was Bob Shaw's mother. Nathan, meanwhile, was visiting his Grandma nearly every day. Lily could still see fine, but she enjoyed hearing Nathan's voice reading the words. "You read it again, Nathan, please." Her favourite part was the passages in the story when Bob was a boy, her husband, Harry, was a working firefighter, and their garden at 44 East 21st won awards. It all seemed to give Lily new life, all the attention perking her up. The series finished at the end of March. Lily died in April.

In August, Jacqueline and Nathan attended a birthday party for Lois, an old friend who had grown up with Bob back in the Concession Street days. Lots of old friends were there, including Ricky Morton, Bob's old junior bowling buddy. It was the first time Jacqueline had chosen to meet socially with her old friends since the funeral a year earlier. After Bob died she did not put herself in a position to see the others, had blocked the rest of the world out. It was how she dealt with it, withdrawing. In some ways that part of her had not changed since the day her mother died. She could still light up a room, but when it was time to be alone, it was time to be alone. The birthday party could have been awkward, but it wasn't. The *Heat* series made it easy, all everyone talked about was the story. It gave them a way to talk about Bob in a relaxed, celebratory way. It was like therapy for everyone, they talked about old times in the context of the story and it was wonderful.

The series was also the talk at a reunion at Hill Park Secondary School. Alum Paul Anderson was there. All anyone wanted to talk about with him was Bob Shaw—and Shawzie hadn't even attended Hill Park. But everyone from the old Mountain days had known each other, and Bob had so many friends from different schools. Seemed like the event was a Bob Shaw reunion more than anything, Paul thought with a smile. One of the guys, Ross Freeman, came to the event from where he lived in Boca Raton, Florida. Had once lived with Bob and the rest of them in the apartment at 43 Forest Avenue downtown.

In some ways the second year after losing someone is worse than the first, Paul thought. In the first year, you're still in shock. But the second, that's when you start thinking about what could have been. Fifty years of friendship, the past is locked in memory, you can go there anytime. But he had lost the future with him, that's what hurt. It happens so often when he's out on the road and sees a motorcycle roar by, or, come the spring thaw in Hamilton, when he drives past a golf course and sees workers out there pulling tarps off the greens—Paul Anderson feels the tightening in his chest.

*****

June 5, 2005
Queen's Park, Toronto
It was hot that day, intense sun, humid, too. There were hundreds at the ceremony to dedicate a new memorial wall honouring Ontario firefighters who had lost their lives in the line of duty, either on the job or from diseases related to their work. The granite walls of the memorial formed the shape of a Maltese cross, the same symbol displayed on a firefighter's badge. There were 344 names etched on the wall, from the first recorded death in 1848 to those who lost their lives in 2004. Ontario Premier Dalton McGuinty spoke, met with the families. Nathan watched it unfold—on the TV news. It was tough to watch an event they should have been at. Jacqueline and Nathan had not been invited. The Hamilton firefighter union told Bob's name wouldn't be on the wall; the Workplace Safety Insurance Board had not accepted the cancer claim, had not recognized that his death had been from his work. Bob's name had made it to the Colorado Springs memorial, but this was different, this was politics. Nathan was bitter. He and his mother should be there, and his dad's name should be on the wall, he thought. Colorado was great, a huge honour, but this was Ontario, their home. Nathan felt like they were denying who Dad was and what he did, denying his life.

Three weeks later, on June 27, Jacqueline received a phone call at work. It was her friend Lois, who worked in Toronto. "You won't believe what I'm looking at right now," Lois said. "Bob's name, on the wall."

EPILOGUE

"No, Lois, you're wrong," Jacqueline said.

"I know what I'm looking at, it says 'Robert M. Shaw.'" Lois used her cellphone to take a picture of the name, then emailed it to Nathan. It wasn't the way they had wanted to find out, but a few days later, Nathan and Jacqueline took the GO train to Toronto, then a subway to Queen's Park to see for themselves. Up the stairs into daylight, and the wall was right in front of their faces. And there was Bob's name, with the others. It felt good, and sad, hit closer to home. Jacqueline and Bob used to go into Toronto all the time.

They never figured out why his name had been included on the wall, but they had not been informed of that fact. Perhaps the *Heat* series had influenced somebody to put Bob's name up there where it belonged, despite the WSIB issue. As for the claim, the fight was far from over. They expected the appeal on the claim to be heard late in 2006 or early 2007. And if the appeal lost, then the case would go to an independent tribunal, which would probably not happen for a couple of years. It bothered Jacqueline, the disputed claim, this denial of Bob's work, of what his health had been before Plastimet. Nathan agitated for his dad's case, researched, wrote letters to local politicians, the Ministry of Labour, the premier. He learned that Ontario lagged behind provinces like Manitoba, Alberta, Saskatchewan, British Columbia, and Nova Scotia in recognizing occupational diseases for firefighters. These provinces had "presumptive legislation" in place that established the link between illness and firefighting, while Ontario still left it up to the firefighters to battle for their claims with the WSIB. He contacted Hamilton East MPP Andrea Horvath and asked for a meeting. It was an emotional one. Nathan and Jacqueline explained Bob's case. Horvath had a special interest in the issue, she had lived in the north end of the city where the Plastimet fire raged, had attended Bob's funeral. Horvath promised the Shaws that she would push the issue forward. On May 4, 2006, Nathan and Jacqueline were at Queen's Park to see Horvath present a private member's bill named in honour of Bob.

The bill called for presumptive legislation to recognize Ontario firefighter disease claims. Private members' bills rarely become law, but

Liberal Labour Minister Steve Peters did stand in the legislature in response to announce that a report would be compiled to review the latest scientific literature on firefighting-related cancers, and also examine how cancer claims had been treated. Nathan, meanwhile, sat under the glare of television lights to urge support for the bill. His picture and words were in newspapers, his press conference appeared on the CTV evening news.

"My dad made the ultimate sacrifice as a firefighter," he told reporters, struggling to keep his emotions in check. "And it's devastating that his own province is saying, 'No, your father did not make that sacrifice, no, your father did not die for that cause.' I'm here to say, yes, he did."

Bob Shaw's boy was now 21 years old, about the age Bob had been when he first met Jacqueline, before he joined the fire department. Come the fall Nathan would enter fourth year at McMaster University to finish his combined degree in communications and politics. Wasn't sure what the future held. Perhaps a career in politics. Maybe a cliché, he reflected, but that would offer an opportunity to make a real difference, help people.

*****

Friday morning, March 24, 2006

She woke that morning, but did not dress for work as usual. Jacqueline had taken the day off. No plans, it was going to be a quiet day. And quiet weekend, too, as it happened. She stayed in, didn't talk to friends, just spent time on her own, and with Nathan when he came home from school. It was how she preferred it at times like this. She always preferred to be alone with her thoughts, not have to give any thought to the face she was showing others. In this respect perhaps her favourite spot was at the cemetery in Hamilton where Bob was buried. She wouldn't even tell others where that was. It was her place, and she would go there to reflect and stare at the stone with the firefighter theme on it.

She thought about something a friend had told her awhile back, trying to offer some advice on coping with the loss of Bob.

EPILOGUE

"Give yourself some time, Jackie, give yourself two years," the friend said. Well, here we are, Jacqueline thought: March 24. Two years to the day that Bob died. Two years, she thought, and nothing's changed. Bob is still not here, she still thinks he's going to be waiting for her one day on the front porch when she comes home from work. People talked about closure. She hated the word. You can't be wrapped in the love they had and then just be—over the loss. In time she had learned that nearly everyone had an opinion on how you cope with it. She also learned not to listen. You just deal with it. It's all you can do. She and Nathan were trying to find a new normal, was how she thought of it You open the front door, and there's the world. You have to keep going, she thought, because what else can you do?

That Friday morning, she got out of bed and walked down the hallway and, just like every morning, looked into Bob's face. It was the watercolour portrait, the same one that hangs in Doc's. Jacqueline had refused to hang it up for a long time. The gift had just sat in the dining room on the floor, leaning against the wall. It had been such a nice gesture, but she couldn't bring herself to put it up. It hurt too much. But eventually she was ready, was strong enough. It was as though she no longer feared seeing Bob as a memory, could celebrate and remember him without feeling like she was letting go—because that would never happen. She hung it right at the top of the stairs, not far from the bedrooms, you can even see it as soon as you come in the front door and look up the winding staircase, a nice high traffic spot, she thought. She absolutely loves it.

So now, two years later, she started her morning like every morning, seeing Bob in his bunker gear walking right towards her, and Jacqueline felt comforted, just like she did every time she looked at the portrait. And then she looked down and saw Buster. One day Bob's father had carried the green-eyed, grey kitten into the house in his pocket, a stray in need of a home, a gift for Nathan. Now Buster is 12 years old. His bed had always been in the living room downstairs, but once the portrait was hung, the cat lay underneath it in the hall. Couldn't budge him from the spot. And that's where he sleeps, every night, right at Bob's feet.

AFTERWORD

It is by no means a job. It is a calling. My father, like his father before him, felt firefighting was what he had to do. *Heat* revolves around my dad, but it also reflects upon all firefighters, people typically too humble to admit their worth.

My dad's story humanizes the profession, gives a face to the faceless—to the unidentified heroes who do their duty without seeking recognition for all that they do. It also illustrates the real dangers of their calling, which so often gets clouded with its impression of invincibility. My dad is evidence that sometimes even those who save others need saving themselves. Even heroes can fall.

So many of us go through life wondering if what we do really matters. Wondering if what we do makes a difference. I believe my dad took comfort in knowing that his life truly did matter. He did make a difference—in my life, in my mother's, and in the countless other lives he touched during his shortened stay on this earth. He was a dedicated husband, father, and friend to many.

We get so caught up in life's minor details we often fail to step back and reflect on the bigger picture of what we are a part of. I know that my dad never wavered in his understanding and appreciation for the bigger picture of life. That it is all too short. That it is precious. That living life is a gift.

Even at his weakest, his attitude to never give up shone through, instilling inspiration and hope to those closest to him. His inner strength and resilience personifies the power of the human spirit. Never before have I witnessed such strength, courage, and determination in the face of unimaginable adversity. One of his firefighting colleagues proudly told me that my dad was their own Terry Fox. I couldn't agree more.

Like all firefighters who put their lives on the line, my dad willingly gave his life for others. In the end he did make the ultimate sacrifice. He gave *his* life so the community where he was born and raised would be safe. He gave *his* life to protect those who needed protection. He gave *his* life so others could have theirs.

The word "hero" can get thrown around often. Through his story, I think my dad restores a rare purity to such a powerful and honourable word. It is a title he did not seek, but one I now hope will be his forever. Because life is unavoidably evanescent, most everything we do fades quickly from our minds. But a person's life depicted in print is perhaps one of the closet things we have to ensuring the great things we achieve remain eternal. This book keeps my father, his story, and his legacy alive. I could ask for no greater tribute.

Nathan Shaw

MEMBER OF SCABRINI GROUP

Québec, Canada
2006